Political Sociology

Political Sociology

A Critical Introduction

Keith Faulks

Edinburgh University Press

© Keith Faulks, 1999

Edinburgh University Press
22 George Square, Edinburgh

Typeset in 10 on 12½ Stone Serif
by Hewer Text Ltd, Edinburgh, and
printed and bound in Great Britain by
MPG Books Ltd, Bodmin

A CIP record for this book is
available from the British Library

ISBN 0 7486 1356 0 (paperback)

Contents

For Stevie

Acknowledgements

I would like to thank John Hoffman and Alex Thomson who both carefully read various drafts of the manuscript, and who made an invaluable contribution to this book through their comments and criticisms. Susan Gray acted as a research assistant during the final stages of the book, and collected numerous sources which were of particular use in writing Chapters 8 and 10. Susan was also a very effective proofreader. The following friends, colleagues and relatives were very supportive in a multitude of ways: Yasmin Ali, Paul Connolly, Neil Faulks, Robert Gibb, James Hamill, Rob Hulme, Joe Ravetz, Colin Wood and Mum and Dad. I would also like to express my gratitude to all the staff at Edinburgh University Press and in particular to Nicola Carr who has been an exemplary editor.

This book is dedicated to Stevie Hallows who, as well as putting up with my obsession with its completion, made a significant input into the development of the ideas it contains. For this, as well as for all her love and support, I am very grateful.

Abbreviations

ACTUP	Aids Coalition to Unleash Power
APEC	Asia-Pacific Economic Co-operation Forum
ASEAN	Association of Southeast Asian Nations
CAP	Common Agricultural Policy
EMR	Economic Management Regime
EU	European Union
FDI	foreign direct investment
GDP	Gross Domestic Product
GNP	Gross National Product
ICT	information and communication technology
IPPR	Institute for Public Policy and Research
IMF	International Monetary Fund
MAIs	Multilateral Agreements on Investments
MNCs	multinational companies
NAFTA	North American Free Trade Agreement
NATO	North Atlantic Treaty Organisation
NGOs	non-governmental organisations
NHS	National Health Service
NSMs	new social movements
OECD	Organisation for Economic Co-operation and Development
TNCs	transnational corporations
UN	United Nations
WTO	World Trade Organisation

Introduction

This book is an introduction to political sociology. It does not, however, attempt to offer an encyclopaedic overview of the numerous perspectives and studies that have been advanced under the banner of political sociology. Instead, it aims to inspire the reader to inquire further into what is a fascinating subject by developing a distinctive argument about the appropriate core of the discipline. In particular, this work is concerned with the impact recent social changes have had upon the relationship between the state and civil society, which this book contends is the primary focus of our subject. This introduction outlines this argument, and explains the structure and approach of the book. Its first task, however, is to define political sociology.

What is Political Sociology?

At its broadest level, political sociology is concerned with the relationship between politics and society. Its distinctiveness within the social sciences lies in its acknowledgement that political actors, including parties, pressure groups and social movements, operate within a wider social context. Political actors therefore inevitably shape, and in turn are shaped by, social structures such as gender, class and nationality. Such social structures ensure that political influence within society is unequal. It follows from this that a key concept in political sociology is that of power, where power is defined as the capacity to achieve one's objectives, even when those objectives are in conflict with the interests of another actor. Political sociologists therefore invariably return to the following question: which individuals and groups in society possess the capacity to pursue their interests, and how is this power exercised and institutionalised?

Because the state is the most powerful political institution, which symbolises and enforces the boundaries between societies, as well as reflecting divisions within its own territory, many political sociologists have focused upon the state's relationship with other sites of power within civil society. This book aims to defend such an approach to political sociology. Therefore, the definition of political sociology advanced in this book is as follows: Political sociology is the study of the interdependent power relationship between the state and civil society.

The concepts of state and civil society are explored in detail in Chapter 1, but at this stage some preliminary definitions are required.

The state is a set of tightly connected governmental institutions, concerned with the administration of a geographically determined population, the authority of which is recognised by other states through international law. The state's dominance over the institutions of civil society is ensured by the state's centralised control of military power.

Civil society is a more specific concept than 'society'. The institutions of civil society all have a political aspect to them. Civil society refers to the multitude of voluntary associations of citizens such as businesses, media organisations, churches, professional bodies, political parties, pressure groups and trade unions. These associations enjoy various degrees of autonomy from the state. Importantly, the institutions of civil society can act as counterpoints to the power of the state and are themselves political actors, protecting and promoting the interests of their members.

The Book's Argument

The main argument of this book entails recognising that the state remains the most powerful political actor in the modern world. At the same time, the state must be subjected to a critique. It is contended that states, and, more specifically, those states of the advanced industrial world, largely remain 'masters' of their own destinies. Recent processes of social change have not proved fatal to the state's unrivalled concentration of military, economic and communicative power.

Globalisation and the rise of a more critical citizenry have, however, highlighted the limitations of statist solutions to human problems, and have changed the context in which states act. If, as I wish to argue, globalisation is defined as the intensification of global risks, which necessitate greater co-operation between states, the prospects for a world beyond the territorially bounded state have never been greater. I therefore wish to contend, somewhat paradoxically, that the primary goal of political sociology is to ascertain the extent to which shifts in the relationship between state and civil society are leading to the transcendence of political sociology's principal point of focus.

Political sociology is thereby transported back to its intellectual origins. It was Hegel and Marx, in the nineteenth century, who first developed sophisticated theories of the problematic relationship between state and civil society. Hegel believed that the two spheres could coexist and their relationship be successfully mediated by public-spirited civil servants. Marx, however, saw the need to move beyond this contradictory relationship if society was to enjoy real social order and justice. Marx envisaged a time when the state would disappear, along with the class antagonisms that required its presence in the first place.

This author sides with Marx against Hegel on the need to look beyond the state and seek a more stable form of governance, one which rests neither upon the threat of force by the state nor upon the inequalities of a civil society conditioned by capitalism. However, it will become apparent that I do not consider such a transcendence as inevitable, as Marx did. Indeed, this book is critical of many of Marx's assumptions. In particular, I believe that the problem of human governance, which is the need to maintain social order and distribute scarce resources, is an ever-present one. It may be possible to move beyond the state; it is not possible, however, to dispense with some form of governance. Marx's has little to tell us about alternative forms of governance, as he unconvincingly reduces the problem of human conflict to social class. According to Marx, once class disappears so does the need for politics. This assumption seems unjustified given the unseen consequences of social change, the finite nature of essential resources, and the fact that, as creative beings, people are always likely to disagree over how society is organised.

If the state is to be transcended, it is likely to be a gradual process rather than as a result of a single revolutionary moment. Neither is this transformation likely to be the result of the actions of any one social class as Marx believed. Ironically, it is more likely to result from the actions of states themselves, as they seek to share their power with other states and the institutions of civil society in response to the social changes examined in this book. Political sociology can best contribute to innovations in governance by critically examining existing forms of power that are located in the state and civil society.

The Book's Structure

Part I develops the state–civil society theme, and critically evaluates the theoretical perspectives on which the foundations of political sociology rest.

The argument that political sociology's focus is upon the state's relations with civil society has not been accepted by all political sociologists. There have been fundamental disagreements within the subject over the significance of the state. For much of the post-war period, this debate seemed to have been settled in favour of those who denied the state's very existence as a meaningful category. The behaviouralists, who dominated political sociology from the 1940s to the 1970s, considered the state far too obscure and ideological to be analytically useful. The political sociologist, it was argued, should instead focus upon the political behaviour of individuals and the institutions of civil society. The key issues for behavioural political sociology were how political values were formed, the nature of a country's political culture, and the reasons why citizens participate politically. In effect, in contrast to the approach of this book, the behaviouralists largely ignored the state.

Chapter 1 therefore begins with a critique of behaviouralism. It is argued that the behaviouralists have a one-dimensional understanding of power, which overlooks both the concentration of power within the state and the impact structural inequalities in civil society play in ensuring that political influence is skewed. The chapter advances an alternative theory of power, which focuses the attention of political sociology firmly back upon the problem of the state. Indeed, the very origins of political sociology lie in a critical engagement with the modern state, and can be located in Marx's critique of Hegel's theory of the state and civil society relationship. The rest of Chapter 1 outlines the historical origins and main characteristics of the modern state.

In Chapter 2, a critique of the three most important theoretical traditions within political sociology is developed. Although Marxism, pluralism and elite theory remain influential, none of them have developed a satisfactory account of the autonomous power of the state and therefore have under-theorised its relationship with civil society. In summary, Part I identifies the state–civil society relationship as the most appropriate focus for political sociology, and critically assesses the theories of this relationship advanced by behaviouralists, Marxists, elitists and pluralists.

Part II assesses the impact of recent social change upon the state.

This section explores whether recent social changes have undermined the state and therefore called into question the argument that the state is the key focal point for political sociology. However, the challenges of globalisation, neo-liberalism and new social movements do not mean we should ignore the state, as the behaviouralists once maintained. Rather, they further highlight the need to study the state in relation to both the institutions of civil society and to processes of social change taking place beyond the boundaries of any single state.

Chapter 3 focuses upon what I call the radical globalisation thesis, which contends that economic and cultural change has created a world economy and global culture that are beyond the state's control. It is argued that many of the claims of the radical globalisation thesis are exaggerated. The theory must therefore be modified to remove its deterministic tendencies, which underestimate the ability of the state to shape its own future. Globalisation is best understood as the development of global security risks, such as ecological damage, which require greater co-operation between states to meet such threats more effectively.

Chapter 4 examines neo-liberalism, which has championed the idea of economic globalisation, and which has sought to defend market freedoms from what its exponents see as an overbearing, inefficient and coercive state. Paradoxically, neo-liberalism has resulted in a more coercive state precisely because of the failure of neo-liberal policies, which have influenced the governments of many developed and developing countries since the 1980s.

Ideological challenges to the state have not only come from the neo-liberal right, they have also been advanced from the political left. Advocates of new social movements see in them the potential for radical social change, which challenges the authority of the state. However, Chapter 5 contends that although such movements have enriched our understanding of politics and power, their uniqueness and impact are overstated. In reality, social movements are forced to interact with the state in their efforts to influence the political agenda. Overall, Part II demonstrates that recent challenges to the state have not undermined its ability to concentrate power to the extent that is often claimed.

Part III explores whether contemporary social changes have weakened the links that bind civil society to the state.

Certain assumptions have underpinned the overwhelmingly positive pluralist and behaviouralist view of civil society as a sphere of voluntary participation and civic responsibility. Liberal democracies are said to rest upon a sense of a shared political culture, a common citizenship and a widespread commitment to representative democracy. Part III examines whether these assumptions are valid in the face of contemporary social change.

A key concept in the behaviouralist lexicon is political culture. The stability of liberal democracies, it is argued, is due to a strong consensus on political values. The theories analysed in Chapter 6 suggest, however, that liberal democracies cannot unquestionably rely on a supportive political culture. Although many of the concepts advanced to explain the growth of anti-social behaviour, such as notions of the underclass or a culture of contentment, are themselves flawed, they do point towards the failure of advanced industrial countries to maintain social cohesion in the light of recent social change.

Chapter 7 explores the related concept of citizenship. The assumption that Western states have achieved a stable set of rights and responsibilities has recently been questioned. The social rights of citizenship, embodied in the welfare state, have been particularly challenged by neo-liberals who have sought to roll back the welfare state in the name of economic competitiveness. Chapter 7 argues that the changing meaning of citizenship is connected to shifts in the relationship between civil society and the state. For communitarians, however, it is liberal democracies' overemphasis upon rights, and the neglect of the citizens' responsibilities, which has undermined citizenship. The final section of the chapter argues that communitarianism is incoherent in its theory of citizenship because of its under-theorised account of the state–civil society relationship. The key to improving the foundations of citizenship lies instead in the opening of avenues of participation, currently blocked by inadequate structures of governance and by social exclusion.

Nonetheless, elite theorists, behaviouralists and pluralists have defended a limited representative democracy. States can only be stable, the argument goes, if they are run by elites and the masses content themselves with issuing occasional stamps of approval through the ballot box. The evidence surveyed in Chapter 8, however, suggests that citizens are increasingly disgruntled with elite forms of democracy. The combination of a more aware citizenry, with the opportunities for participation created by innovations in communication and information technology, may force states to become increasingly participatory and thereby alter the state's relationship with civil society. In summary, the concepts explored in Part III suggest civil society is being transformed by social change in ways which call into question a state-centred system of governance.

Part IV examines how contemporary political sociologists have rethought governance in light of the challenges explored in Parts II and III.

Recent social change requires political sociology to subject the state to a critique which seeks more effective systems of governance. Furthermore, as a consequence of the growth of global risks, it is likely that in the future governance will need to develop at a level beyond the state.

Chapter 9 introduces some influential attempts to rethink the relationship between the state and civil society. A key question explored in Chapter 9 is whether modernist ideologies such as socialism and liberalism are relevant to the problems of governance in the modern world. The chapter concludes that there has been a theoretical convergence in contemporary political sociology towards a radical pluralist perspective which entails various re-conceptualisations of the state–civil society relationship.

The final substantive chapter of this book explores whether we are moving towards new forms of global governance to meet the growing challenge of planetary problems. It will be argued that, although states remain the key actors in world politics, increasing global connections between states and societies suggest both the need for, and the growing possibility of, governance beyond the state.

The conclusion reviews the book's argument and in its final paragraphs assesses the contribution political sociology is making to our understanding of the contemporary problems of governance.

The Book's Approach

This text should be read as if it were a guidebook to a museum, which, while aiming to be informative and stimulating in itself, is bound to be selective and is therefore no alternative to viewing the exhibits themselves. Those readers hoping to find all the answers to political sociology in this relatively small work will therefore be disappointed. Instead, this book should help interested readers to make up their own mind about the issues raised, not by offering definitive answers, but by stimulating thought and encouraging more specialised reading. To this end, all of the chapters in this volume take a critical stance to the questions they raise, in the assumption that a clear line of argument makes for more thought-provoking study than does a spurious attempt at objectively summarising all the issues of a vast subject area. Whenever possible, the discussion is centred upon key contributions to the topics under consideration. It is hoped that this will aid the coherence of my arguments, as well as serving as a guide to further reading. Additional advice on relevant reading for each chapter can be found at the end of the book.

Ideally, the chapters that follow should be read in sequence. Readers are certainly advised to read Chapter 1, which outlines the nature of political sociology in more detail, before tackling any of the other chapters. However, each chapter is relatively self contained and may be read separately, according to the needs of the reader.

Finally, it is worth saying something about the scope of the book. What I have tried to do in this work is to explore some key concepts and theories of political sociology critically and to illustrate their practical relevance through examples of the state–civil society relationship drawn mainly from liberal democratic societies. Where I have discussed non-Western societies, notably in a lengthy case study in Chapter 4 exploring the application of neo-liberalism to Africa, this is aimed at further illuminating particular concepts or theories. I am aware, therefore, that this book is primarily a political sociology of liberal democracy. I make no claim to be offering an account of the diverse ways in which the state–civil society relationship has developed across the globe.

Having acknowledged the limits of this book, I would nonetheless argue that there are sound reasons for focusing upon liberal democratic systems, and that this selectivity is not the product of some misplaced Eurocentric bias on behalf of the author. First, it is indisputable that the power imbalances that exist between the West and the rest have meant that states and societies in the non-Western world have often been shaped directly or indirectly by the actions of liberal democracies. Therefore an understanding of the state's relationship with civil society in liberal democracy helps us to understand the more general problem of human governance. Secondly, as Marx recognised, it is with the development of liberal democracy that the contradictions between state and civil society become most acute. In a book such as this, which seeks to subject the state to a critique, it is therefore appropriate to focus upon its most advanced form.

Many of the difficulties and dilemmas faced by liberal-democratic systems of governance are highlighted throughout this work, and it is hoped that the distinctive approach to political sociology advanced in this text will enhance the reader's understanding of the roots of these problems. In the course of developing the argument that contemporary social changes demand that political sociology explores the possibility of governance beyond the state, many popular and often ill-defined concepts such as globalisation, new social movements and citizenship, are placed in their wider theoretical context. Whoever reads this book should therefore develop a better understanding of the forces that are shaping politics and society in the modern world.

Part I

The Foundations
of Political Sociology

1

Approaches and Key Concepts in Political Sociology

In 1969, Talcott Parsons claimed that political sociology was 'scarcely heard of before the middle of this century' (Parsons, 1969: xiii). Parsons was identifying political sociology with the behaviouralist approach, which dominated the subject from the 1940s to the 1970s. This chapter contends, however, that political sociology has its roots, not in the 1940s, as Parsons implies, but in the early nineteenth century, when the German philosopher Hegel first theorised a clear separation between the state and civil society. The central theme of this book is therefore that political sociology is the study of the interdependent power relationship between the state and civil society.

This theme is established in this chapter, first through a critique of behaviouralist political sociology. The main weakness of this approach is its one-dimensional view of power, which ignores the imbalances of resources that exist both between individuals within civil society and between the state and civil society. If political sociology is to explain why some political interests within society are more successfully promoted than others, then it must develop a more sophisticated theory of power. The second section of this chapter seeks to do just that. It is the question of how power is distributed that leads us logically to focus our attention upon the state, because it is this institution which is the most successful at concentrating power.

The behaviouralists are right to point to the difficulties associated with defining the state, but the state's importance to political sociology compels us to attempt to pin down this enigmatic institution. The discussion of Max Weber's famous definition of the state in section three illustrates the absurdity of an institution which claims both legitimacy and a monopoly of violence. This section also locates the origins of the state in the centralisation of power and the gradual subordination of society through force. Having established the importance of the state to political sociology, the final section identifies the particular characteristics of the modern liberal state.

Limitations of the Behaviouralist Approach

Behaviouralists such as David Easton (1953) aimed to move political sociology beyond the limits of both mainstream political science, with its largely descriptive and historical focus upon the state, and political theory, with its normative and (for the behaviouralists) largely ideological assumptions.

King (1986: Ch. 1) argues that the behaviouralists sought to shift the focus of political sociology towards a micro level of analysis, concerned with individual and group political behaviour within civil society, and away from the theorising of macro problems, such as the distribution of power between elite groups within the state. Behaviouralists insisted that valid conclusions about political behaviour could only be made from the objective analysis of hard data such as statistics on how people voted in elections, as opposed to abstract speculation about the nature of the state (Kavanagh, 1983: 10).

Some behaviouralists even dispensed with the concept of the state altogether. Easton (1953) advocated the use of an alternative concept, the 'political system', which concerned the 'authoritative allocation of values' which may emanate from a variety of sources including religious organisations and political movements, and which Easton therefore argued had much wider significance than the 'state'.

However, for their critics, this neglect of the state was due to the ideological orientation of many behaviouralist thinkers. Their 'objective' analysis of the facts masked a firm normative commitment to 'the development and growth of the capitalist nation-state' (Buxton, 1985: 238). Behaviouralism stressed that liberal democracy was the highest possible form of political system and consequently should be adopted by developing countries if they wished to emulate the success of the West. Behind this argument lay a suspicion of more participatory conceptions of democracy. It was argued that more extensive mass participation in politics may result in totalitarianism, thereby destroying the freedoms of civil society on which the West's achievements were founded.

Indeed, according to King (1986: 8), the behaviouralist dominance of political sociology up to the 1970s represented 'a resolution to the long-standing tension in political sociology arising from competing conceptions of democracy, in favour of democratic elitism'. Thus, the behaviouralists, instead of moving beyond the grand theoretical traditions of political theory as they claimed, came down on one side of the debate on democracy: they implicitly argued against radical conceptions of democracy and in support of sceptics of extensive democracy such as Schumpeter (1942). This necessarily entailed an uncritical approach to the hierarchical power structures found in the political and economic systems of liberal democracies.

For behaviouralism, the success of liberal political systems was due to the maintenance of a distinct civil society characterised by value consensus, a common citizenship, and the wealth created by capitalist enterprises. If one wished to retain a concept of the state this should be seen purely in functional terms, as a neutral, regulatory institution that helped stabilise civil society. As Bottomore (1993b: 6) remarks, such a view entailed the value judgement that liberal democracy is 'maintained in essence by complementary relationships between its various elements, or sub-systems', of which the 'state' is merely one component, or sub-system. Such a functionalist perspective ignored at least two important facts regarding the concentration of power within the state.

Firstly, by the 1970s the state had become more significant than ever before. The behaviouralist denial of the state, which was always unconvincing, became absurd, given the quantitative growth in the state's power. The economic orthodoxy in the advanced industrial world was that growth and stability required extensive intervention into civil society by the state. Newly industrialising countries in Asia relied heavily upon a developmental state, which planned and guided their economic progress. In socialist countries, like the Soviet Union and China, the institution was even more important. It was through the instrument of the state that communist parties closely regulated their citizens, as well as their economies, and the autonomous associations of civil society were suppressed. Cold War hostilities between these communist countries and their Western counterparts further underlined the centrality of the state in international as well as in domestic affairs.

In the 1970s, therefore, the state increasingly took centre stage in critical political sociology. Marxists became more interested in an institution which had stubbornly failed to 'wither away' in the way that Marx had predicted (Jessop, 1982). Weberians too, always clearer on the importance of state power than Marxists, produced a variety of influential theories that sought to bring the state back in as a core area of enquiry for political sociologists (Evans et al., 1985; Skocpol, 1979).

Secondly, despite their distrust of the concept of the state, behaviouralists faced the problem that there 'is no reason to suppose that concepts used in preference to the state, like "political system" or "government", will be any less contestable or ideologically charged in character' (Hoffman, 1988: 20). The state is not just an abstract construct, a fantasy of grand theorists, but rather is a concrete institution, which a mere change of label from state to 'political system' cannot dissolve. Easton's notion of the authoritative allocation of values, for example, fails to address the question of what exactly gives such allocations authority (Birch, 1993: 221). The behaviouralists simply sidestep, rather than solve, the problem of the concentration of coercive power in the state. The state does not passively mediate between the competing claims of the associations of civil society. It has imperatives of its own. Moreover, an important defining characteristic of the state is that ultimately its dominance over civil society rests upon its concentration of the mechanisms of physical coercion. The state must therefore be addressed in any serious study of political sociology.

By ignoring the state, many of the most important questions of political sociology remain unanswered by the behaviouralists. Sanders (1995: 64) identifies this weakness as a 'tendency towards mindless empiricism'. Crucial issues are lost in a sea of peripheral data. What may be easily testable may not be as important as more empirically elusive problems. For example, Sanders (1995: 66) identifies the neglect of the crucial question of conflicting social interests in behaviouralist analysis. As 'it is extraordinarily difficult to observe the "interests" of a particular individual, group or state directly' this pivotal question has not been addressed satisfactorily by behavioural political sociology. This question can only be answered by developing a more advanced theory of power than the one-dimensional approach of behaviouralism, one which moves beyond the observable outcomes of competition between political actors, and which therefore highlights the structural constraints that shape the distribution of resources.

The Nature of Power

Lukes (1974), in his seminal study of power, divides the concept into three dimensions. These can be briefly summarised as follows:

1. *First dimension*: this concerns the capacity of an individual or group to achieve a desired end, even if it is opposed by those with contrary interests. This is relatively easy to measure, since it involves concrete outcomes that clearly favour one actor over another.
2. *Second dimension*: this dimension necessarily assumes hierarchical relationships between different social groups. Those actors in positions of strength have the capacity to further their interests, not only in the direct sense expressed in the first dimension of power, but also by preventing alternative interests from even

being considered. This entails controlling the content of the political agenda. In some aspects of political behaviour (such as formal political participation), the effect of the control over the political agenda by a powerful minority, and the subsequent marginalisation of certain interests, might be measured by exploring the levels of participation and alienation displayed by those deemed most excluded.

3. *Third dimension*: power in this dimension is even more insidious because it not only involves the manipulation of the political agenda, but also entails persuading subordinate groups that this agenda is in their real interests. This form of power involves essentially thought control and the creation of a 'false consciousness' amongst the powerless, who come to identity with and support what may in reality be the exact opposite of their true interests. Due to the often covert and subtle methods used to secure this kind of power, as well as the difficulties associated with ascertaining one's real interests, its measurement is extremely difficult.

Because of behaviouralism's emphasis upon empirically testable phenomena, it has focused overwhelmingly upon the first dimension of power, thereby ignoring what are arguably the more important structural dimensions of power: agenda setting and thought manipulation. However, critics have pointed to the flaws of Lukes's own conception of power, and in particular to the ethical judgements that are entailed in discerning the third dimension of power.

Hay (1997) argues that Lukes conflates an analysis of the distribution of power with a normative judgement about what the distribution of power should be. Moreover, if we follow Lukes's logic, it is difficult to see on what basis any political community could be constructed because, in his account, power is a purely negative attribute. Since all political systems involve, to some extent, the exercise of power, Lukes's theory appears to be underpinned by an unrealistic view of human relations.

Hay's alternative conception of power involves both *conduct-shaping*, where A directly alters the conduct of B through coercion or manipulation and *context-shaping*, where A acts in a way that indirectly constrains B's future actions, but which does not necessarily involve that intention. This marks a considerable advance upon Lukes's theory, because it allows us to analyse power without the need to make a judgement about its distribution: we need not blame A for any restrictions on B's options which result from what may be the unintended consequence of A's actions.

However, Hay's attempt to disentangle power from intent, embodied in his notion of context-shaping, may well meet with the criticism that we are left with an extremely vague notion of power. If we cannot clearly identify who is responsible for the effects of power, what use is the concept? A potential solution to this problem is to consider power alongside the question of agency and structure.

If we assess power purely in terms of individual intent, we are implicitly taking an agent-centred perspective. We are assuming that power results only from the actions of individual and rational actors. This ignores the fact that individuality and rationality are socially constructed, and fails to acknowledge the structural aspects of power. Thus the reasons for the inequalities of power between actors are obscured. Consider, for example, the question of gender inequalities. By any measure, women are disadvantaged in terms of access to resources such as wealth and influence. If we take an agency-based approach, we can identify individual instances of discrimination against women and may quite rightly wish to hold those individuals who perpetuate this discrimination responsible. However, in order to understand the problem of gender inequalities fully we need some way of connecting these seemingly isolated, individual acts of injustice. Thus feminists have advanced the concept of patriarchy, which refers to the structural constraints placed upon women (Walby, 1990). Patriarchy conditions the behaviour of men towards women. The negative portrayal of women in the mass media as passive sexual objects, for example, helps to shape men's attitudes to the women they encounter in their own lives. By acknowledging the structural dimension of power we need not abandon the concept of intentionality. Any sophisticated account of the distribution of power, however, must take into account the structural reasons for individual actions. Power is embodied in and operates through social structures, as well as being exercised by social actors who are conscious of the effects of their actions. However, although individuals may be constrained by social forces beyond their control their actions are not totally determined by such forces.

Hay's theory of power is more nuanced than Lukes's in its account of the relationship between agency and structure and therefore represents a more useful starting point for an examination of power relationships. Building upon Hay's position, I would suggest that any analysis of power should consider the following factors:

1. *Types of Power*: these are military, communicative and economic in form. Military power is the use of organised armed force. It is usually employed by the state, but it may also be utilised by organised groups who seek to change the way in which a society

is governed. Communicative power concerns the control of ideas and the capacity to shape beliefs, such as the ability of a religious leader to influence the actions of their followers. Economic power refers to the control of productive forces and wealth. Politics is not a form of power as such. Broadly defined it encompasses all three types of power. More narrowly, it can be understood as a set of techniques concerned with conflict resolution and compromise between opposing social groups which aims to secure a distribution of power in accordance with the requirements of order and justice. In this sense, politics is the method by which consensual governance is constituted.

2. *Resources of Power*: these include wealth, physical strength, information, ideas, language and technology. The distribution of these resources is crucial in understanding who possesses the ability to exercise their will.

3. *Methods of Power*: these include the use of force, manipulation, persuasion and authority. The most secure form of power is authority, where A recognises the right of B to act on his or her behalf.

4. *Structures of Power*: these include class, ethnicity, generation and gender. Such social cleavages may act as constraints upon the power of some actors to exercise their will, while those individuals who enjoy a privileged class status, for example, are more likely to possess the resources necessary to assert their interests.

5. *Sites of Power*: these include the family, the associations of civil society and the state. Power relationships are played out within these sites. Political sociologists may legitimately focus their attention upon the nature of power within any of them. However, for reasons outlined below, political sociologists have often concentrated upon the institution of the state.

6. *Outcomes of Power*: these may include, on the one hand, increased self-confidence and sense of efficacy amongst those empowered individuals and, on the other hand, feelings of alienation and apathy on the part of those who are the objects of what they perceive to be illegitimate power or who are disempowered owing to a lack of resources. Importantly, the outcomes of any single act of power may have implications for the ability of the actors involved in a relationship to exercise power subsequently. The exercise of power is therefore a dynamic rather than static process that is shaped by previous instances and outcomes of its usage.

Through a reconsideration of power, recent theorists have attempted to shift political sociology back from the micro to the macro level of analysis through a sustained focus upon the role of the state as the most effective 'power container' (Giddens, 1985; Mann, 1986; 1993).

A state-centred approach to political sociology implies that if political behaviour is to be understood the centrality of the state has to be acknowledged. It is the state, more than any other institution, which concentrates those resources of power which influence the conduct of citizens, shape the political agenda, and transform the context in which the activities of civil society take place. The state not only centralises military power, but also possesses considerable communicative and economic power. It is the state that is the actor most able to employ the most effective methods of power such as force, manipulation and, in particular, authority. Moreover, a crucial question for political sociology is how the state, as the most important site of power, reflects and reinforces structures of power such as class and ethnicity.

This book endorses the view that the state requires political sociology's concerted attention. This approach stands in opposition to behaviouralism, which, as we have seen, plays down the role of the state as an institution qualitatively different from other political actors. However, in moving our focus away from the behaviour of actors in civil society, we must ensure that we do not move too far in the opposite direction and end up with a state reductionist argument where civil society is perceived as either totally subservient to the state's power, or the two concepts are seen as unrelated or polarised. This book argues that the most appropriate focus for political sociology is the state–civil society relationship. From this perspective, the state is seen as the primary site of power and civil society is defined as encompassing those institutions and associations, including the media, economic organisations, political parties and social movements, which are not clearly part of the state apparatus and are themselves crucial alternative sites of power. The state and civil society coexist in a relationship that is both dynamic and inherently tense.

We can then reject Parsons's view that political sociology is a post-war phenomenon; rather this book is closer to the view of Horowitz (1972: 4) who contends that 'political sociology as quasi-formal enterprise begins in the eighteenth century' when 'the dialogue between society and state was begun in earnest'. While agreeing on the importance of a distinction between state and civil society as paramount to political sociology, we might wish to dispute the timescale suggested by Horowitz. Classical seventeenth-century political theorists such as John Locke (1924), (although he uses the words 'political' and 'civil' interchangeably) were also implicitly theorising an embryonic state–civil society divide where the state and civil society had their own sphere of activity, with the state being ultimately answerable to civil society that could overthrow its rule if it was seen to be pursuing interests that diverged from its own. However, the most important contribution to political sociology's understanding of the state–civil society divide was made in the early nineteenth century when Hegel articulated a truly modern understanding of the state-civil society divide.

Hegel's discussion of the state–civil society divide in his *Philosophy of Right* (1942) was central to the development of political sociology because it sparked an extremely innovative reply by Karl Marx (1994), the figure most deserving of the label the 'founder of political sociology'.

For Hegel, the relationships between individuals can be understood as operating in three main spheres: the family, civil society and the state. Each of these is seen as a stage in an evolutionary development towards freedom, which Hegel considers to be the opportunity to participate in what he calls 'ethical life'. The first two stages, the family and civil society, are characterised primarily as areas for the advance-ment of self-interest: civil society 'affords a spectacle of extravagance and want as well as of the physical and ethical degeneration of them both' (Hegel, 1942: 123). In contrast, the state 'is the actuality of the ethical ideal', and represents the highest form of human community (Hegel, 1942: 155). However, Hegel comments, 'it may seem hard that the totality of ethical life relinquishes a part of its individuals to the limitations of family life or to the need of civil life. On the one hand that is necessity; on the other [there is] reconciliation in that necessity' (Hegel, cited in Ilting, 1984: 97). Curiously then, Hegel accepts the existence of civil society, despite its clear moral inferiority to the state, because 'a state which will be all-encompassing . . . will be an empty structure' (Avineri, 1972: 167). With this, the paradoxical state–civil society relationship is born. The reconciliation between the two spheres, Hegel suggests, is achieved through the efforts of civil servants who work in the bureaucracy of the state. Although civil servants form a distinct class within civil society, their collective interests are not class interests, but rather they work for the common good: they are the 'universal class'. Moreover, membership of this universal class is open to all members of civil society on a competitive basis, so that the bureaucracy is not socially closed and can therefore truly represent the common interest.

Marx, whilst accepting the analytical usefulness of the state–civil society divide, finds Hegel's argument that the state can reconcile the conflicts of civil society absurd. For Marx, the very existence of the state presupposes social division and indeed has its origins in the develop-ment of private property and social class. Rather than reconciling these conflicts in the universal interest, the state reflects and reinforces economic and social inequality in civil society. Thus for Marx the state can never represent the highest form of ethical life, but instead is a coercive organisation that has, as its main purpose, the maintenance of class divisions. We shall deal with Marx's perspective on the state in more detail in the next chapter. At this stage, it is sufficient to note the very modern concerns raised by Marx's interrogation of Hegel's conception of the state–civil society divide. Questions of the balance of power between the state and civil society, the extent to which economic interests dominate the rationale of state action, and how social divisions shape the institutions of state and civil society, are the very stuff of political sociology. To continue our enquiry, we shall now turn to defining the state in more detail.

The Problem of the State

Defining the state is a notoriously difficult task. This is due in part to the nature of its problematic relationship with civil society, and partly to its undoubted importance in political and social theory. Thus we are faced with a multitude of definitions from which to choose, each one shaped by diverse views on the appropriate functions of the state and what its relationship to society should be. However, it is nonetheless essential to shape a definition of the state if we are to proceed with any degree of conceptual clarity. Probably the best-known definition of the state is advanced by Max Weber, which offers a useful starting point for our analysis. He argues that the state is 'a human community that successfully claims the monopoly of the legitimate use of physical force within a given territory' (Weber, 1948: 78).

Several points of contention strike us about this definition. A discussion of just two issues, the problem of 'legitimate force' and the notion of 'human community', will suffice to show that Weber's apparently clear and logical definition highlights what a problematic institution the state really is. First, Weber appears closer to Marx than Hegel in his acknowledgement of the centrality of physical force to the state. For if the state is, as Hegel suggests, a rational and ethical institution, why does it rely so heavily on violence to control its citizens? Its reliance upon force suggests a denial of its ethical superiority, at least by some individuals. However, Weber's emphasis on violence is also rendered problematic when we explore the juxtaposition of 'physical force' with its 'legitimate use': if the state is legitimate, why do some citizens have to be coerced? This contradiction means that the claim to a monopoly of legitimate physical force can never be made successfully and in fact the state has often been threatened by the terrorist acts of discontented citizens. In the USA, this possibility is enshrined in the second amendment to the constitution, which states that citizens have the right to bear arms. When, in the early 1990s, President Clinton attempted to remove this right, anti-government groups defended it on the grounds that citizens needed to be armed should the coercive power of the state ever need to be opposed.

Second, we may wish to investigate the idea of the state as a 'human community'. In the case of the modern state the term nation is often added to form the term *nation-state*. In this context, the term community generally refers not merely to a group of territorially bound people, but implies that these people are united by common cultural bonds such as language, history and a shared value system. However, according to Oakeshott (1975: 188):

> A state . . . as it appeared in early modern Europe, was not, one may guess from its human composition, very promising material from which to constitute anything properly to be called a community . . . no European state (let alone an imitation European state elsewhere in the world) has ever come within measurable distance of being a 'nation-state'.

Oakeshott's observation is supported by the lack of cultural unity in most of the world's states. For instance, Britain is both multi-national and multi-cultural, including the nations of Scotland, Wales and England, as well as a multitude of culturally diverse peoples drawn mainly from Britain's former colonies. More dramatically, given the relatively peaceful coexistence of these groups in Britain, one can point to many examples in the contemporary world where the imposition of state boundaries upon nationally diverse peoples has led to conflict when, for whatever reason, the imperial power which constituted the state boundary is forced to withdraw. This has been the case throughout Africa in former European colonies such Nigeria, but has also occurred in many of the ex-communist states in Eastern Europe, such as Yugoslavia, whose communist rulers kept only a temporary lid on latent ethnic conflict, which surfaced when communism collapsed in the late 1980s and early 1990s. The terms nation and community, when used in the context of the state, normally refer only to the dominant cultural group, and therefore further highlights the way unequal structures of power in civil society are reflected in, and compounded by, the state.

If the state fails to govern legitimately, regularly resorts to violence, and exacerbates human conflict, why do we need the institution at all?

Indeed, some theorists, ranging from Marxists to libertarians, have speculated on a society free from the state. Whatever the merits of these arguments, they remind us that human beings have not always been statist creatures: the modern state is a historical phenomenon, as well as a political idea, and therefore an exploration of its origins is central to our understanding of the state.

The Origins of the State

For analytical purposes, many scholars have discussed the development of the modern state as a series of historical stages. Such an approach has its uses. However, it can also have its dangers, since it may appear to endorse evolutionary theories of political community, which understand human society as advancing gradually from 'primitive' statelessness towards the present 'civilised' stage of the liberal state. Hall and Ikenberry (1989: 22), in analysing the unique role the state played in the rise of the West, conclude that far from being the result of evolution the state is best conceptualised as a highly contingent and unlikely event: the European state was the product of 'adaptive failure' to a series of social problems which other civilisations in the world had tackled very differently.

To deny the validity of evolutionary theories is not the same thing as suggesting that modern states have not learnt from or built upon innovations found in previous types of state; rather it is to argue that state development has not been linear, and has involved a great many unpredictable actions by historical actors. Therefore, the development of the state was far from certain.

Stateless Communities

Hall and Ikenberry (1989: 16) date the appearance of the first recognisable states in Mesopotamia, often referred to as pristine states, at around 3000 BC. Although, according to other accounts, simple states were found as early as 6000 BC, even this represents only a tiny fraction of the time in which human beings have populated the planet. Given the apparent inevitability of the state asserted in much Western political theory, we can only wonder how the human race made it to the point where, given all those years of 'statelessness', some theorists could complacently assume that the state was 'in the natural order of things'! As Mann (1986: 49–70) argues, the state is in reality a very 'unnatural' development.

Human beings are social animals and despite the fact that for the greater part of human history people lived without states they did not live without rules or indeed without certain forms of coercion based upon non-violent social pressure. Indeed, one way to approach the development of the state is to see it as only one of many attempts to solve two fundamental and inevitable human dilemmas: the problem of social order, and the management and distribution of material and cultural resources. There is much debate concerning whether stateless societies had governments in anything like the modern sense of the word and some have denied that we can even apply the word politics to such 'simple' communities (Raphael, 1990: 32). However, to avoid using the conventional word government, with all its statist connotations, the word *governance* may usefully be employed here to refer to the management of the two perennial political problems identified above, which are common to all human societies whether they possess a state or not.

Anthropological studies of stateless societies that still exist today (though these are growing smaller in number as most have been coerced into becoming part of the states that surround them) have provided us with a large amount of detail on the way these societies are governed. These studies provide valuable insight into the likely methods of maintaining order in the years before the first states appeared. Some stateless communities have systems of authority based upon age, gender or ancestral lineage, whereby order is maintained in part by the recognition of this authority by other members of the community. Alternatively (and more often additionally) clashes of interest between individuals and groups are resolved through the application of well-established methods that each member is made well aware of through kinship and community instruction. Mair's (1962) extensive study of what she terms 'minimal government' in stateless societies gives many examples of the complex and varied ways in which disputes in such communities are resolved. For instance, writing in 1962, she describes how the Anuak people of Africa dealt with violent disputes:

In an Anuak village [disputes] are talked out in the presence of the headman and elders, and the nearest approach to a verdict is the consensus of opinion reached in this public discussion. A headman is entitled to formal respect, and this imposes a certain order upon the proceedings. The idea that revenge for killing could be pursued within the limits of so small a community as an Anuak village is as unthinkable there as anywhere else, but the Anuak way of preventing this is for the killer and his kin to leave the village till the anger of his victims has had time to cool. (Mair, 1962: 49)

Communities such as the Anuak maintained a relatively high degree of social order through a variety of often ingenious methods that were rarely based on large inequalities of status or, indeed, wealth. In stateless societies, those leaders who did enjoy enhanced status did so because they redistributed rather than accumulated wealth (Harris, 1993: 312). Sahlins, in his book *Stone Age Economics*, shows how many stateless peoples remained unstratified and materially egalitarian. Indeed Sahlins (1988: 36) argues that 'the amount of hunger increases relatively and absolutely with the evolution of culture'. Given the success of these stateless communities in maintaining social order and distributing resources, the following question is raised: why did the stateless societies of the past become transformed into states?

The Coming of the State

One of the most common explanations for the origins of the state is that violent conflict between stateless communities led to the subordination of one people by another. De Jasay (1985: 15) puts this view succinctly when he writes that 'states generally start with somebody's defeat'. Oppenheim (1975) offers one of the best known of these 'conquest' theories of state formation. Essentially an anti-state libertarian, Oppenheim is unimpressed with the state's ability to provide for the needs of its members. He sees the inherently warlike nature of states as undermining the peaceful activities of economic exchange. Indeed, for Oppenheim (1975: 27), the pivotal moment in the creation of the first states occurred when 'the conqueror spared his victim in order permanently to exploit him in productive work'. It was this initial act of what might be described as administered exploitation, that 'gave birth to nation and state'.

Other mono-causal theories of the emergence of the state have been advanced, but as Mann (1986: 50) remarks, 'single-factor explanations belong to the kindergarten stage of state theory'. Alternatively, Mann describes how the state can be accounted for through processes of 'social caging'. This idea refers to the restrictions gradually placed on individuals' freedom, who in the past had been able to move away from any centralising processes without suffering significant economic loss. However, it was with the development of alluvial agriculture (as a response to population growth), and particularly the artificial irrigation of agriculture in environmentally enclosed river-valley societies, which encouraged social caging and which led to the development of Mesopotamian civilisation.

In order to co-ordinate the production, funding and defence of the necessary resources, large-scale mechanical irrigation required a much greater level of social organisation than had been the case in previous societies. The opportunity created by artificial irrigation for more intense farming of long-lasting crops, such as rice and wheat, also meant increased storage requirements. Consequently these administrative tasks were 'gradually taken over by a political-religious-military hierarchy, which formed the nucleus of the first state bureaucracies' (Harris, 1993: 165). As Mann (1986: 124) notes, the economic surplus produced by more sophisticated agricultural methods led to economic inequality, which, when combined with the concentration of military power, created stratified societies that meant that the state's 'population was caged into particular authority relations'.

The building up of state power gathered its own momentum as its economic and military advantages became clear. The first states' influence spread because they were more easily able to organise trade and to win military victories than were their stateless neighbours. Also, the population (and therefore the resources) of these states increased because of the circumscription of individuals: people in close proximity to the state were increasingly pulled into the orbit of its power because of environmental factors (such as lack of alternative fertile land), the economic advantages of living within the state, and the development of secondary states which copied the obvious advantages of the pristine states, and which therefore restricted the opportunities for emigration to other regions.

As the state's power expanded, it increasingly fostered a sense of collective identity. This process was reinforced by religious ideology that underpinned the state machine with mystical justification. Huge religious temples, subsidised by the state, dominated the skyline and symbolised military and economic, as well as religious, power. Harris (1993: 317–18) gives a gruesome example of religion's input into one state's sense of internal identity when he describes how the Aztec's religious leaders 'prized out the beating hearts of the state's prisoners of war on top of Tenochtitcan's pyramids'.

The continuation of the state in one form or another throughout subsequent human history can be explained by its unprecedented military capacity: there has simply never been a more effective war machine. As Harris (1993: 313) writes, 'once states come into existence, they tend to spread, engulf, and overwhelm non-state peoples'. In relation to their own respective societies, states were also increasingly able to use their ability to centralise economic, communicative and, above all, military power to pacify their populations. After the first states had survived their uncertain infancy, their importance to human life grew to the point where they 'became permanently useful to social life and to dominant groups, in a way that departed from the patterns of prehistory. Possession of the state became an exploitative power resource, as it had not been hitherto' (Mann, 1986: 124).

Characteristics of the Modern State: Continuities and Innovations

What is revealing about our appraisal of the origins of the state is that many of the processes we associate with its modern form were present, all be it in embryo, in earlier states. Although, as Mann (1986: 102) reminds us, early states were 'diffuse, segmentary, [and] of uncertain boundaries', we can see within them the essence of the state, as a particular way of tackling the perennial problem of governance. All states in history have maintained defences and mounted military campaigns; all states have collected taxes and have tried to create the necessary framework for the production of economic surplus (in part to meet tax requirements); and all states, because they concentrate economic, military and communicative power, have been socially stratified and therefore class based. The state has, of course, taken many forms in the long period between the formation of pristine states and the rise of the modern state, and these different state forms have organised these basic characteristics in extremely diverse ways. Nonetheless, the stability of any state can be determined by how successfully it has institutionalised mechanisms of control over the economy, the military, and its subjects. While not denying the occurrence of institutional innovations (particularly in the modern state), differences between different types of state often involve questions of degree rather than of kind. Moreover, the ability of states to fulfil their functions often rests on factors outside their direct control. These include cultural, technological and economic limitations. For instance, the effectiveness of rule in the feudal era was restricted because communication between ruler and ruled was poor due to 'widespread illiteracy and the decay and insecurity of the road system' (Poggi, 1990: 37).

It is useful to our analysis of the state to understand its development in terms of a certain continuity of function, particularly in regard to the management of resources and the maintenance of social order. However, as political sociologists, whose main focus is upon the modern state's unique relationship to civil society, we need now to consider the main institutional innovations that have made the modern state the most important political actor in the contemporary world, bar none. In exploring the form of the modern state in this section I will avoid describing in any detail those types of the state that preceded it. Rather I will sketch out the main features of the modern state, and where appropriate make comparison with earlier examples only where this aids our understanding of the contemporary state. In discussing the characteristics of the state, it is important to remember the difficulties we encountered earlier when we explored Weber's famous definition. In particular, we cannot successfully analyse the state without considering temporal, spatial and social factors.

1. First, the state is, as we have seen, a historical agent: its form changes through time.
2. Second, the state does not stand in isolation: it exists in relation to other states, and is in this sense a geo-political phenomenon.
3. Third, the state is locked into an interdependent relationship with civil society: that is states are socially structured.

These contexts mean that not only do individual states adapt their internal structures over time, often as a result of conflict or co-operation with other states, but also that there is considerable variety between states in the modern world. For example, as Haynes writes (1996: 20), the state in many African countries is 'qualitatively different from those created in an earlier epoch in Europe'. There are also clear differences between liberal states and authoritarian states, such as China, where state power is monopolised by a single political party and the institutions of civil society are very weak.

The factors outlined above act upon states' structures as both constraints and catalysts to change, and this means that a static definition of the state is highly problematic. As Hay (1996: 8) comments, they demand that we treat 'the essential dynamism and complexity of the state as integral to its very nature'. However, many discussions of the state have often overlooked one or other of these constraints. For example, Mann (1988: viii) complains that 'most political scientists and political sociologists until recently studied politics as an exclusively domestic discipline, conducted without reference to geo-political relations between states'. With these qualifications in mind, we can begin to explore some of the key characteristics of the liberal state as an 'ideal type'.

Impersonal Rule

In the modern liberal state the authority of its agents, such as civil servants, derives not from their individual attributes, but from the rule of law, normally based upon a constitution that constrains the power of any single position of office or state body. The creation of this rational-legal framework of power broke with the traditions of absolutist states where power was to a large extent personalised in the form of the monarchy, enshrined in the doctrine of the 'divine right of kings' (Weber, 1947: 318). For example, the French absolutist monarch Louis

XV claimed in 1766 that 'in my person alone resides the sovereign power . . . The rights and interests of the nation . . . are necessarily united with my own and can only rest in my hands' (Poggi, 1990: 46). In contrast, the modern state's power is claimed as impersonal, legitimate authority.

Legitimate Authority

Legitimacy in the liberal state entails the recognition of state authority by its people. Unlike previous forms of the state, individuals are citizens as well as subjects. Citizenship is a membership status that denotes reciprocal rights between the citizen and the state. The state receives tax revenues from its citizens and may call upon them to defend the state and to perform other duties, such as jury service. Citizens normally expect, as a minimum entitlement, the guarantee of basic civil rights, such as freedom of speech and worship, and normally possess political rights that give them the opportunity to change, through regular competitive elections, the members of the government, which is differentiated from the state as a whole. The government formulates state policy, and is made responsible to the people through the democratic notion that sovereignty resides with the citizens it governs.

Sovereignty

This concept captures the universal and compulsory nature of the state's authority that makes it unique amongst human associations. The state recognises no equal power within its defined territorial boundaries and all those individuals who live within these borders are obliged to obey its laws. If they do not, they are subject to the coercive force of the state machine. The state also claims autonomy from other states that exist in the states system and, following the Treaty of Westphalia in 1648, which ended decades of war in Europe, sovereignty has formed the basis of international law. Many scholars identify this concept as developing first in the sixteenth and seventeenth centuries. However, it can be argued that logically all states have endeavoured to centralise their power: what was missing in earlier states was not the will but the lack of the necessary mechanisms of surveillance to effectively extend political control over their populations. For this reason Giddens (1985: 4) has argued that 'traditional states have frontiers, not borders'. What is clear is that it is the modern state that has been most successful in claiming sovereignty.

Violence

The state asserts the right to inflict violence upon its citizens. This is claimed as a rational necessity to maintain social order, and exists within the context of the rule of law from which no individual is exempt. Previous forms of the state lacked the necessary level of sovereignty to centralise force effectively, often relying on other centres of power, such as nobles, to redress grievances in their individual domains. This characteristic of the liberal state sits uneasily alongside the notion of legitimate authority. Citizens in the liberal state are in the contradictory position of supposedly being the creators of state authority while simultaneously living under the threat of its coercive power.

Integration and Exclusion

Citizenship in the liberal state is both inclusive and exclusive: it defines those who belong to the state and those who do not. Since the French revolution of 1789, citizenship has been closely linked with nationalism, which, although arguably originating well before the development of the modern state, finds its greatest expression in the modern era. As we have noted, the cultural concept of nation does not always coincide with the drawing of legalistic state boundaries and in reality states are often multi-national. However, states have been keen to engender a sense of nationhood amongst their often diverse populations because of the integrative advantages it brings, particularly in times of crisis such as war.

Differentiation

There is a high degree of internal differentiation within the liberal state. Many of its functions are divided into distinct bodies: its welfare system is separate from its court system, which has autonomy from the police, and so on. However, in order for the state to function effectively, these separate organs are co-ordinated by the state's bureaucracy, overseen and directed by the elected government. The term differentiation also refers to the state–civil society divide. In this regard, an important prerequisite for the development of sovereignty claimed by the modern state was the separation of state from church, with the European Reformation in the early modern period being crucial in this. The relatively secular nature of the modern state can be contrasted with the feudal state, where its power was diluted by the presence of the powerful Catholic Church whose claims to absolute religious authority overlapped the state's authority in many areas of social life (Poggi, 1990: 38).

State–Civil Society Distinction

The concept of civil society has had several meanings throughout history. In the seventeenth century, Hobbes and Locke contrasted civil society, which was constituted through a contract between individuals consenting to the formation of a protective state, with a state of nature that was stateless and insecure. In the eighteenth century, Adam Ferguson adapted the term to differentiate between 'civilised' European societies and non-European, despotic regimes. By the nineteenth century, Hegel and Marx were using the concept more precisely to refer to the separation of the state from private institutions (including the economy and voluntary groups), which they argued was unique to the modern state. For liberal thinkers, a clear divide between civil society and the state guaranteed the protection of the universal rights of life, liberty and property. Thus the maintenance of order was no longer enough; the state had to rule in the interests of justice, the nature of which was becoming increasingly defined not by a narrow group of political leaders but by the people as a whole through the growth of democracy. However, for Marx (as for Hegel) civil society is characterised by private property and material inequality because it is shaped by the class struggle inherent to the capitalist mode of production, which developed alongside the liberal state.

Because of the difficulties of conceptualising the relationship between the economy and civil society, and in their desire to see civil society as a 'sphere of (potential) social autonomy' (Axtmann, 1996: 77), some recent theories of civil society have further adapted the concept to exclude the economy altogether (Cohen and Arato, 1992), or have conceived of civil society as being a uniquely harmonious sphere of action, existing as 'the space of *uncoerced* human associations and also the set of relational networks . . . that fill this space' (Walzer, 1992: 89, emphasis added). These arguments are, however, unconvincing, given the coercive power of the economy to pervade, influence and structure civil society. The definition of civil society adopted in this book therefore includes powerful actors such as private corporations and economic interest groups.

Conclusion

This chapter has sought to establish the dynamic power relationship between the state and civil society as the main focal point of political sociology, the systematic analysis of which is rooted in the nineteenth century, when Hegel and Marx first theorised a clear distinction between state and civil society and highlighted their inherently contradictory relationship.

Behaviouralism, which has been prominent in political sociology since the 1940s, has been criticised for its superficial approach to power and its neglect of the state. A more sophisticated theory of power centred upon the state has been advanced in this chapter, and an account of the nature and origins of the state outlined. It has been stressed that the state is a historical rather than an inevitable phenomenon, and represents only one possible approach to the inherent problem of human governance.

It is with the development of the modern state, with its clear division between state and civil society, that the contradictions of the state are most apparent. The liberal state's claim to defend 'universal' rights is absurd in view of the inequalities of civil society, which liberals insist must be clearly separated from the state. The question of how power is distributed between the modern state and civil society is therefore a primary question in political sociology. How this question has been addressed by what I shall call the classical theories of political sociology is the subject of the next chapter.

2

Classical Theories of the State and Civil Society

The state's relationship with civil society was identified in Chapter 1 as the key issue in political sociology. This chapter explores how the three most important theoretical positions of political sociology have analysed this relationship. Marxism, elite theory and pluralism have developed through a dialogue with liberalism, so this chapter therefore begins with a brief overview of the liberal perspective on the state–civil society relationship.

For liberals, the state is a necessary evil that serves civil society, and which is accountable to citizens through political representation. The state's functions are primarily to maintain internal social order and to protect civil society from external threats to its security. The state is often portrayed by liberals as a neutral arbiter between conflicting interests. It is not dominated by any section of society, but instead pursues policies that maximise individual liberty.

Although some liberals allow for a more developed state role in such areas as welfare provision, all liberals prioritise a clear separation between state and civil society. This is contrasted with totalitarian regimes, such as Nazi Germany or the USSR, where the division between state and civil society is dissolved and the state, representing a sectional interest, suppresses alternative sites of power.

In liberal societies, it is argued, the state is a site of formal equality between all citizens. Civil society, in contrast, is characterised by freedom, social diversity and competition in the market place, which results in material inequalities. Such competition, it is contended, promotes general prosperity through the encouragement of individual innovation. This benefits the whole of society by improving the general performance of the economy. Within civil society individuals are free to pursue their own desires, as long as this does not encroach upon the liberty of others. Liberals argue for equality of opportunity and meritocracy, and liberalism is an agency-based theory in that levels of economic success are seen as proportionate to the level of an individual's effort.

This chapter will analyse in turn the Marxist, elitist and pluralist alternatives to this liberal model. In order to map a path through the vast bodies of literature produced by the exponents of these positions, our discussion will be loosely structured around the following five questions, all of which are concerned with aspects of the relationship between state and civil society.

1. Is civil society best defined by value consensus or social conflict?
2. What is the role of the state in generating consensus or reconciling conflict in civil society?
3. Is the state autonomous from or dependent upon civil society?
4. Who controls the state, and in whose interest does the state rule?
5. How can we account for changes in the relationship between the state and civil society historically, and for the many variations in the relationship in different countries?

The final section of the chapter concludes that each of these perspectives, although of continuing influence in political sociology, fails to analyse satisfactorily the autonomous power of the state. Consequently they all present under-theorised accounts of the state's relationship with civil society.

The Marxist Challenge: The State as an Aspect of Class Rule

Marxism is a society-centred theory. It has therefore concentrated upon how the inequalities of civil society shape the imperatives of the state. The development of industrial capitalism, rather than the behaviour of states, is identified as the main driving force behind social change. Individuals' political actions are understood in terms of their relationship to the capitalist mode of production, as members of a social class, rather than as citizens of the state. Since capitalism is an exploitative system, which results in vast inequalities of power, some stand to gain and some to lose. Therefore, capitalist societies are necessarily divided and defined by class struggle. Indeed, in *The Communist Manifesto* Marx and Engels (1962: 34) go as far as to claim that 'the history of all hitherto existing society is the history of class struggles'. This assumption forms the context of Marxist state theory.

For Marx, the state is ultimately a servant of the dominant interests in civil society, however much it seems to have interests of its own, or may appear to serve the 'universal interests' of society. The particular form that the state takes historically is determined in the last analysis by the prevailing mode of production. However, Marx argues that only with the development of capitalism can civil society evolve fully. At this stage of history, the discrepancies between equal citizenship of the state and the inequalities between social classes become acute. The increasing transparency of the state's contradictions ensures that class struggle between the proletariat and the bourgeoisie is inevitable. When this is resolved in the interests of the proletariat the state will become redundant and civil society transcended. This is because the state is explained in class terms. The ruling class, who control the means of production, use the state as an instrument to suppress the working class. Once class disappears under communism, so must the state. In a post-capitalist world, the divisions of civil society are replaced by a collectivist, communist society where property will be owned by the community and all individuals will be equally empowered.

Marxism highlights important tensions in the state's relationship to civil society, which stand in stark contrast to the optimistic view of liberals. All Marxists point to how the structures of power within civil society, based on class divisions rooted in property ownership, prevent the development of the creative potential of all human beings. These inequalities render any formal equality individuals have as citizens impotent, since such political equality is divorced from people's everyday needs. Marxists reject the abstract individualism of liberalism and instead understand human behaviour in its societal context, whereby people's actions are shaped, if not determined, by their place in the economic system. The state cannot but reflect these class divisions: it must either promote them or attempt to reconcile them in the interests of the long-term continuation of capitalism.

There is undoubted insight in the idea that the state cannot be divorced from the class divisions of civil society, and that economic considerations are central to a successful state. But these insights could be accepted without embracing a Marxist framework. However, it has been the task of Marxist state theory to flesh out the detail of the state's relationship with civil society in a way that is consistent with Marx's own holistic theory of human history, which is seen as following an inevitable path towards a stateless society, and which is driven along that path by class conflict. To continue the travelling metaphor, Marxists face the problem that Marx failed to identify, where exactly the institution of the state lies on the conceptual map that leads to communism!

Because of his relative neglect of the state, Marx left a distinctly confused legacy to his many followers. At least two separate theories of the state are normally identified in Marx's writings (Held, 1996: 129). The first of these, which can be found in its clearest form in *The Communist Manifesto*, defines the state as an instrument that is controlled directly by the ruling class to coerce the propertyless class: 'the executive of the modern state is but a committee for managing the affairs of the whole bourgeoisie' (Marx and Engels, 1962: 43–4). This theory has had considerable influence on revolutionaries who have sought to overthrow capitalism. Thus for Lenin, the leader of the Russian Revolution in 1917, the struggle for the control of the state became a goal for which communists should strive. The state's concentration of military power could, in the hands of the representatives of the proletariat, be used to eradicate the remnants of bourgeois society. This entailed first capturing and then 'smashing' the capitalist state and constructing a socialist state in its place.

Lenin, and then Stalin, extended Marx and Engels's phrase, 'the dictatorship of the proletariat' into a dubious rationale for the increasingly centralised state that emerged in Russia after the revolution of 1917. Lenin (1965: 41) argues for the need to substitute one form of partial democracy for another, so that in the aftermath of revolution 'the state must inevitably be a state that is democratic *in a new way* (for the proletariat and the propertyless in general) and dictatorial *in a new way* (against the bourgeoisie)'.

The second theory of the state identified in Marx's work is to be found in his historical writings on France. In *The Eighteenth Brumaire*, in which Marx examines the reign of Louis Napoleon in the middle of the nineteenth century, the state is seen as having an altogether more complicated relationship to civil society:

> Under the absolute monarchy, during the first revolution, under Napoleon, bureaucracy was only the means of preparing the class rule of the bourgeoisie. Under the restoration, under Louis Philippe, under the parliamentary republic, it was the instrument of class rule, however much it strove for power of its own. Only under the second Bonaparte does the state seem to have made itself completely independent. (Marx and Engels, 1962: 333)

This short passage highlights the difficulties in identifying a consistent theory of the state in Marx's work. In the three historical cases Marx cites we have three different interpretations of the role of the state, each of which has been developed by subsequent Marxists. First, Marx refers to the seemingly political motives of Napoleon Bonaparte in his building up of the power of the French state as in fact being in the long-term interests of the bourgeoisie. This is essentially a functionalist and deterministic theory, where the state is seen as acting as a mere agent for the development of capitalism. A version of this position was taken up by writers such as Poulantzas (1978).

Second, under Louis Philippe, the state appears as a direct instrument of the capitalist class and this interpretation is consistent with the theory outlined in *The Communist Manifesto* and developed by theorists such as Miliband (1968). Finally, Marx appears to allow for the possibility that under certain circumstances the state can have complete independence from the capitalist class. Marx shies away from this bold statement of state autonomy a few sentences later when he writes that 'state power is not suspended in mid air. Bonaparte represents a class, and the most numerous class of French society at that, the small-holding peasants' (Marx and Engels, 1962: 333). However, writers such as Jessop (1990) have given serious consideration to the ability of the state to act autonomously, in ways that cannot be reduced to economic imperatives (see Chapter 9). It is Marx's lack of clarity concerning the state that has spawned a huge and often impenetrable literature that arguably makes little headway in making clear the relationship between state and civil society.

As Carnoy (1984: 3–9) observes, the post-war period has seen a growing interest in the state by Marxists. First, this is owing to the huge growth in the state's functions and capacities in capitalist societies. Second, Marxists sought to correct the alleged distortion of Marx's writings by communist parties which had come to power in Eastern Europe and China and whose rule rested upon a highly coercive and centralised state machine. Much of the most interesting discussion by Marxists concerning the state has been inspired by the work of the Italian communist Gramsci (1971). This is because Gramsci's emphasis upon the state as an important site of political struggle appears to allow for a high level of autonomy from the economic structure, which Marx saw as determining the form of civil society. This is attractive to Marxists who wish to avoid the accusation of economism, that is, the view that Marxism reduces all human action to meeting the requirements of the economic base on which all societies supposedly rest.

Gramsci certainly introduces some interesting conceptual variations on Marx's work. In particular, his theory of hegemony highlights the importance of ideological manipulation by the ruling class over the working class. Hegemony is a type of communicative power that refers to an ideological justification for the inequities of capitalism. This hegemony operates through such institutions as the media, the church and political parties. However, although capitalist hegemony pervades both the state and civil society, it is never complete, thereby allowing for the construction of an alternative hegemony.

Thus Gramsci sees the use of communicative power, as well as material class struggles, as being central to the overthrow of capitalism. Hence he stresses the role of intellectuals in constructing an alternative egalitarian 'hegemonic project' to the dominant ideology of capitalism, with its emphasis upon selfish exploitation of the many by the few. This points to the possibility of a political transition to communism in which the mechanisms of liberal democracy are utilised by the working class to transform and eventually transcend the state. Gramsci refers to this type of strategy as a 'war of position', which he contrasts with a 'war of manoeuvre' that emphasises a violent assault upon capitalism (Gramsci, 1971: 238–9). In Gramsci's theory, the state is not an object to be captured, but is itself an arena for struggle (Thomas, 1994: 143). There are several problems with Gramsci's position, however, which highlight more fundamental dilemmas at the heart of Marxism.

First, Gramsci is inconsistent in his definitions of the state and civil society. At times they are identical, on other occasions they are opposed, and in some passages the state is seen to encompass civil society, being distinct from civil society only through its monopoly of physical force (Gramsci, 1971). Second, while allowing room for a more subtle consideration of the relationship between politics and economics, ultimately Gramsci accepts that economic factors are primary in determining political outcomes. This raises the question of whether economism, however carefully it is worded, is essential to all Marxist accounts of the state and civil society relationship. Recent Marxists have attempted to resolve this question. The work of Poulantzas provides the best example.

Poulantzas (1978) takes Gramsci's notion of the state as a site for strategic class struggle and extends this into a general theory of the relative autonomy of the state from civil society. Writing in the context of a hugely increased role for the state in managing the tensions of capitalism, Poulantzas attempts to show how the state's apparent separateness from the direct control of capitalists is functional to the needs of capitalism. For Poulantzas, the imperatives of capitalism exercise an indirect control over the state. The actual class position of the personnel of the state is therefore relatively unimportant. This is due to the fact that the state is dependent upon economic growth for its survival. The state therefore plays a central role in naturalising the inequalities of capitalism as inevitable and desirable. People's needs are portrayed by the organs of state as being identical to the needs of capitalism. The capitalist state takes many forms, such as fascist or social democratic, and this form is dependent upon numerous political and social factors. However, because of the structural constraints of capitalism, the state is always led back to its primary function of maintaining the conditions for capitalist accumulation. These include maintaining social stability, providing infrastructural support, and sustaining an appropriate labour market.

Poulantzas attracts the legitimate criticism that his theory is deterministic and functionalist. The state is merely an institution that is functional for capitalism in its role as the reconciler of class conflict. For this reason a fellow Marxist, Miliband, has accused Poulantzas of a kind of 'structural super-determinism' in which the agency of individuals is rendered irrelevant (Miliband, 1970: 57). If this is the case, Miliband argues, it is difficult to claim there is any real difference between a fascist and social democratic state. The superficiality of such an analysis illustrates, for Miliband, the falsity of Poulantzas's position. It is therefore doubtful how much of a real advance Poulantzas makes on Marx's second theory of the state.

Marx, like Poulantzas, allows for the fact that the capitalist class may at times give up its hold on political power so as to preserve its ability to accumulate wealth: 'that in order to save its purse it must forfeit its crown, and the sword that is to safeguard it must at the same time be hung over its head like the sword of Damocles' (Marx and Engels, 1962: 288). The contradictions that run through the whole of Marx's writings on the state, and which Poulantzas's more extensive treatment only serves to highlight, are well illustrated in this quotation. The first part of the quotation suggests that capitalist accumulation will occur whoever governs the state, the second part suggests that the controllers of the state have at least the potential to use the coercive power of the state against bourgeois interests. This problem is expressed also in Poulantzas's contradictory argument that on one hand the state is structured by the needs of capitalism, but on the other hand the state is itself a site for class struggle. The problem for Poulantzas, as for Marx, is in explaining how these two mutually exclusive points can be reconciled in a convincing theory of the transition to communism (Carnoy, 1984: 107).

Marx's ambiguity concerning the role of the state, and his failure to generate a convincing theory of transition to communism, led Lenin to perceive the state as an object to be captured by the Bolshevik party who would then brandish the 'sword of Damocles' in the interests of the working class. Despite Marx's warning that the 'working class cannot simply lay hold of the ready-made state machinery and wield it for it own purposes' (Marx and Engels, 1962: 516), Lenin's interpretation of the state is not unconnected to Marx's own theories. Although at least two versions of the role of the state can be identified in Marx's writings, these are not distinct positions and often overlap. This allows for the plausible interpretation that not only can the state serve to maintain capitalism, but also it can be used, in certain circumstances, as a means to transcend capitalism.

These theoretical problems are in no small measure due to the failure amongst Marxists to identify the state as an actor in its own right, with resources and imperatives of its own, which cannot be reduced to economic factors. This is not to deny the interdependent relationship the state must necessarily have with civil society, but it is to give more attention to questions such as the potential for the state to be as repressive as economic inequality. Nor can this repressive potential of the state be understood purely in class terms. That is to say, the state is not an oppressive organ of one class, but is an oppressive organ *per se*. This is a point made forcefully by feminist critics and theorists of ethnicity who argue that the state plays an important role in both reflecting and promoting inequalities in civil society between men and women and between different ethnic groups.

The result of the paradoxes of Marxist state theory has been frighteningly illustrated by the repressive use of the state in China and the Soviet Union. If one accepts the essential unity of theory and practice, expressed in the Marxist notion of 'praxis', then Marxist theory must be critically re-evaluated in the light of the historical experience of actual communist regimes. This is not to dispute the power of the Marxist critique of the idealised liberal model outlined at the start of this chapter, but it does require us to question the utility of any theory that reduces the practice of politics to economic factors. Without a developed theory of governance, distinct from his critique of capitalism, Marx laid the seeds for highly repressive states in which a key aim was an end to politics, which is implicitly understood by Marx (particularly in his later work) to be relevant only to class-based societies. The problems of governance would not wither away, even in the stateless society desired by Marx. Nor indeed did they in the authoritarian states that claimed legitimacy from Marx's writings.

Elite Theory: The State as an Aspect of Elite Rule

It is precisely the threat of authoritarian socialism that leads elite theorists to strongly reject both Marxist and liberal prescriptions for the state–civil society relationship. Intrinsic to both theories, according to elite theorists, is a threatening egalitarian logic that flies in the face of historical reality. Mosca (cited in Albertoni, 1987: 12), one of the key elite theorists, describes this 'reality' in the following way:

Those who hold and exercise State power are always a minority, and that below them lies a numerous class of people who never participate in *real terms* in government and are subject to the will of the former; we may call them the ruled.

This captures the essence of the elitist position. Michels goes even further than Mosca in describing the inevitability of elite rule as the 'iron law of oligarchy'. Democracy is paradoxical, and therefore impossible, because democracy cannot exist without organisation, and, for Michels, 'who says organisation says oligarchy' (Michels, 1962: 364).

The question of who governs is a simple one to answer: the state is controlled by those individuals who possess a disproportionate amount of the resources necessary to the process of rule. The two key classical elite theorists, Mosca and Pareto, differ in their view of which resources elites utilise, but both are agreed that the state and civil society are characterised by an inevitable division of power between elites and the masses.

It is because of the inevitability of elite rule that Mosca and Pareto dismiss the notion of popular sovereignty. Mosca contends that even the apparent democratic practice of elections is manipulated by elites: 'those who have the will and, especially, the moral, intellectual and material means to force their will upon others take the lead over the others and command them' (Mosca, 1939: 154).

Although Mosca and Pareto share a low opinion of the masses, they differ on their view of the basis for elite rule. Mosca (1939: 450) denies that the elites are necessarily morally or even intellectually superior, and sees organisational skill as the key to elite rule. Pareto is more militant concerning the superiority of the elite in terms of the psychological and personal attributes suitable for government. He speaks of the political elite in terms of their physical and mental strength. Tellingly, for Pareto, an elite becomes vulnerable to being overthrown when it becomes 'softer, milder, more humane and less able to defend its own interests' (Pareto, 1968: 59). He cites the lack of physical resistance to revolt in Ancient Rome, and by the aristocracy in France prior to the revolution of 1789, as evidence of their weakness (Pareto, 1968: 60). Pareto's theory of elite change, which he calls the circulation of elites, rests upon inevitable degeneration in the qualities of the elite. For Pareto (1966: 249), 'history is a graveyard of aristocracies'. However, the elite is always renewed by superior individuals, who emerge from the ranks of the masses through force of will.

Pareto identifies two kinds of elites: those who are superior in political astuteness and cunning (these he calls 'foxes') and those who possess high levels of courage and military leadership (the 'lions'). Throughout the history of the state, one of these elites, or various combinations of the two, govern, depending upon the needs of the time. Thus, Pareto takes a functional view of the role of elites in that while elites may change, the basic structure of society, with its distinction between elites and the masses, does not, thus maintaining social equilibrium (Bottomore, 1993a: 44).

Manipulation of the masses through the use of communicative power is a strong theme in the writings of both Pareto and Mosca. According to Pareto (1968: 27), humans, and in particular the masses, are largely irrational: 'the greater part of human actions have their origin not in logical reasoning but in sentiment'. Therefore a key element in elite rule is persuasion. Through the creation of what Pareto calls a 'living faith' elite rule is naturalised. Likewise, for Mosca, the ruling class of any state tries to legitimise its control through the creation of a 'political formula' that appears to fit the prevailing historical circumstances. For example, in the feudal period the idea of the divine right of kings lent Godly support to monarchical government. The concept of political formula has some similarities with the Marxist notion of hegemony, but differs from this concept in that it is unconnected to the economic structure of society. Mosca does not believe that political rule is founded upon economic dominance, although confusingly he does use the term ruling class when referring to the political elite. Like Pareto, Mosca is fiercely anti-socialist and indeed argues in his most famous work that 'this whole work is a refutation' of socialism (Mosca, 1939: 447). However, he does acknowledge the importance of the Marxist notion of class struggle and points to the dangers of isolating the masses from the exercise of power whereby a new ruling class 'antagonistic to the class that holds possession of the legal government' may emerge and overthrow the present elite (Mosca, 1939: 116).

Despite his hostility to the extension of the franchise, Mosca did therefore concede that representative democracy may play a role in mediating the relationship between the elite and the masses. Because of this apparent acceptance of liberal institutions, Birch (1993: 185) suggests that Mosca can be classified as a liberal. However, unlike say John Stuart Mill who feared that an uneducated mass would come to govern if democracy was extended but who was nonetheless theoretically committed to democratic principles, Mosca is more interested in representation as a mechanism for social stability. In other words, representation is a particular version of his notion of a political formula. Through representation, 'certain sentiments and passions of the "common herd" come to have their influence' thus avoiding the violent overthrow of one elite by another (Mosca, 1939: 155).

In terms of the analytical questions set out at the start of this chapter, elite theory is clearly under theorised and tells us little about the state–civil society relationship. Regarding the question of conflict and consensus, both Mosca and Pareto point to the importance of each, but fail to construct a convincing theory of the relationship between them. Pareto and Mosca provide little evidence for how or why different 'political formulas' or 'living faiths' are adopted or become redundant. At what point does a ruling elite shift from a reliance on communicative power towards the use of military power?

Neither is the theory strong in its account of changes in elites. For Pareto, elites fail due to self-indulgence, but this theory ignores the importance of class struggles and revolution in explaining change. Mosca's idea of the emergence of new elites from within civil society is incompatible with his low opinion of the masses. Pareto and Mosca also fail to explain how and why a new elite can acquire the resources of power necessary to govern (Bottomore, 1993a: 26).

Elitists fail to explain the relationship between different kinds of power, and in particular the link between politics and economics is left largely unexplored. Pareto does devote some space to discussing the economic elite, which he defines as being made up of *rentiers*, who are property owners and savers, and who therefore desire economic stability, and speculators, who as entrepreneurs are constantly looking to promote and respond to economic change. However, the relationship between the members of the economic elite in civil society and the state is unclear. Pareto briefly mentions networks of 'leading minorities', but the connections between political and economic elites seem to rest in Pareto's view upon an ill-defined temperamental compatibility (for example, lions are close to the *rentiers* in their desire for stability), rather than any sense of a shared class position.

Despite its many flaws, classical elite theory reaffirms the Marxist emphasis upon sectional interest in determining the distribution of power in the state and civil society. The theory appears to offer a realistic account of existing actual power relations in that elites have undoubtedly been important players in the way in which the institutions of state and civil society have been constructed. Elites have institutionalised their influence through the state and resisted radical democratisation for reasons that cannot be reduced to economic interests alone. Elite theory also raises the challenge, which radical democrats must meet, as to whether elites can ever truly be dispensed with, and to what extent pure democratic self-determination by all individuals is both possible and desirable.

The assumptions of classical elite theory also formed the basis for the more sophisticated democratic elitism of Weber and Schumpeter. The concept of a democratic elite would appear at first sight to be an oxymoron. However, this question turns upon the definition of democracy being applied. Weber and Schumpeter accept the 'realist' approach of Mosca and see elite leadership as inevitable. In Weber's words, 'all ideas aiming at abolishing the dominance of men over men are illusory' (cited in Evans, 1995: 232). Elite rule is also desirable, as a barrier to the excesses of the ignorant masses. However, to ensure social stability, elite leadership has to be linked to the people through democratic mechanisms.

Schumpeter (1942) offers an interesting account of how democracy could be made compatible with the reality of elite rule. First, he argues that political rule is always exercised by a minority, and that in complex societies participatory democracy, where the masses play a direct and constant role in decision making, is impossible. There is no one dominant elite in liberal society, but instead there exists a 'dynamic between organised minorities', who each struggle, through non-violent means, to achieve supremacy. Second, democracy is seen, not as an end in itself, but as a method by which elites can be selected by the masses, thus ensuring an orderly circulation of elites. As an economist, Schumpeter feels that the most democratic institution in society is the market and therefore political institutions should be based on this model: just as capitalists compete for customers, politicians should compete for votes. Providing democracy is open to some input by the masses, and membership of elites is based on merit, Schumpeter argues that such a system can be a stable and successful one.

Bottomore (1993a: 90–2) and Bachrach (1967) have subjected democratic elite theory to sustained criticism. The key problem is the impoverished views of democracy held by writers like Weber and Schumpeter. Elites are deemed necessary because of the irrationality, apathy and ignorance of the masses, and democracy is perceived as little more than a cynical exercise in the legitimation of inequality. The problem with this model of elite democracy is that it is a self-fulfilling prophecy. It ignores how reliance upon elites itself deters participation and encourages apathy amongst those who perceive the struggles between elites as remote and irrelevant to their lives. This is reinforced by the fact that Schumpeter sees democratic participation as a limited affair, not applying to economic or social life. Indeed even political democracy is regarded by Schumpeter as being threatened by 'excessive participation' by the masses, such as lobbying representatives between elections. As Bachrach (1967: 100) writes, such a view understands democracy as 'implicitly dedicated to the viability of a democratic elitist system' rather than to 'the self-development of the individual'.

Such a cynical theory runs the risk of alienating the majority from the government of their own lives, and this may threaten the stability of the system. Democracy instead can be viewed more positively, as an ongoing and dynamic process (see Chapter 8). Any society that claims to be a democracy needs to be conscious of its own limits and should strive to extend participation. An example of this is the lack of participation amongst political elites by ethnic minorities and women in most countries throughout the world. In 1992, for instance, women made up only 8 per cent of the legislature in Italy, 6 per cent in France and Greece and 9 per cent in Britain (Evans, 1997: 111). Such exclusions illustrate the danger of complacency concerning the democratic reach of any system. Schumpeter's answer to this is to argue that a state may quite legitimately view a section of civil society as being 'unfit' to vote; for example, 'a race-conscious nation may associate fitness [to participate] with racial considerations' (Schumpeter, 1942: 20). Such an assumption brings us back to the central weakness of elite theory: its tendency to assume that inequalities of power are evidence of the strength, rather than weakness, of a political system. These inequalities are not reflections of the unequal distribution of those attributes suitable for government (as elitists maintain). They are due to structural inequalities such as class, 'race' and gender.

Pluralism: Liberalism Revived?

In the post-war period, political sociologists sympathetic to liberalism attempted to restate and update its central tenets. Pluralism aims to describe actual power relationships in liberal society, as well as normatively approving of the supposedly democratic nature of these relationships. Classical pluralist thinkers such as Dahl and Truman argue that both Marxism and elite theory are wrong in their assumption that the state and civil society are dominated by a minority. Instead power is spread throughout society, with no one sectional interest dominant, and with each power source being balanced by a countervailing force. For pluralists, the political process in liberal societies cannot be reduced to questions of the ownership of the means of production, as in Marxism, or to an unequal distribution of psychological characteristics, or organisational skills, as in elite theory. Neither is power cumulative, in the sense that any one set of individuals can assert their will in every situation and at any given time.

   In his famous study of the distribution of power in New Haven, Dahl (1961: 228) reaffirmed the liberal belief in human progress by arguing that there had occurred in New Haven a historical shift from 'a system of cumulative inequalities in political resources to a system of non cumulative or dispersed inequalities in political resources'. Pluralists generalised the conclusions of such studies to describe the distribution of power in civil society as a whole. Greater stress was placed upon the reality of sectional interest than in classical liberalism, reflected in pluralism's emphasis upon the formation of pressure groups and parties that institutionalise such divisions. However, the central point is that a democratic system, with a free civil society based on basic rights (as found in the USA), allows for all interests to organise politically, thereby ensuring no one group always prevails. As in liberal thought, the state is seen both as mediator between clashes of interests and a reflection, in constitutional form, of the general consensus that underpins civil society (Dahl, 1956: 132–3). Pluralism also shares with liberalism the view that civil society must be free from excessive interference from the state, which should at all times respond to the needs and demands that originate within civil society.

Dahl does not claim, however, that in a pluralist system the majority rule. Instead he uses the term 'polyarchy' to describe how in liberal democracy, 'government by *minority*' (as occurs in oligarchies) is replaced by 'government by *minorities*' (Dahl, 1956: 133, emphasis added). Schwarzmantel argues that pluralism is an attempt to resolve the tension between the values of liberalism, with its emphasis upon a limited state, and the values of democracy. The solution to this tension entails rejecting direct forms of democracy and instead 'lies through participation in a network of groups and associations' (Schwarzmantel, 1994: 48).

However, like the behaviouralist theory examined in Chapter 1, and with which pluralism shares many ideas and leading thinkers, classical pluralism is criticised for being an ideological justification for the inequalities of the capitalist system, rather than a realistic account of the relationship between the state and civil society. First, social changes in the 1960s exposed the lack of value consensus assumed by pluralists to underpin political systems like the USA. Mass social movements associated with asserting rights for blacks and women, coupled with the campaign against the Vietnam War, also highlighted the continued structural inequalities of American society (McLennan, 1984: 84). The classical pluralist framework could not account for these very visible signs of alienation from the 'democratic' process. Widespread social problems seemed to provide evidence of the exclusion from the political agenda of many issues that affected the lives of ordinary Americans. This threw doubt upon the ability of the capitalist state to be truly inclusive. If the political system was as open as pluralists argued, how could the dominance of political positions by white, middle-class males be explained?

Secondly, the pluralist account of interest group participation is criticised for underplaying the inequality of these groups, particularly in regard to the kind of economic resources necessary to the exercise of power. Business and financial interests possess the economic and institutional structures to organise themselves into influential groupings. Because of politicians' reliance upon economic growth in creating a 'feel good factor' amongst voters, they are more likely to influence policy making than are the socially excluded. Truman's (1951) notion that even such groups as the poor, who may fail to organise formally, nevertheless have to be taken into account by powerful forces within the state and civil society, because of their 'latent' capacity to organise, seems particularly unconvincing. Most of the interchanges of influence between interest groups and the state rest on a basis of mutual benefit; for example professionals, such as doctors, trade technical advice to government in return for influence over policies that impact upon them. Excluded groups lack these tradable skills and are therefore of little interest to powerful economic and political forces.

In response to such criticisms, many pluralists have, since the 1960s, reworked their ideas. Classical pluralists like Dahl have been more willing to look at structural constraints upon participation by certain groups; for example in 1991, in recognising the problem of gender inequality, he wrote, 'throughout recorded history in all parts of the globe women have been subject to domination by males' (Dahl, 1991: 114). The neo-pluralism of some of Dahl's later writings also allows for a more nuanced account of inequality between interest groups. He recognises that, in the context of a capitalist civil society, business groups will have a greater leverage on the state concerning economic issues. However, a degree of plurality is maintained in other policy areas.

Other pluralists, such as Richardson and Jordan (1979), have developed a position that is close in some respects to the democratic elitism of Schumpeter. Elite pluralists argue that liberal society is democratic because even though elites do dominate individual parties and pressure groups, and despite the fact that some elites are more powerful than others, there is no single coherent ruling class. Elites are therefore forced to compromise with other powerful groupings and to seek support from as wide a social base as possible to lend democratic weight to their interests. Elite pluralists have also placed more importance upon the state than classical pluralism. The state is seen as fragmented into various 'policy communities' through which influential interests groups can help shape policy in consultation with government and bureaucratic elites (Smith, M. 1995: 220). In such a revised form, however, pluralism is even more vulnerable to critics who advocate direct participation by all members of society as the only way to guarantee that all voices in civil society are heard. Also, like classical pluralism, elite pluralists do not place policy making into the context of the prevailing ideologies of civil society. They also fail to give sufficient consideration to the constraints that economic conditions place upon the options of policy communities, constraints that may, in times of crisis, restrict or negate the influence of less powerful groups.

Rethinking the Power of the State

The principal weakness of all three theories is their treatment of the state. Both pluralism and Marxism suffer from being society-centred theories: neither gives sufficient weight to the state as an actor in its own right. Pluralists stress the dispersal of power between multiple actors and ignore the ability of the state to assert its autonomy from civil society. Marxism emphasises the importance of economic and, to a lesser extent, communicative power in civil society. It overlooks, however, the importance of military power and the concentration of all three types of power in the state. Elite theory has been more ready to acknowledge the importance of the state, but because of its concentration upon the supposed individualised nature of elites it has seriously underplayed important issues such as the state's role as an institution of violence, its relationship to economic forces, and the interaction between states. This neglect has formed the basis of an important critique of these theories by political sociologists who urge that the state requires much more detailed theoretical attention (Mann, 1988; Skocpol, 1979). Five points can be made in support of this argument, all of which relate to the theory of power developed in Chapter 1.

1. The state is a unique institution that can 'territorially centralise' its power, thereby making it a relatively strong and coherent 'power container' in comparison to the fragmented nature of civil society. In particular, the state concentrates military power, economic and communicative power. This makes the state distinct from other human institutions and forms the basis for its autonomy (Mann, 1988).
2. The state possesses a number of resources of power, particularly those relating to its surveillance capabilities over its citizens, which gives it the capacity to penetrate and influence civil society (Giddens, 1985).
3. The state cannot be understood in isolation, but exists within a states system. In the context of mutual suspicion between states, the importance of the state's military capacity is crucial.

4. The modern state relates to its population not just as a mediator between interests, or as an economic manager, but as a symbol and defender of the 'imagined community' that forms the dominant cultural identity of any particular state–civil society relationship (Anderson, 1983). The close relationship between the state and nationalism gives the state an invaluable communicative power to unify disparate elements of civil society, particularly in times of war or during other crises that might face the state.

5. Through its coercive and centralised power, the state may act to exacerbate as well as mediate social divisions. The structures of power that pervade civil society are embodied and reflected in the state. These divisions are multifaceted and include gender, 'race' and religion, as well as class. The state has been an agent of patriarchy and ethnicity, as much as it has been an oppressor of classes (Walby, 1990).

The general point that these arguments highlight is that factors such as the maintenance of internal order or threats from beyond the state's boundaries will sometimes predominate over the sectional interests of civil society.

To understand the nature of the state–civil society relationship we are therefore required to explore the extent to which the state is able to control its population through surveillance techniques. In the late twentieth century, this is of growing relevance as the speed of innovation in computer technology allows states to gather and retain much more detailed information on any group or individual in civil society, thus potentially threatening basic civil freedoms. This suggests the need for detailed examination of the constitutional protections of privacy and accountability in any given state, if its coercive relationship to civil society is to be understood.

We also have to consider how foreign affairs impact upon the power of the state, the rights enjoyed by individuals in civil society, and processes of social change. None of the classical theories give sufficient consideration to the fluctuations in the influence of the state caused by its fortunes in geo-politics. A state that fails in war may be overthrown. For example, as Skocpol (1979) notes, the collapse of the authoritarian tsarist state in 1917 was due more to the appalling conduct of the war with Germany by Russia's military leaders than it was to class struggle. War has also impacted upon the development of citizenship, particularly through the development of political and social rights for women and workers as a result of their contribution to the war effort. This was illustrated by the development of the welfare state in Britain in the years following the Second World War.

Such considerations do not mean that we should shift from society-focused theories to purely state-centred models. Rather they suggest a need to reassess the balance between the two. As was argued in Chapter 1, the state and civil society are in an interdependent power relationship. What is required is more detailed analysis of specific historical and contemporary examples of the relationship. This does mean being more humble in our theoretical generalisations. Ideas such as the state always serves dominant economic interests or that the state can never act in the interests of class must be abandoned in favour of a more nuanced approach that focuses on specific cases. This involves treating the state and civil society as interrelated problems. For example the relationship between the modern state and the economy is a reciprocal one. The state requires a dynamic economy to maintain its legitimacy in the eyes of the members of civil society, and to maintain its competitive edge with other states, not least through the production of military hardware. The economy requires the state to provide a framework of laws to maintain social cohesion and protect property. The state also provides infrastructural support, such as transport, training and education, to facilitate market exchanges.

However, both the state and capitalism are prone to crisis. Any individual state exists in tension with other states: one state's security is another's insecurity. Consequently, diplomatic relations may break down and states plunged into war. The result of this might be a regime's demise, as happened in Russia in 1917. Alternatively, a state's relative power may be increased, as in the case of the USA after the First World War. Capitalism, like the states system, is also inherently unstable, being prone to periods of economic boom and slump. History has shown how states have often adapted their relationship to the economy according to these shifts in economic fortunes. So, for example, in the 1880s, when Britain experienced relative economic decline, the state increased its interventionary role in the economy in an attempt to reverse this decline (Hall and Schwarz, 1985). The central argument being made here is that both political and economic change can significantly alter the relationship between the state and civil society. This point highlights the need to make the dynamic power relationship between the state and civil society the focus of political sociology, and to explore the impact of social change upon this relationship.

Conclusion

The classical theories of the state–civil relationship explored in this chapter have laid the foundations for contemporary political sociology, and their insights therefore remain worthy of our continued attention. Indeed, in Part IV of this book, we shall see how Marxism and pluralism, in particular, have influenced recent attempts by political sociologists to rethink the problem of governance. Nonetheless, it has been argued in this chapter that each of these classical theoretical positions is flawed, particularly in relation to the question of the state.

Marxism has been unable to free itself from economism and therefore has not recognised the many resources of power that are at the disposal of the state, which give it potential autonomy from any single section of civil society. This economism has also meant that Marxists have equated politics solely with the state. Despite its willingness to look beyond the state, therefore, Marxists have failed to see that even if the state were to wither away the problem of governance would remain.

Elitists naturalise elite rule and fail to relate this convincingly to the relationship between state and civil society. They therefore are unable to account for how and why this relationship changes over time. For this reason, elite theory is the least likely of the three theories to find a solution to the problems of the state's relationship with civil society.

Pluralism also fails to acknowledge how unequal structures of power pervade both the state and civil society. Consequently they naively consider the state to be neutral in its relationship to the competing interests of civil society. Classical pluralism is therefore poorly placed to identify and transcend the problems of a system of governance centred upon the state.

If political sociology is to move beyond the problematic relationship between the state–civil society relationship then it must transcend the classical theories explored in this chapter, where it is has been argued that this means taking the power of the state more seriously than has been in case in many theories of political sociology. However, for some theorists, recent social change has diminished the importance of the state and thereby challenged the relevance of political sociology's focus upon it. Part II explores this argument by analysing the challenges to the state presented by globalisation, neo-liberalism and new social movements.

Part II

Challenges to the State

Part II

Challenging the State

3

Globalisation

During the 1980s and 1990s the state appeared besieged by challenges both externally and from within its own boundaries. Consequently, a huge literature has developed, proclaiming the state's demise (see Horsman and Marshall, 1995, for an excellent review). But have recent social changes really undermined the state and thereby invalidated political sociology's focus upon it? This question is addressed in Part II of this book. Chapters 4 and 5 explore the challenges to the state presented by the ideology of neo-liberalism and the growth of new social movements. This chapter looks at globalisation.

As with so many concepts of interest to political sociology, Marx was one of the first thinkers to develop a theory of globalisation. In *The Communist Manifesto* Marx and Engels famously observed that capital inevitably expands beyond the boundaries of the state in search of new markets. Does the recent popularity of concepts of globalisation therefore support the Marxist thesis that the forces of capitalism will create a global economy leading eventually to international communism?

The recent history of globalisation does suggest that the concept is closely connected to changes in the world economy. The economic crisis of the 1970s, which saw profits fall dramatically throughout the whole industrialised world, led to an attempt by capitalist companies to expand the international nature of their production processes and trade patterns (see Box 3.1). Viewed in this context, globalisation marks the attempt by capital to move beyond the shackles of largely nationally based systems of production to a more flexible and global regime (Harvey, 1990: Part II). Many theories of globalisation have, then, concurred with Marx and Engels' insight into the globalising effects of capitalism. Overwhelmingly, though, radical theories of globalisation have had at their core the celebration of capitalism, rather than its demise.

Moreover, Amin argues that Marxism's tendency to equate globalisation purely with the advance of the capital mode of production means the theory is 'poorly equipped to face the challenge of globalisation' (Amin, 1996: 226). This is because globalisation is as much a cultural

Box 3.1 Capitalism in Crisis

The post-war history of capitalism can be divided into two main periods. From 1948 to the early 1970s the advanced industrial countries experienced unprecedented and sustained levels of economic growth. World trade also accelerated rapidly during this period. For example between 1963 and 1968 the annual rate of growth in trade reached a staggering 8.6 per cent. However, by the early 1970s this long boom was at an end and capitalism entered a period of decline and uncertainty. The oil crisis of 1973, which saw the Arab oil producing countries raise their prices fourfold, is often considered pivotal to the decline of capitalism. However, this event only exacerbated more fundamental problems. The long boom had been built upon the Bretton Woods agreement of 1944 that had constructed a stable monetary system of fixed exchange rates centred upon the US dollar. The interdependent nature of this system meant that, once the American economy began to experience problems, the rest of the capitalist world was affected too. The huge expenditure of the USA on the Vietnam war, along with increased international competition, rising wage levels and commodity prices throughout the world led to the decline of the American economy. In 1971 the America trade account fell into deficit for the first time since the nineteenth century. The USA was therefore forced to abandon the Bretton Woods system and shift to floating exchange rates. Other countries soon followed suit. This had the effect of destabilising the world economy and led to a large drop in the profitability of the major industrial countries. Between 1960 and 1981 the net profit rate in the USA fell from 22 per cent to 10 per cent, in France from 18 per cent to 1 per cent and in Japan from 44 per cent to 13 per cent. Consequently, in the 1980s and 1990s capitalist corporations have sought to maximise their share of uncertain global markets by seeking to take advantage of a more deregulated world financial system by moving capital from country to country in search of cheaper wage costs, weak unions and low tax rates.

Sources: Dicken (1998: 24–6); Armstrong et al. (1984)

phenomenon as it is an economic one. Individuals as well as corporations are becoming conscious of, and influenced by, a world beyond their immediate locality (Giddens, 1990: 64). The guiding thread of globalisation seems to lie in the acknowledgement 'that a proper understanding of the complexities of social life can no longer be extracted from an analytical focus on "society", especially where that is seen as equivalent to the quintessentially modern form of the nation-state' (Axford, 1995: 25).

Axford is of course correct to stress the limitations of a state-centred approach which ignores the external constraints upon states and the cultural and economic ties that connect diverse civil societies. None-theless, the central argument of this chapter suggests that globalisation has not been as damaging to the power of the state as is often claimed. In fact, many developments associated with globalisation can only be understood in terms of the relationship between the state and institu-tions of civil society. The evidence surveyed in this chapter will show that states still remain the focal point for cultural and economic activity and that the institutions of civil society, such as multinational com-panies, rely upon the political frameworks which states provide.

My focus in this chapter will be upon the supposed cultural and economic aspects of global change, while the political dimensions of globalisation will be analysed more fully in Chapter 10, which discusses the extent to which governance is becoming globalised. In the first section of this chapter, the central tenets of cultural and economic globalisation are outlined. In particular, what I shall call the radical globalisation thesis will be summarised. After an examination of the main criticisms of this thesis, the chapter will conclude with an assessment of the concept of globalisation.

Theories of Globalisation

Moderate accounts of globalisation acknowledge that 'nation-states continue to be key players in the contemporary global economy' (Dicken, 1998: 7). Radical versions of the thesis, however, stress the decline of the state as an autonomous decision-making body. Such radical theories include writers who embrace globalisation, and who argue that it is multinational companies (MNCs) and not states that are the most effective providers of economic prosperity (O'Brien 1992; Ohmae, 1995). They also come from staunch critics of globalisation who nonetheless accept that globalisation has led to dramatic social change (Korten, 1995; Sklair, 1995). The radical globalisation perspec-tive stresses the following factors:

1. The development and wide availability of low-cost telecommu-nications technology such as fibre-optic cables, fax machines, digital transmission and satellites, which has meant that the populations of states are increasingly becoming subjected to a

'global culture' that is beyond the power of individual governments to control.

2. The rise of MNCs which now have the resources to rival many
   states, but unlike states are not rooted in geography and are easily
   able to relocate their plants according to shifting demand and the
   availability of local advantages such as cheap wage costs, low
   business taxes and weak trade unions.

3. The increasingly global nature of trade, which has rendered states
   unable to develop effective economic policies. States increasingly
   have to respond to factors beyond their control such as imperatives of MNCs and the fluctuations of the world's financial
   markets. Overall, it is claimed that world markets and MNCs
   are more powerful forces in international affairs than states and
   that these new forces of globalisation cannot be effectively
   governed.

Such alleged trends have become almost hegemonic in their influence
on management theorists, business leaders and neo-liberal politicians
during the 1990s. Two key figures from the business world who have
contributed to the radical globalisation thesis are the Japanese business
guru, Kenichi Ohmae, and the President of The People-Centred Development Forum, David Korten. In 1995 both writers produced key texts,
which set out in stark terms the huge impact globalisation is supposedly having upon the power of the state. As examples of the radical
globalisation thesis, written in jargon-free prose, they are hard to beat
and therefore merit some close attention in this chapter. Despite their
very different conclusions concerning the desirability of global change,
both writers broadly agree on the main areas of social life where
globalisation has impacted, and their books provide a useful framework
through which we can explore the evidence that supports, or contra-
dicts, the globalisation thesis.

Ohmae (1995: 2–5) defines global change in terms of what he calls
the four 'I's': investment, industry, information technology and individual consumers. He argues that investment via financial markets
has grown rapidly in recent years, as technology has greatly increased
the opportunity for speculators to bypass national government controls. Opportunities for investment are provided by globalised corporations, which unlike the old geographically bound firms are able to
move shiftily into newly developing markets such as India and China.
Large successful companies attract individuals' investments via large
pension funds, which target well-known, global companies whose
reputation is a guarantee of a good return.

Not only have innovations in information technology increased the mobility of capital, but also they have made expert labour in engineering, medicine or design more widely available across states' borders via sophisticated computer interfacing with customers thousands of miles away. These developments are supported by a growing consumer awareness of the variety of lifestyles and products open to them on the world markets. Thus calls for national loyalty in customer patterns are increasingly falling on deaf ears, as consumers seek the best deal for their money, from whatever source is most competitive and convenient.

The central thesis of Ohmae's book is that the leaders of states have failed to accept that the forces outlined above are beyond the control of governments (Ohmae, 1995: 7). The key to these developments is the rapid expansion of the global economy. For Ohmae, this is to be welcomed because it brings with it increased prosperity and opportunity across and within national cultures. The globalising forces identified by Ohmae cannot (he argues) be resisted by narrow-minded political leaders for long. Political barriers will increasingly be prone to leaks as global flows of information ensure that people will become more aware of a shared global consumer culture, defined as 'Californiaization' by Ohmae (1995: 15). Individuals have already begun to assert their consumer sovereignty above their bonds to national sovereignty. As Ohmae writes, 'the well-informed citizens of a global marketplace will not wait passively until nation-states or cultural prophets deliver tangible improvements in lifestyle . . . They want their own means of direct access to what has become a genuinely global economy' (Ohmae, 1995: 16).

The sheer speed of technological advancement is creating a deep change in the mindset of those exposed to it. Ohmae cites the example of Japan, where a new generation of 'Nintendo kids' is becoming resistant to rules handed down by their parents and grandparents whose thinking was shaped by Japan's experience in the Second World War. Life opportunities can, like the interactive computer games that have reshaped their consciousness, be 'explored, rearranged, reprogrammed' (1995: 36).

A decline in stifling national cultures is, argues Ohmae, to be welcomed, as is the weakened abilities of states to trade off economic success for political survival through expensive and dependency creating welfare systems. Because the state has failed to move with the global current of our times, it has become, not the protector, but the 'enemy of the public at large' (1995: 56).

The logic of Ohmae's argument brings him to the conclusion that governments now have a useful role only as facilitators of what he calls *region states*. He defines these as 'natural economic zones', which have evolved through market forces operating both beyond and within national boundaries. Many of these regions have huge economic capacities; for example the Shutoken region in Japan would alone rate as the third greatest economic power behind the USA and Germany (1995: 80). These region states are economic rather than political units and therefore welcome unconditionally foreign direct investment and foreign ownership. As such, they provide a much greater chance of meeting the changing needs of the people who reside in them than do traditional states. The challenge for states is to develop more flexible federal structures of co-ordination to ensure that these regional states are maintained and fostered (1995: 100).

However, even this limited role is transitionary because the rationale for the existence of states is disappearing. For Ohmae, the militaristic logic of states has been shown to be a mask for vested interests; the control of territory is increasingly irrelevant in an economy that values knowledge over natural resources, and political independence is increasingly a sham in the context of a global economy.

While other 'radical globalists' may largely accept the description of the global forces outlined by Ohmae, not all agree with his optimistic appraisal of their effects. Ohmae's neo-liberal position has been contradicted forcibly by David Korten in his excellent book *When Corporations Rule the World*.

In describing the development of what he refers to as the 'full world', Korten stresses the global nature of world problems, accelerated by the very forces Ohmae identifies as positive (Korten, 1995: 28). Thus, Korten notes the disintegrative effects of the ecologically unsustainable quest for continued economic growth, and the extremes of inequality between the world's rich and poor. In the face of these pressures, traditional forms of governance seem incapable of resisting the process of 'economic globalisation that is shifting power away from governments . . . toward a handful of corporations and financial institutions' (1995: 12). Far from being beneficial, as Ohmae argues, these developments are 'a modern form of the imperial phenomenon' whereby the undemocratic and short termist drive for profit, at the expense of people, is the principle force guiding globalisation (Korten, 1995: 28).

For Korten, corporations have ceased to be merely economic entities and have become the 'dominant governance institutions' (Korten, 1995: 54). As such, they are barriers to, rather than champions of, free markets and genuine competition. Korten cites Adam Smith's famous treatise on the benefits of trade, *The Wealth of Nations*, in support of his argument that modern corporations are 'instruments for suppressing the competitive forces of the market' (Korten, 1995: 56). Smith has a much more sophisticated approach to trade than many of his neo-

liberal followers would have us believe. Smith's wariness of the oppressive tendencies of the state was matched by his fear of unfettered
corporate power, which if allowed to develop would inevitability
distort the laws of supply and demand.

In a fascinating discussion, Korten shows how the political disrup-
tions caused by the American Civil War led to the reduction of democratic constraints on the power of American corporations. In a pivotal
judgement in 1886, the Supreme Court decided in favour of the
Southern Pacific Railroad in its case against Santa Clara County, and
declared that corporations should be treated henceforth as individuals
with all the protections of the constitution, rather than as economic
units (Korten, 1995: 59). In this historical event, Korten sees the roots
of the present dominance of corporations across the globe because from
that point on, the 'constitutional intent that all citizens have an equal
voice' could no longer be upheld, owing to the huge resources at the
disposal of huge private companies. Less than a hundred years after this
ruling, American companies have shaped the world economy in an
image suited to their needs, and against the interests of the bulk of the
world's population.

These firms have become increasingly global in their outlook to the
point whereby they have 'grown beyond any national interest' (Korten,
1995: 124). Such corporations have played a central role in undermining indigenous cultures which are barriers to global consumer
patterns. In this way advertising jingles, product symbols and corporate
sponsored popular music are replacing national identity and community values as the driving force behind human interconnectedness (see
Sklair, 1995: 87–97). Korten cites the Chairman of Coca-Cola, who
argues that 'people around the world are today connected by brand
name consumer products as much as by anything else' (Robert Goi-
zueta, cited in Korten, 1995: 153). This point is illustrated by the
sponsorship of street signs in Tanzania by Coca-Cola's biggest rival,
Pepsi!

The pictures that Ohmae and Korten paint may be composed in very
different ways, and the impact upon the viewer contrasting, but their
subject matter is essentially the same. According to the radical globalisation thesis, the state is being replaced as the key actor in the world
by corporations which operate in a world economy underpinned by a
universalised consumer culture. All of these tenets of the globalisation
thesis have been refuted or substantially qualified by writers who
dispute that globalisation is as pervasive as Ohmae and Korten claim.

Criticisms of the Radical Globalisation Thesis

The central problem with the thesis is a lack of a clear definition of what globalisation entails (Hirst and Thompson, 1996: 1–17). Globalisation has obtained a mythical status and appears to encompass a vast number of related, unrelated, or even contradictory processes. Its effects are nonetheless often portrayed as irresistible. Will Hutton (1995b) has pointed to how globalisation has been 'naturalised' by neo-liberal governments, which seek to justify the deregulation of the economy. Such policies can be asserted as the 'only alternative', in an economic climate where it has become impossible to 'buck the market'. Globalisation is in this sense a self-fulfilling prophecy. It demands a set of policies that ironically create the social conditions that are said to result from the inevitable logic of global capital. It can be argued then, that processes of globalisation are promoted more by neo-liberal political ideology than economics. An assessment of the available evidence certainly suggests that the effects of globalisation are far from certain.

The Development of a Global Culture?

No one could dispute the growing significance of telecommunications and information technology in increasing the ability for companies to spread their messages more widely and quickly. However, important qualifications need to be made to the view that an increasing ability to communicate will necessarily lead to an homogeneous global culture. First, several practical qualifications can be made to the 'global culture' thesis. As Cable has argued, states are beginning to respond to the new technologies with increased regulation:

> Access to global media requires equipment – satellite dishes, modems – which can, in varying degrees, be controlled, as the Chinese authorities and others are trying to do. Surveillance techniques are catching up. The US law enforcement agencies are developing a 'tessar' which will help them maintain effective surveillance over computer networks. (Cable, 1996: 133)

It is also wrong to assume that technological advances are necessarily detrimental to the power of states to control their citizens. Increased technology in communications equipment may in some instances increase the ability of the state to control immigration, and monitor its populations through the use of computer databases, identity cards and surveillance cameras. As Giddens (1985) has noted, innovations in surveillance have historically been crucial to the development of the state and recent developments may well enhance, rather than detract from, states' ability to police their citizens. Additionally, states which are best able to utilise technological advances to enhance their military power are well placed to assert their will in international affairs, as witnessed by the huge variety of technological weaponry used by the USA and its allies in the Second Gulf War. Moreover, Hutton (1995a) has argued that in many areas technological innovation is not increasing in pace. He insists that 'it is possible to view the change that confronts this generation as the least transforming of this century'. This is because many of the technologies we use today, from the telephone to the television, are 'broadly the same as 30 years ago'.

Secondly, Smith has insisted that the deep-rooted identities of nationalism and ethnicity are unlikely to be replaced by a rootless global culture built upon the consumer capitalism of Disneyland, Coca-Cola and Power Rangers:

> The fact remains that cultures are historically specific, and so is their imagery. The packaged imagery of the visionary global culture is either trivial and shallow, a matter of mass-commodity advertisements, or it is rooted in existing historical cultures, drawing from them whatever meanings and power it may derive. (Smith, A., 1995: 23)

Notions of a hegemonic global culture are asserted rather than proven. Cultural interchanges are by their nature two way in nature. Thus the spread of Western-style capitalism or European ideological systems across the globe is unlikely to lead to cultural homogeneity (Ahmed and Donnan, 1994: 1–5). This point is supported by Hebdige's work on the alleged Americanisation of British culture since the 1950s. Hebdige (1982) found that American cultural forms in dress and popular music were not adopted passively by British youth, but instead were creatively adapted. This led to new hybrids of popular culture that in turn were influential on American culture. For example the 1960s rock band The Beatles successfully integrated elements of the English music hall tradition and Anglo-Celtic folk ballads into a distinctively British version of Rock n' Roll music. This was then successfully exported back to the USA. Culture, then, can be seen to develop through a process of cross-fertilisation as external cultural forms are mixed with indigenous forms of expression.

Thirdly, Hall (1995: 200) argues that the present era is characterised, not by cultural uniformity, but by the resurgence of ethnic identities. Hall cites the rise of racism in Western Europe, the growth of neofascism in Russia, the influence of Islamic fundamentalism throughout the Middle East and Africa, and the jingoist nature of anti-Europeanism in Britain, as examples of these developments. Communication across the globe may, in some quarters, increase and accent difference, rather than create a global market of passive 'Americanised' consumers.

Cable contends that technological advances can aid the promotion of sub-national or ethnic identities. For example in the USA the various mediums of privately owned television programmes, VHF vernacular radio and cheap videos and CDs have helped minority groups maintain their identity. As Cable (1996: 133) argues, 'the medium may integrate people globally, but the message may promote political and social fragmentation'. The growth of fundamentalism, religious cults and ethnic nationalism can in part be explained in terms of a rejection of Western capitalistic values that are seen as hollow and corrosive, in favour of more deeply held belief systems which are forcibly reasserted at the national or sub-national level. Beyer, for example, concludes his study of the relationship between globalisation and religion by arguing that 'a great many people in global society, perhaps the majority, will continue as almost exclusive adherents and practitioners of the traditional systematic forms, a fact that the abiding vitality of conservative religion only seems to underscore' (Beyer, 1994: 226).

A Global Economy?

Few commentators would argue with Lanjouw (1995: 4) when he writes that 'an ever increasing proportion of world output is being traded internationally'. As Hirst and Thompson (1996) note, however, the distinction between internationalisation and globalisation is an important one because the latter implies not just increased trade across the globe but also that the world economy has moved beyond the capacity for states to govern. In reality, the international economy has for decades operated in the context of the states system, and therefore 'self regulating economies independent of politics are a myth' (Anderson, 1995: 79). Hirst and Thompson agree that 'the world trading system has hitherto never just been an "economy", a distinct system governed by its own laws. On the contrary, the term "international economy" has been shorthand for the complex interaction of economic relations and political processes' (Hirst and Thompson, 1995: 418). Furthermore, an increase in the volume of world trade, or in the growth of foreign investment, does not necessarily mean that we are witnessing globalisation. In fact, many of the trends that are cited as evidence in support of globalisation illustrate just how concentrated the world's economic activity is.

One of the key measurements of globalisation is the amount of foreign direct investment (FDI) in the world system. As Kozul-Wright (1995: 157) suggests, the stock of FDI in the world economy actually peaked in 1914. Although in the 1990s the potential exists for many industries to be more global in the future, the patterns of these developments are complex and therefore we cannot easily generalise about the world economy as a whole. FDI is also dominated by a few powerful economies. As Hirst and Thompson observe, in the early 1990s, 70 per cent of FDI was by the top five economies of the world (1996: 196).

Hutton has argued that recent developments suggest that 'multi-nationals are deglobalising their production and pulling back into their home regions' (Hutton, 1995a). Indeed, much export and import activity is intra-firm in nature. For example, in 1993, 45 per cent of the USA's import value and 32 per cent of its exports could be accounted for by intra-firm trade (Eurostat, 1995: 7–9). The concentration of economic activity by relatively few MNCs, located in a small number of states, cannot be classed as persuasive evidence of globalisation.

The exaggerated claims for global markets ignore the fact that most international trade is still between the industrialised nations and a few favoured newly industrialising countries such as South Korea and Taiwan. Much of the apparent global economic activity can be explained in terms of the evasion by MNCs of high costs incurred by national regulation or taxation. For example although total FDI levels grew considerably between 1991 and 1993 this could largely be accounted by inward investment by Chinese enterprises taking money out of their own country and bringing it straight back in, thereby securing the favourable treatment afforded to 'foreign investment' (Hutton, 1995b).

In reality, the development of the 'free market' associated with globalisation has marginalised many economies in terms of trade. Inequality between the developed and 'developing' nations is wider than ever. For example 14 per cent of the world's population accounted for 70 per cent of world trade in 1992 (Hirst and Thompson, 1995: 425). Between 1980 and 1994 the percentage of the world's exports going to Africa actually fell from 3.1 per cent to 1.5 per cent. During the same period Latin America's share of world exports decreased from 6.1 per cent to 5.2 per cent (United Nations, 1996c: 318). These figures hardly provide evidence of a trend towards globalisation.

In many regions of the world the supposed benefits of globalisation are difficult to detect. In 1995 the annual rate of growth of Gross Domestic Product (GDP) in Latin America fell by 0.9 per cent, while in

Africa it stood still at 0 per cent (United Nations, 1996c: 7). Although South-East Asia showed high rates of growth in the early 1990s, by the end of 1997 many countries in the region were forced to devalue their currencies against a background of falling growth rates and a collapse in confidence in their underlying economic strength (*Financial Times*, 1998). In Central and Eastern Europe during the 1990s, the position was dire. In Romania, levels of GDP in 1995 stood at 86.5 per cent of what they had been in 1989. In Bulgaria and Albania the economic situation was even worse (United Nations, 1996c: 24).

Importantly, political considerations have also been central to the economic marginalisation of many Third World countries. With the ending of the Cold War, during which the USSR and the USA fought the conflict through proxies in the developing world, the strategic dimension that ensured some economic support to the allies of the superpowers disappeared. Financial aid from the developed world going to low income countries has actually fallen in recent years, as funds have been used to cut public spending by developed countries eager to compete in the new 'global economy' (United Nations, 1996c: 73). At a meeting of the G8 (the world's seven strongest economies plus Russia) in May 1998 the debt crisis, which cripples many underdeveloped economies, was on the agenda for discussion. Little firm action was taken, however, even to relieve the problem. Such neglect has led to extreme 'global imbalances' and 'unsustainable levels of indebtedness' (Kirdar, 1992: 3). The United Nations Conference on Trade and Development (United Nations, 1996c: 27–32) concluded that many Third World countries have 'been unable to benefit from, and meaningfully participate in, the globalisation process'. These inequalities suggest that economic globalisation might be more accurately described as economic polarisation.

Even amongst the industrialised nations, patterns of investment and trade differ greatly. Countries such as Britain and Japan are less dependent upon trade now than they were eighty years ago (Cable, 1996: 135), and, as Kozul-Wright (1995: 157) contends, Germany and Japan have not been significant 'host' countries for external investment, suggesting great variation between states based on different political strategies towards economic change (Weiss, 1998).

The extent to which globalisation of the economy is genuinely occurring varies not only between states, but also between industrial sectors. In those sectors which are bound up with national identity, there is strong resistance to the opening up of markets. Examples of this include industries like cinema and agriculture where the shift to free trade in a global setting may be seen as a threat to the social fabric of the nation (Lanjouw, 1995: 16–17). Such resistance to global change has had a large impact upon the shape of the European Union, which spends much of its income on the Common Agriculture Policy (CAP) largely to protect inefficient, but politically significant, farmers in France and Germany. This policy has been highly controversial within and outside the Union. There is much agreement amongst economists that not only does the CAP distort the world market in food it greatly hinders development of successful agricultural sectors in the developing world (Leonard, 1994: 120–8).

As well as the growth in world trade and increased FDI, supporters of the globalisation thesis argue that the world economic system has witnessed 'increasingly volatile globalised financial markets in which speculative financial movements are a major source of instability and disruption' (Korten, 1995: 196). Certainly the levels of speculation on the world's currency markets are staggering; in 1996 around $1.3 trillion a day was being traded. This is over ten times the amount necessary to support the volume of world trade (OECD, 1996: 2). However, Hirst and Thompson (1996: 197) insist that the openness of the money and capital markets is not new. In this respect, 'the international economy was hardly less integrated before 1914 than it is today'. They point to the development of international submarine telegraph cables from the late nineteenth century, which facilitated fast currency exchanges, and conclude that new technologies have not transformed the economy to the extent the radical globalisation thesis suggests. As Cable (1995) notes, the openness of the financial system is largely due to political decisions by neo-liberal governments, such as the deregulation of markets and privatisation. Importantly, therefore, Hirst and Thompson argue that the international markets could be regulated much more efficiently if the political will amongst the top economic powers existed (Hirst and Thompson, 1996: 197–201).

MNCs as the Dominant International Actors?

The third element of the radical globalisation thesis centres upon the role of MNCs as the principal vehicles of global economic change and the chief rivals to states. On closer inspection, many of the powers attributed to these companies are shown to be mythical or exaggerated.

There certainly is substantial evidence to suggest that the largest of the world's corporations are increasing their economic strength and therefore, in some instances, their political influence. In 1993 it was estimated that multinationals controlled 70 per cent of the world's trade. The combined sales of the top 350 companies accounted for almost one third of the total Gross National Product (GNP) of the industrialised countries (*New Internationalist*, 1993: 19).

Such is the significance of MNCs to the radical globalisation thesis that some theorists have advocated the use of the term transnational to describe many modern corporations. This is because multinationals are still firmly rooted in their home country and are 'deeply integrated into the individual local economies in which they operate' (Korten, 1995: 125). Transnational corporations, in contrast, are companies which are 'geocentric' in their outlook (Albrow, 1996: 121). These companies are concerned with increased profitability, regardless of national interest, the location of their plants, or the origins of their workforce. However, there is reason to remain sceptical about the true transnational character of the majority of these companies.

The first point of criticism is that corporations are not rootless economic actors, but are still firmly entrenched in and dependent upon states. Most of the assets of even the largest MNCs are contained in their home country. For example Ford has 80 per cent and Pepsi-Cola and McDonald's over 50 per cent of their fixed assets located in the USA (Hutton, 1995a). In the crucial area of technological research, American companies conduct only 9 per cent of this in foreign countries (Cable, 1995: 31).

In many cases, the culture of MNCs is also very firmly rooted in the home state. The management personnel of these companies have their cultural origins in states, and globalisation has not eroded national sentiments. The desire for home control of the management of corporations means that very few have 'attained a really global dimension' because 'the economies of scale or location are often balanced by the loss of co-ordination' (Eurostat, 1995: 5).

It is the national context which provides the wider setting for the development of corporate cultures. MNCs are unlikely, by themselves, to be able to generate such strong allegiances as states. Local cultural factors also retain a strong resistance to convergence towards globalised models of management practice (Hofstede, 1981). Moreover, Hirst and Thompson note how states provide companies with important support mechanisms, such as 'networks of relations with central and local governments, with trade associations, with organised labour, with specifically national financial institutions orientated towards local companies, and with national systems of skills formation and labour motivation' (Hirst and Thompson, 1995: 426).

MNCs by themselves are unable to provide the necessary stability and regulation necessary for continued economic growth, and are still very much reliant upon states to manage global change. The particular institutional framework, the political culture and the dominant ideology of a state at given time will help to shape the form and success of this political management. In the relationship between

MNCs and the state, it is the latter which still tends to hold sway. As Berridge contends:

> It is one thing to concede that multinationals have influence with the state, even, on occasions, great influence; it is quite another to accept that they exercise uninterrupted control over even micro-states and small states, let alone middle or major powers. Only sleight of hand has allowed this impression, and it is no more than that, to become established. (Berridge, 1992: 49)

An Assessment of the Globalisation Debate

The evidence examined in this chapter suggests that the claims of the radical globalisation thesis need to be qualified in the following ways.

1. A global culture, in the sense of a homogeneous set of essentially Western values accepted universally across and within states, has not emerged in recent years, and is unlikely to develop in the foreseeable future. Ethnic, religious, and local belief systems still exercise a tremendous pull on individuals and communities across the globe.

It is true to say that many people throughout the world are becoming increasingly exposed to other cultures, and technological advances have largely been responsible for this (Ahmed and Donnan, 1994: 4). This may well result, however, in greater cultural diversity rather than less. Old traditions may themselves become reworked and globalised as they compete with other visions of how the good life can be best obtained. Religion, for example, may gain a 'recontextualized salience', that involves a movement 'away from the particular culture with which that tradition identified itself in the past', so that 'religion within the global system can be antisystematic and prosystematic at the same time: it can further globalisation in opposing its effects' (Beyer, 1994: 3, 10, 100).

A good example of the complex ways in which the local and global interact is the Salman Rushdie case (Beyer, 1994: 1–4; Ahmed and Donnan, 1994: 1). Rushdie's alleged attack (in his novel *The Satanic Verses*) upon the Islamic faith placed in opposition his Westernised defence of 'universal' values such as free speech and the globalising tendencies of Islam, which like any world religion strives to universalise its perspective. The global telecommunication network allowed this value conflict to spread rapidly around the globe so that demonstrations against Rushdie's book in cities in England sparked an immediate reaction thousands of miles away in Bombay and Islamabad.

2. The world economy is best described as internationalised, rather than globalised, since its main actors and benefactors are heavily concentrated. The term globalised economy also implies that economic actors have a level of independence from states that does not exist. However, the fluctuations of the international financial markets are an increasing source of political and economic instability.

The world economy has undoubtedly grown in volume and intensity. Particularly significant has been the vast increase in currency flows via the world's stock markets. This has to some extent reduced states' autonomy in the management of their economies. However, the notion of a global economy significantly underestimates the concentration of trade and investment in a few powerful states and MNCs. The benefits of the growing international economy have not been global, as they virtually exclude large regions of the world. Neither does the term globalisation capture the interdependent relationship between states and firms. For these reasons, Hirst and Thompson (1996) persuasively argue that the present economic climate is probably best described as internationalised rather than globalised. Moreover, patterns of trade illustrate the polarisation of the world economy. Regions such as Sub-Saharan Africa are all but excluded from the benefits of trade.

However, critics of globalisation often underestimate the impact of new technologies on the world economy and the difficulties associated with regulating its effects. Indeed this is where Hirst and Thompson's critique of globalisation is at its weakest. They argue that the development of submarine telegraph cables in the mid-nineteenth century ensured that financial markets in the pre-1914 period were 'not fundamentally different from the satellite-linked and computer-controlled markets of today' (Hirst and Thompson, 1996: 197). This greatly underestimates the quantity, quality and speed of information which computer technology has given to financial traders. Successful traders have to make use of available technology if they are to be successful. In contrast, in the pre-1914 period some stock exchanges made little use of technological advancements, such as the telephone and telegraph. In 1913, an American stockbroker, Van Antwerp, observed that on the London stock exchange telegraph machines were 'limited in number, almost nobody looks at them, and many really enterprising houses do not install them at all' (Morgan and Thomas, 1969: 163). Van Antwerp also remarked upon the hundreds of letters and telegrams from investors that lay unopened on brokers' desks. This would be unthinkable today, where computer technology allows fortunes to be made and lost in seconds by dealers speculating on often momentary fluctuations in currency values.

3. Large companies, operating beyond the boundaries of their home state, are still overwhelmingly multinational rather than transnational, relying as they do upon the political and legal frameworks provided by states. However, the 'global reach' of many companies is likely to increase with further advances in communications technology and through the influence of globalisation as an almost hegemonic ideology in business and management circles.

The evidence would suggest that states committed to market economies do have to consider carefully the needs and interests of MNCs. Although to some extent this has always been the case, most commentators would agree that states now operate in a new context where MNCs increasingly, directly or indirectly, influence government policy (Anderson, 1995: 82). As Hirst and Thompson (1996) have argued, however, there is nothing inevitable about this. Most states retain enormous economic, military and communicative power particularly when acting together in regional bodies such as the European Union. Moreover, many of the freedoms and frameworks necessary for successful operations by MNCs are guaranteed or supplied directly by states. The opportunity therefore does exist for further political regulation if states wish to redefine their relationships with the economic organisations of civil society.

Conclusion

The radical globalisation thesis introduced in this chapter suggests a growing interdependence between cultures and economies, and a subsequent weakening of the power of the state. If this thesis were accepted uncritically, grave damage would be done to our argument that an analysis of the state is pivotal to political sociology. However, a very different picture of globalisation emerges from the evidence explored in this chapter.

Globalisation is in fact a product of the interactions between the state and the institutions of civil society, such as multinational companies. Individuals and associations within civil society are still dependent upon the state's unique ability to centralise and concentrate military, economic and communicative power. Greater awareness of other cultures has often intensified rather than minimised clashes between belief systems, and increased not reduced calls for statehood. Economic corporations depend upon states to provide infrastructure and legal support and economic management is still shaped by political culture and ideology. In short, states still provide the framework for cultural and economic activity.

Globalisation, in the form asserted by writers such Ohmae, is an ideological assertion rather than a description of inevitable economic and cultural processes. In this sense, the radical globalisation thesis shares a crude economism with some versions of Marxism. Such economism ignores the important question of governance that is raised by globalisation: how can states, acting individually and collectively, regulate the associations of civil society more effectively?

In Chapter 10, I will argue that the concept of globalisation best describes, not the triumph of capitalism, but a set of global risks. Defined in this way, globalisation is changing the context in which states govern and is creating the opportunity, if states are willing to seize it, for the creation of alternative forms of governance. Global risks highlight the need for a global system of governance to regulate the environmental damage and material inequalities caused largely by the economic liberalisation championed by many exponents of globalisation. However, since the 1980s, the influential ideology of neo-liberalism has advocated the promotion rather than regulation of economic 'globalisation'. Neo-liberalism is therefore the next challenge to the state that we shall explore.

4

Neo-Liberalism

The radical globalisation thesis discussed in the previous chapter has at its core an economic determinism, which greatly underestimates the role political ideology has played in promoting the 'virtues' of the free market in recent decades. That is to say economic globalisation is not an inevitable set of processes, but has instead been actively promoted by neo-liberal theorists and politicians suspicious of state interference in civil society. The ideology of neo-liberalism therefore presents another important challenge to the power of the state and is the subject of this chapter.

Neo-liberals seek, above all, to transform the balance of power between state and civil society. In particular, they believe that the economic institutions of civil society are more effective in creating order and distributing resources than is the state. For neo-liberals, human potential is best realised, not through power being centralised in the state, but by the promotion of a free economy, where power is dispersed throughout civil society.

However, this chapter will argue that neo-liberalism is deeply flawed, both conceptually and in practice. The central paradox of neo-liberalism is that it is critical of the state but at the same time accepts the state as a necessary evil. So while neo-liberalism rightly highlights the limitations of a system of governance centred upon the coercive and bureaucratic state, it fails to find a convincing alternative. Instead, neo-liberals seek to regulate society through the laws of supply and demand. In practice, however, the 'free market' creates high levels of social inequality and therefore social conflict. To manage these problems, the limited state that neo-liberals embrace is forced in practice to become increasingly coercive. The deregulation of the economy therefore ironically leads to a strong state. Furthermore, their suspicion of political interference with the market makes neo-liberals wary of democracy and therefore the strong neo-liberal state is also an increasingly unaccountable state as well. The chapter therefore concludes that the challenge to the state presented by neo-liberalism is a bizarre one, given that its policy prescriptions result in an even more coercive and unaccountable state. Moreover, as the world economy is structured in the interests of powerful states, the dominance of neo-liberalism in the international arena also has enormous negative implications for the fortunes of developing countries and for the management of global problems generally.

The chapter is structured as follows. First I summarise neo-liberal theory and consider its policy implications. Next, a case study of the application of neo-liberal ideology in Africa will be used to illustrate the difficulties of putting such an abstract doctrine into practice. Finally, the chapter concludes with a critical assessment of neo-liberalism, focusing upon its implications for the state–civil society relationship.

An Outline of Neo-Liberalism

Since the 1980s, neo-liberal doctrines have been influential in two ways:

1. They have formed the ideological core of international economic organisations such as the World Bank and the International Monetary Fund (IMF), particularly in their advocacy of such ideas as 'structural adjustment' as a 'cure' to the economic problems of the underdeveloped world.
2. They have been highly influential upon the governments of the developed world from the 1970s onwards, particularly in the USA under Ronald Reagan and George Bush, and in Britain under Margaret Thatcher and John Major.

The key thinker of neo-liberalism, from whom many other theorists derive their ideas, is the Austrian philosopher Frederick Hayek. Of particular significance is his seminal work *The Road to Serfdom* (1944). This book not only provides one of clearest accounts of the neo-liberal perspective, but also is especially interesting because it outlines a radical theory that was at odds with the prevailing mood of its time. Written in 1944, during a period when industrial societies were enthusiastically embracing state intervention and the growth of the public sector, Hayek's polemic on the inefficiencies and dangers of the large state seemed strangely out of place.

Lash and Urry (1987) argue that because of the widespread realisation of the limits of the market in the latter half of the nineteenth century the years from the 1870s to the 1970s saw the development of an increasingly 'organised' capitalism. As Hall and Schwarz (1985: 10) contend: 'the tempo of state intervention increased sharply in the 1880s and 1890s; the boundaries between state and civil society began to be redefined; and the nightwatchman role of the state began to be steadily eroded'.

Social liberalism, with its acceptance of the need for state intervention to provide training, economic stability and a state welfare system, replaced classical liberalism (with its advocacy of *laissez-faire* economics) as the dominant ideology in much of the capitalist world from the late nineteenth century onwards. The development of organised capitalism identified by Hall and Schwarz grew in pace at the time when Hayek was penning *The Road to Serfdom*. This was due mainly to the industrialised nature of the Second World War, which required extensive planning to mobilise the whole of the societies of the participants, and therefore further increased the need for state intervention in civil society. It was such intervention that led Hayek (1944: 15) to write that the dominant trend was towards 'an entire abandonment of the individualist tradition which has created Western civilisation'. However, as had occurred in the 1870s, it was an economic crisis that led to a reconsideration of the relationship between the state and the market at the end of the 1970s (See box 3.1). It was at this time that Hayek's theories appeared to resonate with the prevailing economic and social conditions and to offer a clear way forward for capitalism.

Hayek's work provides a scathing attack upon collectivist theories, such as social liberalism, which have advocated the expansion of the power of the state at the expense of the market. Neo-liberals rejected the explanation that capitalism's problems were due to the inherent weaknesses of the capitalist system. Rather, such problems were best explained by a number of factors, which to varying degrees were undermining capitalism in the USA and across Europe in the second half of the twentieth century. These included:

1. A commitment to Keynesian economic management that involved the interference of the state with the operations of the free market.
2. Increased welfare spending, which meant higher taxes and therefore lower investment in industry and less consumer spending. The welfare state also created a dependency culture that undermined personal responsibility, enterprise and innovation.
3. The development of corporatism and, in particular, the increasing influence of trade unions in the making of economic policy. This led to the artificial inflation of wages, increased industrial unrest that disrupted production, and the pursuit of full employment which could not be sustained economically.

The solution to the decline in profitability and the rise in social unrest and political disillusionment was the reversal of these trends. Neo-liberal economists such as Friedman (1980) and political scientists like Brittan (1976) built upon the insights of Hayek and advanced an alternative strategy to the statist economic management of the post war period. Such writers argue for a minimal state that provides for internal order and for protection from invasion by hostile states, but which leaves economic affairs almost exclusively to the market. In this way a 'spontaneous order' will be created whereby society needs will be met by the laws of supply and demand. Prosperity for all will be increased because the most gifted individuals will be freed from political interference and excessive taxation and will be increasingly innovative and creative, thus resulting in a 'trickle down effect' whereby the efforts of the few will result in opportunities for everyone.

At the centre of this philosophy is the rejection of abstract notions of society, community and the 'public good'. According to Hayek, the dominance of the West in modern world history can be attributed to an emphasis upon individuals' freedom to choose (Hayek, 1944: 11). For neo-liberals, individuals are perceived as autonomous, self-governing and rational actors who enter into voluntary political, economic or social contracts within civil society. Neo-liberals argue that inequality is both inevitable and desirable. Attempts to offset inequality through state interference will inevitably lead to the erosion of human freedom, preventing individuals making choices about how to spend their income. The inevitability of human diversity within civil society will ensure that the state acts on only a partial, and therefore distorted, understanding of individuals' needs. This will, argues Hayek, lead at worst to totalitarianism, and at best to an increased conflict between ever-more expectant citizens and a state unable to fulfil its promises. Voluntary exchange within the free market is a far more reliable way of ensuring the fulfilment of individuals' talents because it does not discriminate between people on the grounds of prejudice or ideology, but merely reflects the ability of individuals to manipulate the market to their advantage.

Neo-Liberalism in Practice

One of the effects of the radical globalisation thesis, explored in Chapter 3, has been to help erode, in some countries, social liberalism as the cornerstone of political management of the economy. Consequently, in the USA and Britain, there has been an ideological shift towards neo-liberalism, which was seen by the Republican Party of Reagan and the Conservative Party led by Margaret Thatcher as the ideology most suited to the new 'globalised' conditions in which such governments found themselves during the 1980s.

Like all ideologies that are applied to actual societies, the policy outcomes of neo-liberalism are far removed from the apparent coherence of Hayek's work. However, neo-liberalism did provide a clear set of policy alternatives to the Keynesianism of the post-war period. When the profitability of capitalist society declined dramatically during the 1970s, political parties on the right of the political spectrum in Europe and the USA turned to neo-liberalism to provide a blueprint for restructuring their societies. As we shall see in the next section of this chapter, the adoption of neo-liberalism by Western economic institutions was also to have serious repercussions in the developing world. The main features of a neo-liberal programme of reform follow from two core principles:

1. The superiority of markets over politics in providing for human need, generating prosperity and enhancing personal freedom.
2. The need to defend individuals' market rights, including property rights, the right to assert one's inequality and the right to choose from a diversity of goods and services in the market place.

From these guiding dictums a number of policies logically follow. These include:

1. Deregulation of the economy, including greater openness in international trade and investment, reduction in business taxation, and the slashing of any bureaucratic 'red tape' that hinders private accumulation and profitability.
2. The reduction of trade union rights and the creation of a flexible labour market where wages find their own level.
3. Cuts in public expenditure in social services such as health, welfare and education.
4. Privatisation of public services whenever possible and the creation of 'quasi-markets' which apply market principles such as internal competition for services, contracting out of peripheral work tasks, and performance related pay in other state-run services.
5. A redefinition of citizenship where limited civil and market rights are emphasised at the expense of social entitlements, and citizens are expected to take greater personal responsibility for themselves and their dependants.

It is essential to stress that the influence of such neo-liberal principles has not been uniform across all countries that have been influenced by them. The application of such policies is mediated through such factors as the political institutions and culture of any given state and a state's relative strength in the world economic system, as well as its social and economic characteristics. For example, in Britain the rise of the neo-liberal agenda of Thatcherism in the 1980s and 1990s can be attributed to a number of complex factors which, when combined at a particular juncture, created the possibility for the Thatcherite project to supersede social liberalism. These factors included:

1. A political culture which stressed individualism, associated with developments such as the early growth of basic rights through such developments as Magna Carta in 1215 and the establishment of Habeas Corpus in 1679, and the political theory of liberals such as Thomas Hobbes and John Locke in the seventeenth century. This meant that Britain's political culture, with its emphasis upon individualism, was conducive, in ways which other European countries were not, to the arguments of neo-liberalism.
2. A political constitution that was unwritten and rested largely upon the self-constraint of governments to respect the many conventions of British politics. This, therefore, allowed for the possibility of a radical government to assert a neo-liberal agenda by ignoring the largely informal constraints of tradition.
3. A political and economic history that placed Britain at the heart of the development of the world economic system and that made it, paradoxically, both vulnerable to, but supportive of, processes of free trade and deregulation in the post-war period, when its underlying economic performance was in decline.

A key weakness of neo-liberalism, however, is that its highly abstract formulations blinds it to historical and structural constraints which may render its implementation highly unsuitable. To illustrate the difficulties of applying neo-liberalism in states less structurally conducive than Britain to its doctrines, and to highlight some of its theoretical flaws, I shall next examine in some detail its influence in Africa since the 1980s. It should first be stressed, however, that in exploring the failure of neo-liberalism in Africa I am in no way suggesting that all of Africa's problems can be attributed to the neo-liberal policy of structural adjustment. Africa's problems are, of course, long standing and deep rooted and result from the problems of securing stable governance, imperialism and the failure of political leadership, amongst many others (see Thomson, forthcoming). However, Africa's experience of neo-liberalism does help to illuminate neo-liberalism's general inability to solve the problems of governance as well as its failure to acknowledge the structural inequalities that are built into the states system and which prevent sustainable development throughout the developing world.

Neo-Liberalism in Africa

In Africa, the application of neo-liberal policies has been led by the IMF and the World Bank in their role as what Susan George has called 'collection agencies for the creditor countries' (George, 1993: 63). Following the decline of the European empires after 1945, many newly independent African countries found that a downside of their new-found 'freedom' was the legacy of a massive burden of debt. This debt continued to grow, particularly following the world recession of the 1970s, so that by the late 1980s the value of the continent's debt relative to its export earning was 500 per cent (Watkins, 1995: 74). Consequently, the IMF and World Bank, acting in the interests of the industrial countries that had created them, began to look for new ways to make Africa pay back its creditors.

In 1981 the World Bank produced the Berg Report that blamed Africa's economic problems firmly upon the failure of African states to manage their own economies effectively. The Report set out the alleged need for what was called the 'structural adjustment' of African states. This primarily involved the assertion of neo-liberal reforms of Africa's economic and political structures in an attempt to render them efficient and thereby enable them to honour their debts. Loans from the IMF and World Bank were to be made only on the condition that those states accepting them would manage their economic affairs according to neo-liberal principles.

The central strategy dictated by structural adjustment was the notion of comparative advantage, whereby states would maximise their economic potential by focusing upon the export of one or two specialist commodities such as copper or cocoa that they had a history of producing. In this way, it was argued, African states could gain greater access to world markets. Such a strategy needed to be supported by the reduction of state interference in industry, privatisation programmes, the removal of barriers to international trade, and the deregulation of the labour market. The Berg Report assumed that Africa's failure to modernise itself could overwhelmingly be attributed to political mis-management. Therefore, the only solution open to them was to roll back the frontiers of the state, thereby freeing the much more effective mechanisms of market forces. Underdeveloped states could only succeed if they reformed their systems in line with the needs of the global economy.

The high level of indebtedness of African states ensured that many did, albeit often reluctantly, pursue structural adjustment. Since the early 1980s, around thirty African states have embarked on all or some of the neo-liberal reforms set out by the IMF and World Bank (Watkins, 1995: 74). For example, in Nigeria between 1991 and 1993 some thirty-five public enterprises were privatised (Moser et al., 1997: 43), in Kenya unions were subject to government restrictions under pressure from the World Bank, and in Ghana there occurred an extensive liberalisation of trade mechanisms (Brown, 1995: 76).

Those organisations promoting neo-liberal policies in Africa were convinced of their success and, in line with the neo-liberal orthodoxy of writers like Hayek, claimed not only economic benefits but also an increase in individual freedom and opportunity for the citizens of Africa's states. The IMF asserted that in countries like Ghana which 'effectively implemented comprehensive adjustment and reform pro-grams', such policies have decreased poverty as well as leading to increased income levels, the modernisation of economic structures, and an increased share of world trade (Hadjimichael et al., 1996: 44; Dixon et al., 1995: 6). The World Bank concurs with this positive assessment of neo-liberal policies in Africa. A report by the Bank in 1994 concluded that the more countries have embraced structural adjustment, the greater have been the economic and social benefits (World Bank, 1994).

However, many aid organisations and academics have been critical of structural adjustment policies. They have questioned the true extent of the economic gains claimed by neo-liberals, and have pointed to the huge social costs associated with such policies. The IMF and World Bank's claim that, if implemented correctly, structural adjustment results in economic growth, has been questioned by Schatz. In an alternative statistical analysis of the World Bank's 1994 report, he concludes that the data presented 'fail[s] to support this claim and even bolster the contrary thesis' (Schatz, 1994: 679). Watkins contends that any benefits created by adjustment in some areas of the economy are normally more than offset by decline in other sectors. Zimbabwe, for example, did experience average annual growth rates of 2.7 per cent in the 1980s, but this was accompanied by 'deteriorating living stan-dards', brought on by increased population growth and an 'increasingly untenable budget deficit' (Watkins, 1995: 76).

One weakness of neo-liberalism is its obsession with narrow econom-ic criteria as a measure of a state's success, without taking into con-sideration the wider social impact of reform. As Logan and Mengisteab

(1993) contend, it must be remembered that even in countries such as Ghana, which has had some success in attracting overseas investment and increasing its trade, such developments should not be seen as ends in themselves but rather should be aimed at the general well being of the country as a whole. They argue that the policies of neo-liberalism have the effect of excluding 70 or 80 per cent of the population and are socially divisive. Contrary to the IMF assessment of Ghana as a flagship example of the benefits of neo-liberalism, Haynes (1996: 88) argues that the results of adjustment in Ghana have amounted to 'social failure'. Despite extensive adjustment policies, ordinary workers found that in 1993 the minimum day's wage of 46 cedis was equal to $0.33 and could purchase only a single bottle of beer! Even the IMF's positive assessment of Ghana's performance conceded that 1996 rates of economic growth would mean that those in absolute poverty would require from thirty to forty years to move out of poverty (Hadjimichael et al., 1996: 44–5). Moreover, even this prediction seems optimistic if one considers that the mild alleviation of poverty claimed by the IMF is more likely to be attributable to the increase in state spending on health and social services in the late 1980s, after they had been slashed in the early years of structural adjustment, rather than the result of the 'trickle down of economic wealth' suggested by neo-liberals (Hadjimichael et al., 1996: 45).

The policy of concentrating upon export-led growth has also been heavily criticised. Such concentration has been extensive in many African states; for example in the 1980s copper accounted for 83 per cent of Zambia's exports while cocoa made up 63 per cent of Ghana's total export earnings (McMichael, 1996: 129). As Brown (1995: 5) argues, the result of such a policy has been 'gross over-production and growing stocks of commodities, which has led to sharply falling world prices of primary commodity exports and thus to a collapse in the earnings of African countries'. The policy of devaluation of currency that often accompanied this export-led approach also meant that any benefits of this strategy were offset by the lowering of earning capacity of workers in real terms and the increase in the cost of imports (Logan and Mengisteab, 1993).

Structural adjustment policies have also had an adverse effect on social cohesion in many states. One of the problems here is the neo-liberal assumption that the answer to Africa's problems is to ape the industrial world in order to emulate its economic success (Brown, 1995). This has often meant adjustment policies have been insensitive to the traditional indigenous cultures of African states and have exacerbated social tensions. Even a state like Tanzania, with 'a long history of ethnic, racial, and religious cohesion', has 'begun to fray as the Government attempts to reform its ailing economy' (Kaiser, 1996: 227). In Tanzania, racial tension has emerged largely as a result of the 'benefits' of reform disproportionately accruing to the minority Asian community. As Watkins (1995: 78–9) argues, the failure of market regulation to provide 'a framework for poverty reduction' coupled with the fact that social welfare programmes have 'not been adequately protected', has meant that the gap between rich and poor has grown under neo-liberal policies. Kaiser (1996) concludes that, in states with a greater history of unrest than Tanzania, adjustment policies are likely to result in even greater social conflicts.

Ironically, although market reforms have significantly undermined the strength of the state to govern effectively, the World Bank and the IMF have often blamed the lack of success of neo-liberal policies on 'poor governance'. For example, in assessing Nigeria's abandonment of structural adjustment in 1994, the IMF blames the inability of the government to win popular support for economic reform (Moser et al., 1997). Neo-liberals such as Hayek have emphasised the superiority of market forces over state planning, but political and economic factors cannot be so easily detached. As Mackintosh (cited in Kiely, 1995: 129) suggests, 'there is no such thing as a free market: *all* markets are structured by state action'. This brings us to the key problem of neo-liberalism in practice. Individuals and states engage in market activity, not as autonomous and unconstrained actors, but act in the context of social and economic structures. For individuals, their ability to compete in the market is shaped by such factors as their 'race', gender and class position. Similarly, countries exist within the context of a states system that privileges some countries over others. In the case of African states, their ability to compete in world markets is greatly restricted by such structural factors, as well Africa's own historical, political and economic circumstances. In ignoring such conditioning factors, neo-liberalism displays a profound lack of understanding of the nature of power. It was highly unlikely that Africa's long-standing problems in constructing effective mechanisms of governance could be solved by importing a highly abstract economic theory which was blind to the multiple sources of Africa's problems.

Any solution to the continent's problems has to begin therefore by acknowledging this fact and dealing with the many factors that hold back Africa's development such as a lack of access to technology, poor internal infrastructure, political instability and the related difficulties of attracting foreign investment (United Nations, 1996b: 27–32). However, one of the paradoxes of the West's promotion of structural adjustment has been its insistence that states in Africa have all too often been self-serving and inefficient, and have therefore been impediments to capitalism, while at the same time displaying geo-political expediency in supporting some of the most corrupt African governments. A classic example of this can be found in the former state of Zaire, renamed the Democratic Republic of the Congo in 1997. As Brown (1995: 111) argues, the 'hideous regime' of Zaire's dictator Mobuto Sese Seko was sustained by the USA as a convenient base for the Angolan rebels the USA supported in their struggle against the Marxist government of Angola. The result of this was that the corrupt Mobuto plundered his country's extensive natural resources for personal gain. Mobuto, who once claimed that 'I owe Zaire nothing. It's Zaire that owes me everything', came to power in 1965 promising to live on his soldier's income, but was thrown out of power by the rebel leader Kabila in 1997 having plundered an estimated $4 billion for himself from his often starving people (*Observer*, 1997). Such examples illustrate the *naïveté* of neo-liberalism in ignoring the constraints that external and internal political factors have played in maintaining Africa in a state of underdevelopment. As the IMF has itself recognised, even in countries with some evidence of benefiting from neo-liberal reform, a key question has been the ability of unstable states to attract sufficient private investment (Moser et al., 1997). Such organisations as the IMF have failed, however, to understand the way in which economic disadvantage and political crises in many African states have reinforced each other, thereby making it unlikely that investors can have sufficient confidence to make a long-term financial commitment. Moreover, recent examples of political instability, corruption and civil war have occurred, not as a result of Africa's inherent 'primitive culture' as has often been implied by the West, but largely as a consequence of the contradictions in Western policy to Africa. As Brown (1995: 6) writes, 'the outbreaks of civil violence and internecine wars in Africa seemed to be more the result of the impasse of accumulating debt and the destruction of old forms of community action than of any irreconcilable differences between ethnic groups'. The combination of extreme indebtedness, political interference from the developed world and inappropriate Western-inspired economic reforms, have all hindered Africa's ability to compete in the world market and to maintain the living standards of its people, thereby increasing social unrest and creating a vicious circle of structural exclusion.

As the World Development Movement has argued (1993), it is not just Africa's geo-political position that prevents its development, it is also its relationship to the world trade system, which operates in a manner that is far from 'free'. The structure of world trade constructed during Africa's colonial period is partly still in place; for example in 1993 over half Africa's trade was with the countries of the European

Union while only 7 per cent was between African states themselves. Africa is therefore dependent on its trade links with Europe that are structured in ways that disadvantage African states. One of the problems with Africa's reliance upon primary commodities has been that the continent has little control over the price of these commodities. Satellite technology means that the West often has greater knowledge of the extent of mineral reserves and the performance of cash crops in Africa than do the Africans themselves. This aids the West in fixing price levels to its advantage (Spybey, 1996: 84). In addition, in 1993 many trade tariffs still existed on goods manufactured in Africa and this helped to prevent a shift away from a dependence upon primary commodities (World Development Movement, 1993).

The myth of the free market is not the only untruth that has driven neo-liberal policy in Africa. The ideological emphasis the IMF and World Bank have placed on the benefits of the market has led them to claim falsely that in South-East Asia, economic success during the early 1990s could be attributed to market forces alone (rather than being led by the state), and that this should be the model broadly followed in Africa. As Dixon and his colleagues have argued:

> The international agencies have indulged in a considerable measure of 'double think' with respect to the role of the state in the development of the Pacific Asian economies . . . attributing the economic problems they experienced during the early 1980s to state involvement in the market, and their subsequent rapid economic recovery to successful liberalisation. (Dixon et al., 1995: 3)

When such organisations as the World Bank argue that the state should play an indirect and limited 'enabling' role in support of economic development they ignore the fact that in South-East Asia the state has often played a much more direct developmental role in economic growth (Ramesh, 1995). Many writers have claimed that such a developmental role for the state may be much more appropriate for many African economies. Such a judgement rejects the highly abstract neo-liberal view of state intervention as being wrong in all places and at all times, and instead asserts a 'balanced pragmatism' where policy should be led by 'an even handed weighing of probable costs and benefits of government involvement on the one hand, and reliance on the market on the other' (Schatz, 1994: 692). As Kiely (1995: 132) argues, such a practical perspective 'does not deny that many states in the developing world are inefficient, but this must be demonstrated rather than theorised on an a priori basis devoid of any historical or social content'. This lack of empirical rigour lies at the heart of neo-liberalism and goes a long way to explaining its lack of success when applied to practical economic and political problems in both the developing and developed world.

Neo-Liberalism and the Problem of Governance

Neo-liberalism does raise fundamental questions about governance. In particular, neo-liberals have been right to highlight how the concentration of power in the state means that the state is often an oppressive, bureaucratic institution which fails to serve the diverse interests of its citizens. Therefore the state can never be a guarantor of order and an effective distributor of resources. Neo-liberals therefore argue for a greatly reduced role for the state and turn to the market to govern the economic interactions of individuals. The illusion that the state can create social justice by over regulating the market should be abandoned and the state put firmly back in its proper place. This neo-liberal challenge to the state has forced many on the left to reject the interventionist state as the solution to the problem of governance, and to consider how the balance between the state and civil society can be transformed (see Chapter 9).

However, as our case study of Africa has highlighted, neo-liberalism has been shown to have weaknesses both theoretically and in practice. Consequently, despite neo-liberal rhetoric about the need to roll back the state, it is unlikely that the real problems of the state identified by writers like Hayek can be resolved in the way he suggests. Some of the clearest deficiencies of neo-liberalism are its flawed conception of the relationship between the state and civil society, its promotion of extreme inequalities of wealth and income, its failure to acknowledge the adverse effect of deregulated markets upon forms of human community, and its lack of understanding of the structures of power. When these weaknesses are considered in combination a number of tensions are revealed in neo-liberal theory, which account for its failure in practice.

The problematic position of the state in neo-liberalism arises from the fact that while wishing to severely limit its operations, neo-liberals accept the need for a state to protect the rights of the individuals and assert the rule of law. However, this leaves unanswered the question that if a state, albeit a limited one, is necessary, how and in whose interests is it run? The importance of this question is heightened by neo-liberalism's embrace of inequality. Neo-liberals argue that such inequality will be accepted by individuals with good grace, since in a society governed by neo-liberal principles such inequality will be the product of a fair struggle within the neutral and undiscriminating market place rather than a result of a prejudiced political judgement by the state. Moreover, the detrimental effects of inequality will in time be offset for the majority because of the huge economic gains created by the free market and the effects of wealth from the most successful 'trickling down' to the rest of the population.

However, the neo-liberal judgement that market forces should be extended at the expense of the state assumes that all individuals begin the race to succeed in the market at the same starting point. As our example of Africa starkly illustrates, this is plainly not the case. The free market does not take into account structural disadvantages such as 'race', gender and class that prevent a fair race from being run. Once this point is accepted neo-liberal theories collapse into contradiction. Structural inequalities lead to social conflict which cannot be resolved by the market. Consequently the state is forced to become increasingly coercive to assert the rule of law. Such social conflict is also exacerbated by the adverse effect that economic deregulation has upon traditional forms of community. As Giddens (1994: 40) has contended, 'neo-liberal political philosophy unleashes detraditionalising influences of a quite far reaching kind' and this undermines possible social and moral barriers to social disorder and conflict, such as traditional family and community structures. The failure of neo-liberalism to produce the large economic growth it promises, the growing gap between rich and poor in both the developed and developing world, and the lack of any evidence of a 'trickle down' effect have meant that, in countries which fell under the neo-liberal spell, the state introduced draconian measures through police and criminal justice reform in order to combat disorder and rising crime rates. For example in Britain the Thatcher and Major governments introduced a number of legislative measures from 1979 onwards which ironically greatly increased the coercive power of the state. Expenditure on the police and prisons grew rapidly, the police were given greater powers to restrict demonstrations, and basic civil rights, such as the right to remain silent in police custody, were removed (Benyon and Edwards, 1997).

This last point brings us back to the question of the state and its relationship to civil society. The inevitable outcome of neo-liberal economic policy, which generates vast and unjustified inequalities, is a strong state that operates in the interests of those who prosper from the operations of the market and which, contrary to the libertarian aspirations of neo-liberalism, entails extensive state interference in civil society. To take Britain as an example once again, the Thatcherite attempt to assert the market often led the state into high-profile conflicts with the associations of civil society, including disputes with professional groups such as teachers and doctors, who protested against the introduction of market reforms into public services (Gilmour, 1992: 184–216).

Finally, not only is the neo-liberal state a highly coercive state, it is also an unaccountable one. Hayek's (1944) hostility to democracy reinforces this interpretation of the outcomes of neo-liberalism: a state that exists to serve the interests of the market rather than being served by it cannot but act in a coercive and undemocratic manner. Because Hayek is so wary of democracy leading to what he sees as anti-market legislation (such as the extension of social rights guaranteed by the state), he argues that a liberal society does not necessarily have to be a democratic one. This view has been echoed in the application of neo-liberalism in Africa; for example one neo-liberal economist stated that in order to successfully enact market reforms, 'a courageous, ruthless and perhaps undemocratic government' was required to 'ride rough-shod' over the democratic wishes of the people (cited in Brown, 1995: 110). The logic of neo-liberalism necessarily entails restricting democracy, precisely because the democratic majority is likely to perceive a deregulated market to be socially and morally unacceptable in its consequences.

This has meant that in practice the neo-liberal state has centralised power rather than dispersed it throughout civil society. To return to our example of the British experience, the neo-liberal state under Thatcher and Major increasingly reduced the power of local government, and greatly increased the number of government appointed 'quangos' which took the place of elected bodies in regulating industries and public services (Coxall and Robins, 1994: 169–203).

Conclusion

This chapter has highlighted the many contradictions of the neo-liberal challenge to the state. While highly critical of the state's interference with the associations of civil society, and therefore advocating the 'rolling back of the state', neo-liberals have ironically embraced an increasingly coercive and unaccountable state. This is because the problems of maintaining social order and distributing resources according to the requirements of justice become acute where the forces of the market are left unregulated. Neo-liberal prescriptions have therefore led to social division and unrest in the developed and developing world. This has required greater state interference in civil society, through the growth in the powers of law-enforcement agencies.

The dominance of neo-liberal principles in powerful, Western-led, international institutions such as the IMF and World Bank, means that such institutions have perceived an extensive role for political institutions as part of the problem of, rather than the solution to, underdevelopment. Such an abstract approach to economic development ignores the ways in which the world economy is structured in the interests of developed countries. Powerful states have been 'the midwives' rather than the victims of economic deregulation and have shaped international trade, not in ways consistent with the 'free' market, but rather in their own interests (Weiss, 1998: 204).

The apparent critique of the state in neo-liberal theory is revealed as in reality a critique of democratic governance. Domestically, the neo-liberal state is not a weak state, but a strong and unaccountable state. Internationally it is powerful states, as much as the laws of supply and demand, which have shaped a distinctly undemocratic system of global governance (See chapter 10). In effect, neo-liberalism is a particular state strategy which serves the interests of those individuals and actors who stand to gain from economic deregulation, both domestically and internationally.

This anti-democratic tendency, inherent to neo-liberalism, has been a major factor in redoubling the efforts of new social movements to oppose the coercive statism that paradoxically emerges from the application of neo-liberal policies. The challenge to the state presented by new social movements is the subject of Chapter 5.

5

New Social Movements

The most distinctive feature of new social movements (NSMs) is their anti-statism. They are therefore of particular interest to our analysis of the relationship between recent social change and the state. This chapter will outline the main elements of the NSMs thesis, before moving on to explore some criticisms that have been made of this thesis. The chapter will conclude with an assessment of the significance of NSMs.

NSMs have undoubtedly helped to highlight the limitations of a state-centred system of governance. In particular they have enhanced our understanding of the ways in which the state privileges certain identities over others. However, this chapter will argue that in their eagerness to stress the novelty and significance of NSMs theorists have overstated their discontinuity with 'old' social movements, have failed to define the relationship between NSMs and other political actors clearly, and have therefore been unable to satisfactorily tackle the dilemma of how NSMs can radically transform systems of governance without wholeheartedly engaging directly with the state. NSMs are, by themselves, therefore highly unlikely to present a serious challenge to the power of the state.

The New Social Movements Thesis

It is through the actions of social movements, which can be defined as groups of like minded individuals combining in a variety of organisational forms to attempt to enact or to prevent social change, that the relationship between the state and civil society is often transformed. For example since the nineteenth century, the labour movement in Western Europe has helped to increase the control civil society has over the state by extending political and social rights. This has ensured that the state has to attempt to (at least) be seen to operate in the general interest of the majority of its citizens. Despite the widespread acknowledgement of the importance of the workers' movement, the study of other social movements was relatively neglected in the first two decades of the post-war period (Scott, 1990: 1–3).

However, ever since the rise of important movements of protest in the late 1960s, such as the Black Power movement, the anti-Vietnam War campaigns, and the student protest movements in Western Europe in 1968, social movements have become the subject of increased scrutiny by political sociologists. For many theorists, contemporary social movements are fundamentally different from those of classical industrial society. They have therefore been christened new social movements. Examples of NSMs include: feminist groups, such as the women in Britain who during the early 1980s set up a peace camp at Greenham Common and campaigned for nuclear disarmament; movements concerned with issues of sexuality such as the Gay Liberation Front and the Aids Coalition to Unleash Power (ACT UP); animal rights activists such as the Animal Liberation Front, which has resorted to the use of letter bombs and other acts of violence in their efforts to publicise the plight of animals; and ecological groups such as Earth First which have protested against the destruction of nature (see Box 5.1).

The novelty of NSMs can be seen in their disillusionment with the statist politics of the socialist left and the neo-liberal right, and their explicit rejection of the state as a tool that can be utilised to create social justice and ensure democratic accountability. Indeed, NSMs' most distinctive defining characteristic is their wariness of any centralised and hierarchical form of governance. In contrast to the workers' movement, NSMs therefore do not seek to control the state. Instead, NSMs, it is argued, display novel forms of democratic organisation which are rooted in the defence of a pluralistic and autonomous civil society.

Linked to their suspicion of the state is the global focus of many NSMs. A good example is environmental groups, such as Friends of the Earth, which have stressed the impotence of state solutions when faced with problems such as pollution, global warming and the erosion of the ozone layer, which are geographically boundless. Consequently, many environmental groups are increasingly global actors and have raised awareness of the growing global nature of many of the problems facing humanity. As Melucci notes (1995: 114), one of the defining characteristics of NSMs is that 'even when the action is located at a specific and particularistic level, actors display a high degree of awareness of planetary interdependence'.

Awareness of the failure of statist solutions to human problems is also common to the other movements normally identified as NSMs, such as anti-racist groups, like the Anti-Nazi League, and gay and lesbian liberation movements, such as Outrage and ACT UP. More generally,

Box 5.1 Anti-Roads Campaigns in Britain

In the 1990s, environmental protests against the government's road building programme in such places as Twyford Down, Fairmile and Preston provided a good example of NSM activity. They differed from previous anti-roads campaigns in three main ways. First, protesters consciously bypassed the formal consultation process in favour of direct action. Second, many activists asserted a counter-culture centred upon anarchistic and anti-modernist ideals. These activists were often critical of what were seen as 'establishment' environmental groups such as Greenpeace, who in turn saw such radicalism as potentially undermining the support amongst the general public for environmental causes generally. The 'eco-warriors' who participated in the anti-roads campaigns believed in spontaneous action rather than formal political organisation. The Brighton-based group Justice, for example, referred to themselves as a 'disorganisation'. They also aimed at a radical shift towards an ecologically sustainable lifestyle, rather than piecemeal political changes. During the campaign against the extension of a motorway through Wanstead and Leyton in East London, for instance, protesters set up squats along the route and declared them 'Free States' for the promotion of alternative lifestyles. Third, campaigners utilised headline grabbing tactics, such as preventing roads from being built by occupying trees and digging tunnels under land which was threatened by road construction. Such campaigns were co-ordinated in part by Earth First, which was set up in the early 1990s. This group had no national organisational structure and no formal leadership. Anti-road campaigns were instead set up via e-mail, newsletters and through direct contact in colleges and universities. Individual campaigns quickly dispersed when a particular road had been either built or stopped. Earth First had considerable success in raising the profile of Britain's transport problems through extensive media coverage of their high-profile protests. Even more significantly, they directly influenced the Conservative government, which cut their 1989 road building programme to one-third of its original size.

Source: Doherty, B. (1998)

this anti-statism can be seen as part of a wider rejection of authoritarianism, associated not only with the state, but also with coercive practices by other social movements, such as fascist or racist groups.

For example the anti-racist movement in Britain, which developed in the late 1970s, lacked faith in the ability of the state to counter effectively the emerging neo-Nazi groups threatening the security of many of Britain's ethnic minorities (Brittan, 1987). Thus informal coalitions of anti-Nazi groups organised protests, petitions and media events to counter the rise in popularity of racist groups such as the National Front.

The rejection of authoritarianism by NSMs can also be seen in their relationship to the workers' movement and Marxist theory. The goals of NSMs are very different from traditional socialist movements and mark a 'shift from a vision of a sudden and total transformation of the social order to the hope that partial, local, and continuous changes will add up to a transformation as profound as a revolution' (Garner, 1996: 101).

In terms of social composition, NSMs are, it is argued, not rooted in the working class in the mould of the labour movement. Instead, 'new social movements are typically either predominantly movements of the educated middle classes, especially the "new middle class", or of the most educated/privileged section of generally less privileged groups' (Scott, 1990: 138). Theorists of NSMs have either stressed that these groups cannot be reduced to their class interest, and therefore should be seen as transcending class relations, or alternatively they have radically redefined class, thereby allowing for the adaptation of class analysis to the study of these movements. Interesting examples of the attempt to rethink the relationship between Marxism, social class and NSMs can be found in the work of Touraine (1981) and Eder (1993).

For Touraine (1981: 77), social movements represent the 'organised collective behaviour of a class actor struggling against his class adversary for the social control of *historicity*'. However, Touraine is using the concept of class in a very different way to Marxist thinkers. The problem with Marxist analysis, for Touraine, is that it reduces the actions of social movements to either furthering or trying to prevent the inevitable forward march of history towards communism. Thus social movements are seen as unreflective and only dimly aware of the deeper social processes by which their actions are driven. Touraine instead wishes to reassert the importance of social action, with social movements lying at the heart of his theory of social change. He therefore begins his most important contribution to the NSMs debate in the following manner: 'Men make their own history: social life is produced by cultural achievements and social conflicts, and at the heart of society burns the fire of social movements' (Touraine, 1981: 1). The use of the term *historicity* by Touraine refers to the object of social movements' struggle, which is not to seize the state and use it to oppress the movements' class enemies, but rather is centred upon the conflict over the competing value systems through which the architecture of society is constructed: that is the *historicity* of a social system. When Touraine speaks of class conflict then, he has in mind a struggle over the 'symbolic representation' of experience, the construction of which cannot be reduced to antagonisms over the means of material production. Therefore the workers' movement of the nineteenth century, as described by Marxism, was not a social movement in terms of Touraine's definition because it was not guided by 'normative orientations, by a *plan*, in fact a call to historicity' (Touraine, 1981: 78). The worker's movement was, according to Touraine, understood by Marxists as a pawn in a game of chess in which the result and the strategy deployed, if not the direction of every move, was already known, not necessarily by the movement itself, but certainly by the Marxist theorist! The teleological assumptions of Marxism must be rejected if the true natures of social movements are to be revealed as 'culturally oriented forms of behaviour, and not as the manifestation of the objective contradictions of a system of domination' (Touraine, 1981: 80).

Like Touraine, Eder (1993) stresses the need to analyse social movements in terms of culture, while, at the same time, retaining a revised concept of class. First, Eder rejects the idea that class conflict can be reduced to the struggle between capital and labour. Second, the concept of class nevertheless retains a utility because the struggles of NSMs are not simply concerned with the demand for universal and equal inclusion in the social system: they are also about the struggle between 'antagonistic and even incommensurable interests' (Eder, 1995: 22). Third, the use of class in a way that emphasises cultural (as well as material) conflicts, allows for the possibility of accounting for as yet unknown or undeveloped social conflicts, which may be based upon social divisions other than those that exist between the owners of the means of production and the exploited workers. For Eder, NSMs can be understood in class terms as examples of 'middle class radicalism' (Eder, 1993). This notion allows us to move beyond the naturalistic definition inherent to Marxist theory where class is 'tied to natural forces, the forces of production' towards a conception of class tied to the problem of cultural identity (Eder, 1995: 36).

It is argued that to maintain their independent cultural identities the struggle for the recognition of diversity cannot be centred singularly upon the state. For writers like Melucci, a central prerequisite for the redefinition of democracy by NSMs is the creation and maintenance of 'public spaces independent of the institutions of government, the party system and state structures' (Melucci, 1989: 173). This is because NSMs are concerned with diverse and profound objectives, which are often centred upon issues of morality, rather than the extension of political citizenship (Eder, 1993: 149). For Melucci (1989), NSMs bring to prominence social struggles that have been ignored because of an over concentration upon workers by Marxists or by an obsession with formal equality on behalf of liberals. Thus conflicts over gender, sexuality, the ecology and animal abuse have been central to NSMs. These areas of social struggle have often been referred to as post-material by NSMs theorists, since they do not focus primarily upon issues of income, wealth or formal political representation and have therefore been defined as social or cultural, rather than political in nature (Scott, 1990: 13). For this reason, NSMs' main arena of struggle is located within civil society rather than oriented towards the state, which is seen by NSMs as having failed to guarantee social justice and freedom from discrimination. NSMs have provided powerful critiques of the welfare functions of the state, pointing towards their basis on patriarchal, homophobic and racist assumptions, as well as being connected with ecologically unsustainable economic growth and the maintenance of destructive 'defence' systems (Pierson, 1991: Ch. 3).

Touraine (1981) has identified how an increasingly technocratic state moves to colonise civil society in order to exercise social control. From this perspective, NSMs are important defenders of civil society from the increasingly coercive state machine. This coercion takes the form, not just of physical force, but is asserted through discourses of power which attempt to inhibit the self-management of social problems and create dependency upon the agents of the state such as the health service, education system and social security providers. It is for this reason that Melucci (1989) argues for maximum independence for NSMs and the deliberate distancing from the organs of the state. If allowed the necessary freedom from state interference, NSMs can be 'social laboratories', creating innovative life styles. They focus not upon confronting state power, but on changing human relationships at the micro level. Consequently, 'interactionist and cultural resistance is an ongoing process and may take the form of play, performance, and style rather than political organizing' (Garner, 1996: 392). Through these strategies of resistance within civil society, the technocratic state is revealed as 'no longer the all-powerful god it was made out to be' (Touraine, 1981: 6).

As well as presenting fresh ideological challenges to the state then NSMs have also adopted novel forms of organisation and tactics to promote themselves. NSMs place great stress upon non-hierarchical systems of organisation, which are often highly flexible and involve the interaction of loose networks of self-aware and egalitarian individuals who consciously reject the aggressive centralisation of traditional parties, trade unions and pressure groups. The fluid organisational forms taken by NSMs are concrete statements of the democratic values that they espouse. Organisationally, NSMs do not rely upon an elite group of professional campaigners, that are common to most pressure groups, and have instead a fluctuating and dynamic membership. Activists signal their support, not through the payment of a subscription, or by the holding of a membership card, but through sporadic actions such as organising petitions, attracting media attention, demonstrating in favour of or against policy changes by government and by protesting against ideologically opposed groups such as racist, homophobic or other socially conservative forces. Advocates of NSMs see such loose networks of affiliation as a strength. By resisting the institutionalisation of their various causes, they can more easily retain their independence and their ideological purity, as well as allowing space outside formal and oppressive structures for the building of confidence and solidarity amongst their members. Tactically, their innovative efforts to influence public opinion and to assert alternative discourses that challenge the bureaucratic orthodoxy of traditional parties and pressure groups deliberately go beyond narrow political actions. As Garner (1996: 99) writes, NSMs' tactics have included such diverse acts as: 'Mass peace demonstrations, squatter takeovers of buildings to protect housing shortages and gentrification, the formation of feminist collectives, experiments in media and the arts including cultural protests like punk, and many local actions against nuclear power plants and industrial pollution'. For example the Greenham Common Women, mentioned earlier, relied on non-violent direct action such as removing fences, street theatre and spinning webs around the military base at Greenham. The British gay and lesbian group, Outrage, have advertised their message through mass gay weddings, 'kiss-ins' and by bombarding schools with leaflets about safe sex (Studzinski, 1994: 17, 50).

Many of these actions are concerned with the assertion of heterogeneous identities as symbols and signs of alternative lifestyles. They are a reaction not only to the coercive power and disabling discourses of the state, but also to the increasing commodification of all spheres of life and the promotion of junk culture associated with the assertion by neo-liberals of the free market as the main arbiter of success in late modern societies. Attempts to classify NSMs in terms of the old language of political discourse, such as left versus right, or reform versus revolution, is (it is argued) to miss the distinctive nature of these movements. NSMs attempt to transcend the traditional emphasis of the workers' movement upon the promotion of the rights of white

male able-bodied workers, as much as they do the conservative emphasis upon patriarchal private property. They reject the 'soviet type
revolutionary state' as much as they do the paternalistic and dependency creating liberal state (Touraine, 1981: 17). Theorists of NSMs
point to the dangers of seeing such movements as mere appendices to
the greater struggle of workers against capitalists, and stress the failure
of the old social movements to take into account the diverse needs of
other members of society. For instance, as Campbell and Oliver (1996:
176) argue in relation to the disability movement, the idea that the
disabled can achieve their aims through a closer link with the workers'
movement 'flies in the face of history' since it has often been the
workers' movement that has hindered progress towards the extension
of rights for the disabled.

The recognition of the inevitability of difference, and the celebration
of cultural pluralism, is central to NSMs conception of democracy, in
contrast to essentialist liberal and Marxist accounts of the universality
of the individual (liberal) or of the proletariat as a universal class
(Marxist). Whilst many NSMs might fight to receive recognition on
the terrain of human rights, ultimately Touraine (1981: 18) sees this as a
tactical move: 'We shall have to live with cultural modernisation
movements linked to a liberal critique before we are able to assist
the renaissance of social movements'.

It is important to stress that theorists such as Touraine and Melucci
do not believe that the new experiments taking place in these 'social
laboratories' are marginal or doomed to failure. The prevailing view of
the relationship between NSMs and social change amongst NSMs
theorists is captured by Marable (1997: 11) who, in commenting upon
developments in the black liberation movement in the USA, writes
'liberation begins by winning small battles . . . creating confidence
among the oppressed, building ultimately towards a democratic vision
which can successfully challenge the very foundation of this system'. It
is the sum of these 'small battles' which will transform society by
destabilising the coercive state and delegitimising its dominant discourses of power. As Melucci (1995: 114) contends, 'the very existence
of collective action is a message sent to the society: power becomes
visible because it is challenged by the production of different meanings'. In the longer term the successes of NSMs will not be marked by
the replacement of one dominant discourse by another, but rather by
the 'recognition of diversity': a culturally plural society (Melucci, 1989:
178). The notion of a progressive evolution towards a more advanced
society is bound up with the outdated ideologies of modernity such as
socialism and liberalism, and therefore the principle for social change
in the contemporary world must be that the 'idea of superseding must

be replaced by the search for an alternative', because, 'we are moving quite simply into a type of society in which no transcendence . . . will any longer force collective action to take on a meaning by which it is surpassed' (Touraine, 1981: 2, 80). By this, Touraine implies that the value of NSMs lies in their existence as alternative sites of democracy to the state, rather than merely as a means to a greater end.

The NSMs thesis, the main elements of which are summarised and contrasted with an 'ideal type' definition of the labour movement in Table 5.1, presents an interesting and multifaceted challenge to definitions of governance centred upon the state. However, both the conceptual assumptions of the NSMs theorists and their description of the practical realities of NSMs have been challenged from a variety of perspectives. The next section of this chapter will examine the most important of these critiques.

Criticisms of the New Social Movements Thesis

Political scientists have been especially critical of the notion that NSMs are clearly distinct from conventional pressure groups. The problem here is that the NSMs thesis has paid too much attention to the alleged cultural and social novelty of these movements and has not properly addressed exactly how these groups are organised, what resources they use to assert their aims, and in what ways they interact with the state and other political actors. Because these issues have not been fully considered by NSMs theorists, these movements can appear to have 'something ethereal or unrealistic about them' (Garner, 1996: 14).

Without more precise definitions, there is the danger of lumping together, under a single term, groups that have very different ideological perspectives, levels of commitment to the 'cause', varied organisational forms and a variety of political as well as cultural objectives (Jordan and Maloney, 1997: 48–52). It may not be appropriate, for example, to group together formal groups such as Friends of the Earth, which offers relatively little opportunity for participation by ordinary supporters, and more radical and decentralised groups such as the anti-road campaigners like Earth First and Justice. Scott supports this point through a study of the development of the Green movement in West Germany. He finds that there is a great deal of ideological diversity, which can usefully be divided along conventional left- and right-wing lines. The fact that much NSMs theory has often failed to acknowledge these distinctions has meant that the NSMs thesis has tended to centre upon the 'most fundamentalist expression' of a particular movement, thereby giving a distorted view of the movement as a whole (Scott, 1990: 150).

Table 5.1 Ideal Types of Old and New Social Movements

Characteristics	Labour Movement	New Social Movements
Principal objective	Control of state	Maintenance of autonomy within an expanded and highly pluralistic civil society
Principal opponent/ threat	Deregulated capitalism	Technocratic state
Type of movement	Primarily political but unions provide important social/economic function	Primarily cultural/social but engaged in redefining the political: 'the personal is political'
Key Issues	Questions of inequality of material goods, social justice, poverty and unemployment	Ethical questions of personal autonomy, libertarianism, protection of nature, and the maintenance of peace
Organisation	Centralised and hierarchical parties and unions	Loose networks of like minded individuals
Tactics	Participation in elections, campaigns and industrial action aimed at increasing economic and social rights	Sporadic mass demonstrations, protests, cultural expressions of alternative lifestyles and identities
Orientation to international sphere	International solidarity offset by nationalistic sentiment	Awareness of interconnections between the local and the global: 'act local, think global'
Approach to democracy	Social democracy/ industrial democracy	Democracy of difference/ deliberative democracy
Approach to citizenship	Extension of liberal citizenship (civil, political and social rights) to all members of the polity	Promotion of group rights/ protection of general human rights
Main social base	Working class and socialist intellectuals from other classes	Middle class, particularly professional and public sector workers, and university-educated working class

Jordan and Maloney (1997) also question the extent to which, in reality, NSMs can be both non-institutional and successful. This takes us to the fundamental issue of the relationship between the state and NSMs, and whether NSMs are to be understood as political or cultural entities. A consideration of these questions exposes the major weakness of the NSMs thesis. Theorists like Touraine and Melucci assert that NSMs are cultural rather than political phenomena and should therefore not overly concern themselves with conventional political issues like the extension of citizenship. From this perspective, success is measured by the extent to which NSMs can maintain their autonomy from the state and retain their loose-knit organisation. As we have seen, however, the NSMs thesis does not assume the marginality of these groups, but instead argues that it is through these groups that society will be transformed and governance redefined. The problem with this observation is that the nature and method of this transformation are extremely vague. This is due in part to an exaggerated importance being placed upon the transformative power of the new emancipatory discourses associated with the NSMs. Such 'discursive resistance' fails to take into account the problem of how the very real material power that the state commands could be dismantled or successfully opposed, and how the coercive inequality of the market could be transcended. Therefore, NSMs theorists, who contend that such movements can have a revolutionary impact upon the social system, are forced into the position of trying to identify an appropriate harbinger of this transformation in a manner not far removed from the structuralist thinkers they criticise. For instance, Touraine (1981: 95), while asserting the need for movements to retain autonomy and to define their future though their own social agency, searches (in vain) for a single movement to 'occupy the central role held by the workers' movement in industrial society' and by doing so he falls into the teleological trap that he identifies as tripping up Marxism. He asserts that it is 'mistaken to believe social movements are by definition agents of *historical change*' while at the same believing that 'society is animated by *a single* social movement for each social class' (Touraine, 1981: 94–5). If, as Touraine argues, individuals make their own history through their social actions, then this last assertion has all the theoretical power of wishful thinking.

Similarly Melucci, although disputing the idea that the NSMs can form a single transformative movement, is caught in the dilemma of wanting to grant great significance to the actions of NSMs while failing to overcome the problem identified by Scott (1990: 67) that 'social movement activity is unstable to the extent that there is no effective third course between sporadic action around specific questions and formal political organisation'. The problem here for Melucci revolves around the false dualism he asserts between cultural and political movements. By defining NSMs as cultural, Melucci is in danger of missing one of the most original aspects of social movements, which is their redefinition and extension of the field of politics that has occurred in a practical as well as theoretical sense. In societies that are governed by the state, which has compulsory and universal jurisdiction, NSMs have little choice to, at some stage, interact with the state and its agents, often in alliance with more formal groups such as pressure groups. It is only by challenging the state directly, rather than ignoring it, that the state may be reformed and democratised.

Box 5.2 Classifying Social Movements

The social movement concept may be best used as an umbrella term to refer to a coalition of groups at various stages of institutionalisation which each aims to further a shared cause. A social movement may include political parties and pressure groups, as well as more informal groups. For example, in the British context, the environmental movement embraces organised political parties such as the Green Party and pressure groups such as Greenpeace and the World Wildlife Fund, as well as informal new social movements such as anti-road construction campaigners. Within this framework, NSMs can best be understood as the ideological and politically innovative subsector of a wider social movement.

Generally, then, the NSMs thesis overstates the autonomy such movements can or may wish to maintain. In reality, the dilemma of ideological purity versus increasing institutionalisation is an ever-present one for NSMs. Their ability to join together in the first place and to maintain their independence cannot be understood outside of the wider political system. Contrary to Melucci, many of the issues raised by such movements have focused upon the extension of citizenship of the state, either in terms of civil rights, for example issues of the age of sexual consent for gay men, or social rights, for instance women's struggle for changes to tax and benefit systems. Moreover, these struggles are ongoing.

A related criticism is that many theorists have failed to analyse the continuing constraints upon the actions and resources of NSMs. Political scientists have attempted to address these problems of constraints and resources through the theories of Resource Mobilisation and Political Opportunity. McAdam (1996: 27) gives an example of the political opportunity approach when he outlines the factors that shape the ability of NSMs to influence the political agenda. These include:

1. The relative openness of the state to changes that arise in civil society
2. The stability of elite alignments

3. The presence of elite allies, sympathetic to the proposed social changes
4. The nature of social control mechanisms and the state's willingness to suppress protest and the formation of new movements

This approach, along with the resources mobilisation model, which points to the need to consider how NSMs utilise such resources as time, money and leadership skills, suggests that the formation and actions of NSMs have to be understood in their political context: NSMs theory, in its desire to assert the importance of social agency, has often forgotten the importance of structural constraints. This problem is very apparent in authoritarian countries, where the autonomy and relative freedom of civil society, often taken as given by the NSMs thesis, is largely absent. Thus as Gledhill (1994: 181) notes, Touraine often displays a Eurocentric approach because he assumes that the 'explosion of "social movements" as he defines them is conditional on a society reaching a certain stage of development not yet reached in "dependent" peripheral countries'.

In fact, social movements in authoritarian regimes have to struggle to gain, rather than simply maintain, a level of autonomy. This will often only be won if for some reason the coercive powers of the state become weakened. For example Zhao (1997) has argued that the rise of the student movement in China in 1989 can be attributed mainly to the decline of state legitimacy within universities, which in turn helped to loosen the controls on student mobilisation normally undertaken by student activists in co-operation with paid party workers. As the economy was gradually liberalised, and alternative careers for the young opened up, the status and number of such loyal student activists declined and consequently the student movement was able to develop. In the Latin American context, Foweraker (1995: 42) contends that 'the very different relations between state and civil society . . . do make a difference: the challenge [of NSMs] cannot be mounted at a great distance from the state'.

If the over emphasis on emancipatory ideology and culture has led NSMs theorists to underestimate the need for empirical research into the relationship between NSMs and the context in which they evolve, it has also led them to overstate the discontinuity between 'old' social movements and NSMs. Calhoun (1993) maintains that the early nineteenth century witnessed the formation of a whole host of social movements throughout Europe and the USA that were based on non-material issues such as temperance, lifestyle issues, and religion, many of which had characteristics very similar to the NSMs of the late twentieth century. It can also be argued that the workers' movement of the nineteenth century had a strong base in civil society through their union organisation. Nor is the emphasis on building confidence and self-worth amongst their members new to contemporary movements, as the following statement from Sylvia Pankhurst, one of the leaders of the British women's suffrage movement in the early twentieth century, illustrates:

> The existence of a strong self-reliant movement amongst working women would be the greatest aid in safeguarding their rights on the day of settlement. Moreover, I was looking to the future: I wanted to rouse these women of the submerged mass to be, not merely the argument of more fortunate people, but to be fighters on their own account. (cited in Durham, 1985: 186)

The failure to include groups such as pro-family, pro-life or racist movements in most discussions of NSMs also raises suspicion as to the academic rigour being applied in the NSMs thesis. This criticism can be successfully met, however, if new social movements are defined as emancipatory and anti-statist in orientation. Nevertheless, Jordan and Maloney (1997: 57) are right to suggest that 'the NSMs term is often used as a mark of approval of the (radical) goal rather than a statement about organisational structures that usefully distinguishes the group and the movement'. This comment summarises the view of some critics that NSMs are barely more than abstract and ideological constructs, which tell us little about the true nature or objectives of collective action. As such, it could be argued that the term NSMs should be abandoned and instead collective action should be considered through conventional concepts like pressure groups and political parties.

The Significance of New Social Movements

Given these extensive criticisms of the NSMs thesis, does the concept of NSMs have any utility for the political sociologist's concern with the state–civil society relationship?

Where the NSMs thesis seems weakest is in its concentration upon the cultural aspects of movements at the expense of understanding the significant contributions some movements have made in redefining the concept of the politics. In this sense, NSMs have mounted an important symbolic challenge to the state and highlighted the ways in which the state–civil society relationship reflects deep social divisions and depoliticises important issues. For example the often innovative methods of protest adopted by ecological and women's movements have helped to place many new issues firmly on the political agenda in many developed and developing countries. These include exposing the essentially ideologically constructed division between a male-dominated public sphere and a private sphere, where the operation of patriarchy attempts to keep women in a subservient position. Increasing awareness of the constant threat that industrial society poses to the global environment is also due in no small measure to the activities of NSMs.

As Scott (1990: 25) has argued, if NSMs are analysed in their proper political context, clearly they have helped to increase political participation amongst young people in Europe and the USA who have felt alienated from bureaucratic and increasingly similar political parties. The adoption of many of the issues championed by NSMs by political parties and pressure groups, argues Scott, should be seen as a success for these movements. Indeed, even the demise of a movement, rather than signalling its failure or its institutionalisation into a hostile system, can instead often signal the achievement of its goal (Scott, 1990: 10). The relationship between the state and social movements will be shaped by numerous economic, political and social factors that cannot be easily accommodated into a single grand theory as is often attempted by the NSM theorists. The course of events will sometimes mean that a particular movement can gain prominence and significantly influence the political debate, and at other times their prominence and relevance will fade: that is, NSMs are often cyclical in nature. A good example of this process is provided by Ruzza's (1997) study of the relationship between the Italian peace movement and the state. Ruzza observes that at times when issues of defence were high on the agenda in Italy, such as in 1981 when the government proposed deploying Pershing and Cruise missiles or in 1991 during the Second Gulf War, the peace movement had a considerable impact in shifting public opinion towards support for nuclear-free zones and draft objectors. In the absence of such galvanising events, the inherent tendency towards fragmentation displayed by such groups might lead to a decline in their influence. Such reliance on political events, the difficulties of maintaining anti-hierarchical structures while retaining coherence, and the problem of sustaining media coverage, means that many NSMs are perhaps best perceived as catalysts that sometimes spark action by more formal political actors. However, as Ruzza contends, this role can at times be of considerable importance in legitimising new areas of political concern as a basis for public debate and policy formulation.

The West European focus of much NSMs theory has obscured how, in the developing world, and throughout Eastern Europe, mass social movements have had an even more direct impact on the governance

of these countries, playing an important role in breaking down authoritarian regimes. Foweraker (1995: 91) has shown, for example, how
NSMs in Latin American countries have acted as 'schools of democracy
in the form of intellectual caucuses, popular assemblies, demonstrations, sit-ins and negotiations with political authorities'. By playing
such a role, NSMs have strongly contributed to democratic transition in
many countries. In Chile during the early 1980s, for example, a mass
women's movement was formed independently of conventional political parties and through campaigns such as the Women for Life
demonstration in December 1983 the movement played a central role
in the development of democracy (Foweraker, 1995: 110).

NSMs have considerably improved our understanding of the multifaceted operation of power. In this regard, they have highlighted the
importance of discourses of power and the way in which specialist
systems of language can be used by the agents of the state in ways that
contribute to very real inequalities in areas such as health care and
education. Women's groups have highlighted how the symbolic portrayal of women in popular culture through pornography, advertising
and cinema has helped to create an atmosphere of oppression for
women and encouraged male violence towards them.

The NSMs thesis has also highlighted the difficult issue of how
fundamental differences within democratic systems are to be accommodated and raised important questions about whether the state can
ever be truly inclusive. NSMs have contributed to our understanding of
the importance of social agency in shaping the relationship between
the social and the political, and the ways in which individuals' conscious actions can help to subvert and transform social structures. In
this sense, they have shown how the state–civil society relationship is
shaped by the agency of individuals as well as by structural forces.
Consequently, political sociology has benefited from engaging in the
NSMs debate, which has helped to expose the limits of a purely state-
centred or society-centred approach to understanding the state's relationship with civil society.

Conclusion

The activities of new social movements have thrown considerable light
upon the problematic relationship between the state and civil society.
Their very emergence as a political force can be explained by a distrust
of the ability of the state to govern civil society in ways which are
democratic and inclusive. Through their novel campaigns NSMs have
highlighted the way in which the state is not neutral but in fact

embodies the inequalities that pervade society. Our understanding of the nature of communicative power has therefore been deepened through a consideration of new social movements. They have shown how our state-centred and therefore exclusive and hierarchical definitions of political problems reflect deep-seated power relationships.

However, like the challenges of globalisation and neo-liberalism, NSMs have served to highlight the problems of the state rather than significantly diminishing its power. In this sense, in their desire to maintain the purity of NSMs, champions of NSMs, such as Touraine and Melucci, are in danger of ignoring rather than than engaging actively with the power of the state. By themselves, the informal and sporadic actions of NSMs cannot hope to transform the relationship between state and civil society in the way Touraine and Melucci suggest. In reality, the state remains the central focal point of power, and social movements of all kinds need to interact directly with the state if they are not to be permanently marginalised politically.

The central argument of this part of the book then has been that in order to find effective systems of governance beyond the state it is first necessary to acknowledge the power of the state. We cannot prematurely announce the state's demise, as some exponents of globalisation have done. Nor can we ignore the state and find refuge in the market or in self-governing social movements. This would be to gravely underestimate the power of the state.

Nevertheless, recent processes of social change have been significant in changing the context in which the state operates and highlighting its problematic relationship with civil society. This had led political sociologists to reconsider the problem of governance. Part IV explores some ways in which the state–civil society relationship has been rethought by contemporary political sociologists. First, however, Part III continues my analysis of the impact of social change upon the state–civil society relationship through a consideration of political culture, citizenship and political participation.

Part III

Challenges to Civil Society

6

Political Culture

Within prominent schools of thought in political sociology, such as behaviouralism and pluralism, it has long been assumed that a stable system of governance is necessarily based upon a strong and cohesive civil society. In this sense, civil society not only rests upon a legal and political framework provided by the state, but also upon the political orientations, attitudes and goals of its citizens. It is often assumed that it is a set of common political attitudes, universal citizenship and respect for representative democracy within civil society that makes liberal democracy such an attractive form of governance. Indeed it is for such reasons that writers such as Fukuyama (1992) have argued that liberal democracy is becoming the universally accepted model of governance across the globe. In Part III we explore whether such optimism is justified in the light of recent social changes. These changes have raised doubts over whether the current forms of political culture, citizenship and political participation within liberal democracy are able to successfully underpin civil society. Each chapter has two main aims. First, each will explore how the concept under discussion has been variously defined by political sociologists. Secondly, each chapter will explore how recent social change has affected the role the concept plays in mediating civil society's relationship to the state.

One of the most influential theories of the relationship between individuals' political attitudes and systems of governance can be found in the behaviouralist concept of political culture. In this chapter I shall therefore analyse this concept. Of particular importance in developing the concept was Almond and Verba's *The Civic Culture* (1963). In this study, the stability of liberal democracies was explained in terms of their supportive value systems. However, as early as the mid-1970s, writers such as Daniel Bell (1976) were observing the development of a schism between the cultural values of modern society and the economic and political systems of liberal democracy. The second section of the chapter introduces various theories of crisis that were advanced to explain the decline of civic culture. In the 1990s, concerns about the onset of a moral crisis are even more widespread amongst commentators from many intellectual traditions. In the third section of the chapter I shall therefore explore the supposed replacement of a civic culture by a new culture of anomie, characterised variously as the demoralisation of society, the rise of a dangerous 'underclass' and the development of a culture of contentment. The chapter will conclude with an assessment of the connections between political culture and governance.

The Concept of Political Culture

In 1956, the behaviouralist Gabriel Almond (1956: 396) defined political culture as 'the particular patterns of orientations to political action', which for him underpinned all systems of governance. The political culture approach asserted that a particular system needed to be seen as legitimate by its citizens if it was to survive. As Fukuyama (1992: 215) has recently insisted, 'no real-world society can long survive based on rational calculation and desire alone'.

In 1963, in collaboration with Sidney Verba, Almond published an extensive study of the political cultures of five very different political systems: the USA, Britain, Mexico, Italy and Germany. On the basis of interviews conducted with one thousand citizens in each of these states, Almond and Verba drew extensive conclusions about the impact of diverse political cultures upon democracy. Their findings appeared to support Fukuyama's observation that for democracy to work, its values must be assimilated 'into the citizen's sense of his own self' (Fukuyama, 1992: 215).

Of the countries studied, Almond and Verba concluded that the 'civic culture' found in the USA and Britain was the most conducive to stable governance. States that had failed to develop such cultural support for democracy were prone to authoritarianism, as demonstrated by the rise of Nazism in Germany in the 1930s. This Anglo-American civic culture was characterised by a balance between citizens' deference for established authority on the one hand and their willingness to actively participate in the political process on the other. Britain provided perhaps the best example of a stable civic culture, with its high degree of cultural homogeneity, a broad consensus on the rules underpinning parliamentary democracy and a respect for government that was often deferential. Thus, Almond and Verba reject the notion that political behaviour is best explained by the rational choices of individual actors. Instead it is shared core values and 'social trust' between individuals and political institutions that underpin a successful civil society: the question of how people feel about their political institutions is, for Almond and Verba, a crucial question of political sociology. Political culture then is seen by the behaviouralists as an important mediator between civil society and the state. It provides a link 'between the behaviour of individuals and the behaviour of systems' (Almond and Verba, 1963: 300).

Criticisms of the Political Culture Approach

The first set of criticisms of Almond and Verba's study relates to the methodology employed, and in particular the supposed objectivity that Almond and Verba claimed informed their study. Welch (1993) has identified a tension between the notion of political culture as a socio-logical concept used to evaluate attitudes within a particular civil society and its use as a comparative tool to analyse differences between political systems. In its sociological usage, a range of sociological variables is said to account for the level of democracy within a state, whereas in their comparisons across states the stability of democracy is explained 'in terms of pre-existing political cultural conditions' (Welch, 1993: 15). This suggests a rather vague conception of the actual relationship between a particular culture and any given state. As Barry (1978) has argued, it is not clear if the value system leads to a successful system of governance, or whether political culture is itself a product of a set of stable institutional relationships. More fundamentally, it suggests that Almond and Verba begin with a preconceived view of what constitutes a successful democracy. Their study is shaped by their normative support of liberal democracy.

Pateman (1989) has provided an extensive critique of Almond and Verba's definition of democracy. Despite linking their study to the classical view of democracy, by referring to Greek notions of 'civic virtue' in the preface to their study, the vision of democracy that underpins *The Civic Culture* is a far cry from the extensive participatory model of the ancient Greek polis. Almond and Verba's celebration of deference and limited participation is more in keeping with the demo-cratic elitist position of Weber or Schumpeter. Indeed, for Almond and Verba, deference to elites is crucial in sustaining the 'myth' of the democratic citizen. For the state to run effectively, this myth 'must never become more than an unrealized potentiality' (Pateman, 1989: 147). Thus political culture is an illusion that sustains what is in reality a highly centralised and hierarchical system of governance.

That behaviouralists start with a preconceived idea about what kind of democracy is both desirable and viable is supported by Almond and Verba's interpretation of their own, often crude, data. Despite the fact that only 46 per cent of the British interviewees said they were proud of their system, Almond and Verba see Britain as perhaps the most successful democracy in the world (Held, 1996: 210). Almond and Verba further betray their preconceptions when they describe the civic culture as Anglo-American tradition's 'gift to the world'. Other studies in the behaviouralist tradition have also produced bizarre interpretations of data that might more accurately reflect a lack of faith in representative democracy. For instance, Rosenbaum, in his 1975 book on political culture, somehow managed to conclude that in the USA democracy was reasonably healthy. This, despite the fact that in the surveys he draws support from (1975: 84–8), 61.5 per cent of respondents asked in 1964 agreed with the statement that 'nothing I ever do seems to have any effect upon what happens in politics', while in 1970 only 27 per cent professed to having voiced a political opinion!

The concept of political culture has also been criticised for ignoring important social cleavages based on gender, class and 'race'. As Pateman (1989: 143) contends, large differences in levels of political activity and political competence between men and women, and between different social classes, are largely ignored by the authors of *The Civic Culture*. However, accounting for such differences is crucial if one is to ascertain how truly democratic a system of government is. Despite their claims to be objectively analysing politics by questioning the actual participants in the political process Almond and Verba's study is both highly abstract and particularistic. It is abstract because although they deny the rational activist view of the citizen, Almond and Verba do in fact embrace an atomised view of individuality: citizens are abstracted from the economic and social structures that in practice constrain and influence political participation. As Pateman contends, Almond and Verba assume that 'systematically structured inequalities appear as *individual* psychological and personal attributes that happen to be distributed in a particular way' (Pateman, 1989: 174, emphasis added). It is particularistic because their limited definitions of politics and participation highlight their ideological commitments. For example, issues of gender exclusion from mainstream politics are not addressed by Almond and Verba. This may be accounted for by the implicit assumption in behaviouralism that the active citizen is, and should be, predominately male. Almond and Verba's own figures on the importance of participation in 'non-political' institutions in building subjective feelings of political competence suggest that a truly democratic system depends upon a much wider definition of politics than the narrow and gendered conception employed in *The Civic Culture* (Almond and Verba, 1963: 348–54; Pateman, 1989: 151–4). This reinforces the point made by feminists, that effective democratisation necessarily entails a breaking down of the public–private distinction that under-mines women's opportunities to be active citizens.

In largely overlooking the class differences evident in their study, Almond and Verba also ignore the possibility that political culture may be much more fragmented within a state than they suppose. Mann (1970) argues that it is precisely the lack of a value consensus amongst the working class in countries like the USA that explains the absence of a revolutionary consciousness that might threaten the dominant values of the ruling class. This suggests that a high degree of ideological cohesion may be necessary for the rulers, but not the ruled. For critics like Jessop (1974), this means that 'civic culture' best describes an ideological aspect of class rule, rather than a set of shared values that transcend social divisions.

The abstract nature of *The Civic Culture* divorces the notion of a set of core values from the power relationships that shape such values within liberal democracy. Almond and Verba tell us little about how or why a particular political culture develops, and just how it may support existing power structures. In my discussion of Gramsci's concept of hegemony in Chapter 2, I noted how a set of value orientations towards a political system may not be the product of historical accident, but may represent a conscious attempt by the ruling class to legitimise their rule through the promotion of a set of supposedly universal values. In this sense, concepts of nationalism, citizenship or legitimacy are useful tools of social control, which undermine working-class consciousness and thereby ensure the survival of the system. In their analysis of the relationship between the state and culture in Britain, Lloyd and Thomas (1998) illustrate just such a point. They trace the development of the increased state involvement in civil society from the 1860s onwards as part of a 'transition from a predominantly coercive to a hegemonic form . . . in order to contain the demands of a highly mobilized and articulate working class' (1998: 115). The conscious creation of a shared political culture involved 'drawing or eliciting the formal or "representative" disposition in every person out of the real, particular conditions of a person's life', thereby creating the illusion that the state was an 'ethical' project that acted for the common good and not in the interests of a particular class (Lloyd and Thomas, 1998: 146).

Abercrombie et al. (1980) have challenged the importance given by behaviouralists and Marxists to the formation of a value consensus. They argue that the acquiescence of the working class is best explained in terms of pragmatic acceptance, economic necessity and the fear of the state's coercive power, rather than by a common political culture or the creation of 'false consciousness' by a ruling class hegemonic project. Abercrombie and his co-authors (1980: 57) cite a phrase from Marx's *Capital* in support of their argument: that it is the 'dull compulsion of economic relations' which is the key to understanding the survival of liberal democracy.

However, in their desire to assert the importance of material considerations in conditioning working-class behaviour, Abercrombie and his colleagues overstate their case. In putting cultural values in their proper context, it is important not to fall into their trap of dismissing their importance in shaping political and social behaviour. For example, some of the sociological studies that Abercrombie, Hill and Turner cite in support of their case are ambiguous concerning the importance of cultural values. For instance, they utilise Willis's (1977) famous study of working-class teenage boys' experiences in a secondary school in England. Willis shows how such boys creatively resist incorporation into the wider values of the school, thereby illustrating the point, argue Abercrombie, Hill and Turner, that working-class experience is shaped by material, rather than cultural factors.

The problem is that the 'lads', as Willis calls them, end their school days with few qualifications and (as Abercrombie et al. acknowledge) are ready to 'accept the nature of the economic system and their place in it' (Abercrombie et al., 1980: 151). What this suggests is not that cultural factors are unimportant, but rather that material and cultural factors combine to seal the fate of many members of the working class. The lads may develop a counter-culture that 'inverts' the values of the school, but paradoxically it merely helps to prepare them for a life on the factory floor. Ironically then, the lads' counter-culture is of little emancipatory benefit because it develops in the context of a wider 'dominant culture'. Abercrombie and his co-authors implicitly accept this point when they employ the phrase 'dominant culture' in this context, which appears to run against the logic of their thesis (Abercrombie et al., 1980: 150). Willis's study suggests that while individuals are far from being passive actors, determined by ideological forces beyond their control, they are not completely beyond ideological influence. The central point here is that the 'dull compulsion of economic relations' cannot be easily divorced from the cultural limitations such material necessities promote. Although individuals may not fully internalise the dominant culture, the context in which they act is shaped by it. A useful concept in explaining this is Bourdieu's (1977) notion of cultural capital, which refers to the cultural resources necessary to succeed in a particular society. In liberal democracies, cultural capital is clearly unevenly distributed, which means that the resistance of marginalised groups is often only of limited impact. As Willis argues, although the lads manage to penetrate, to some extent, the ideological veneer of capitalism, this penetration is incomplete. Consequently, their resistance to the elements of the dominant culture is partial and of limited effect. Willis's findings then arguably lend weight to the Gramscian notion of a dominant, but contested, notion of hegemony, rather than supporting Abercrombie, Hill and Turner's thesis that class domination rests on material factors alone. As Coates (1991: 130) argues, because of the impact of ruling-class ideology, 'resistance to the inevitability of "capitalist social life" has been, and remains, very vestigial, ephemeral and episodic'.

The political culture perspective of the behaviouralists, despite its many flaws, does then usefully draw our attention to the importance of cultural values and their relationship to social order. How people feel about these issues will help to determine the attitudes they adopt in exercising their citizenship and political participation, and in their relationship with others within civil society. What is required in analysing these issues, however, is a much wider approach to the notion of culture than that employed by Almond and Verba. Thus some commentators have provided broader definitions of political culture, such as Topf's notion that political culture refers to 'the moral order', the nature of which lies at the heart of 'the core problem of cultural renewal and change' (Topf, 1989: 68). Such a view acknowledges political culture as a dynamic process that is intimately connected to social change (Welch, 1993: 164). Contemporary political sociologists are again making the concept of political culture central to their analysis of the state–civil society relationship: 'growing disillusionment with . . . purely materialist or individualist accounts of politics has allowed political culture to re-emerge as an important topic' (Street, 1997: 128). Indeed, since the 1970s, and particularly in the 1990s, questions concerning the health of the moral order in liberal democracy have been centre stage in political sociology.

From Civic Culture to Cultural Contradictions

By the mid-1970s, the cosy assumptions of Almond and Verba seemed increasingly misplaced. A series of political, economic and social crises, which affected the greater part of the industrial world, called into question the symmetry Almond and Verba found between the value systems and institutions of liberal democracy. As was discussed in Chapters 3 and 4, the period of the 'golden age of capitalism', which followed the end of the Second World War, and which led to unprecedentedly high levels of economic growth, came to an end in the 1970s. Politically, the state seemed to be besieged by a vast array of vested interests, as unions, businesses, pressure groups and other lobbyists sought favours. Government was increasingly unable to live up to expectations that had grown enormously during the period of boom. Social movements highlighted the failure of the state to protect their rights, and their demands placed further strain upon the legitimacy of liberal democracy. It was such events that formed the context of the neo-liberal backlash in the 1980s in countries like the USA. For neo-liberals like Ronald Reagan, America's problems could be accounted for by the excessive state interference with the freedoms of civil society. Programmes like affirmative action for blacks and women, plus extravagant welfare spending and the growth of federal government, had it was argued created too many vested interests vying for the state's attention. This had undermined civic culture, and in particular America's emphasis upon self-help.

Writers from the right of the political spectrum in the 1970s therefore began to talk of political overload and the ungovernability of Western societies. Commentators on the left, such as Habermas (1976), spoke of a crisis of legitimacy, where the incompatible state goals of providing increasingly extensive (and expensive) public services, while at the same time attempting to provide a framework for increased economic growth, became impossible to reconcile.

Despite their differences in emphasis, both right and left theories of crisis contained a cultural dimension. The ungovernability thesis held that the problems of liberal democracies could to some extent be accounted for by a decline in deferential attitudes amongst the masses, which Almond and Verba had identified as central to political stability. In a sense liberal democracy seemed to be hoisted by its own petard, for the creation of more educational opportunities, social mobility and the promotion of greater individual liberty had (it was argued) undermined the moral fabric of society. One theorist detected 'a general drift toward alienation, irresponsibility and breakdown of consensus' and 'the near collapse of the traditional authority structure' (Crozier, 1975: 18, 25). Habermas's (1976: 74–5) thesis also contained a strong cultural element in the form of a perceived 'motivation crisis' where the ability of the system to reproduce itself through the promotion of supportive values was undermined by an increasingly disillusioned citizenry.

One of the most influential theories of the crisis of liberal democracy in the 1970s can be found in Daniel Bell's *The Cultural Contradictions of Capitalism* (1976). As the title of his book suggests, Bell places great significance upon what he saw as the increasing tension between the political culture of modern societies and the institutions of state and civil society.

The central thesis advanced by Bell is that processes of modernity have created an individualistic, hedonistic and instrumentalist culture at odds with the requirements of the polity and the economy. For Bell (1976: 28) 'the real problem of modernity is the problem of belief'. With the decline of tradition, and in particular the demise of religious belief, modern societies increasingly face a 'spiritual crisis' which has undermined the foundations of economic growth and political stability. Bell follows Weber in believing that the economic successes of the West are attributable in no small measure to the Protestant work ethic, which emphasised investment, the virtues of saving and the development of a sense of self through 'doing and making'; rather than the modern tendencies towards conspicuous consumption, the pursuit of pleasure and instant gratification (Bell, 1976: 70). The implication of Bell's argument is that the values of civic virtue, which underpin a successful republican system of governance, are being eroded. The 'goodness morality' that involved self-restraint and self-discipline has been replaced by a 'fun morality', where obligations to perform one's civic duties are undermined (Bell, 1976: 71). Bell locates the roots of many of these problems in the culturally radical 1960s, which, in its urgency to debunk all that was traditional,

'added something distinctly its own: a concern with violence and cruelty; a preoccupation with the sexually perverse; a desire to make noise; an anti-cognitive and anti-intellectual mood; an effort once and for all to erase the boundary between 'art' and 'life'; and a fusion of art and politics. (Bell, 1976: 121)

Bell's thesis contains many conservative elements, but interestingly he develops ideas that are extremely close to the post-modernist ideas of the 1990s. Bell (1976: 102) discusses the 'lack of centre, geographical or spiritual' to provide a focal point for authority. Such notions as the decentred self, popular in post-modern theory, can in part be traced back to Bell's observations about the blurring of the distinction between reality and image, or, as Bell puts it, between 'art and politics'. However, unlike many post-modernists, for Bell these trends are threatening rather than liberating. His proposed solution is to place conscious limits on the disruptive impact of modernity and to 'return to the sacred' where society can again be grounded on the firm foundation of shared belief.

Political Culture in the 1990s: The New Anomie?

During the 1990s, the anxieties expressed by Bell have been repeated in many forms, as liberal democracies face the apparent demise of civic culture. Commentators have pointed to such phenomena as rising crime rates, 'racial' tensions, widespread abuse of drugs, family break-down and the decline of deference as evidence that liberal democracies are, as Bell predicted, facing a collapse of value consensus with danger-ous results for the health of their societies. Such concerns are not unique to the twentieth century, however. In the nineteenth century the sociologist Emile Durkheim used the term anomie to describe a state of normlessness and the decline of shared values that regulate and maintain social order. Anomie was, for Durkheim, the consequence of the development of modernity that disrupted traditional patterns of community life, and that led to family decline, helping to create a rootless individualism. Thus, like the behaviouralists, Durkheim argues that any successful system of governance is grounded in a set of shared moral values within a community. Weber was also concerned with the detrimental effects of modernity upon systems of belief. For Weber, the rationalisation of society, despite the material benefits it may bring, also poses a danger to the values that give meaning to human life. Weber fears that rationalisation may become an 'iron cage' where science and technology have allowed humanity to understand the mechanics of everything and the value of nothing.

Contemporary debates concerning the value systems of modern society echo the work of Durkheim, Weber and Bell. The rest of this section will critically examine three such interpretations of the state of the 'moral order' in the 1990s. All the theories explored below share the view that the value systems of liberal democracy are increasingly at odds with the requirements of its economic and political institutions.

Neo-conservatism: The De-Moralisation of Society

Given their negative view of human nature, which is characterised as selfish and prone to evil, conservatives have always placed a great deal of importance upon the role of moral values in constraining humani-ty's self-destructive urges (Nisbet, 1986: 68–74). Therefore conserva-tives like Burke see loyalty and devotion to the institutions of civil society and the state as central to the maintenance of social order. Recent neo-conservatives, such as Gertrude Himmelfarb, have identi-fied the decline of such virtues as lying at the centre of the moral crisis that threatens to destroy Western societies in the 1990s. For Himmel-farb (1995: 257), 'as often as not' moral and cultural factors are 'a determining factor in their own right', and have an autonomous role in shaping economic and social change.

Himmelfarb traces the replacement of Victorian virtues by modern values. Victorian virtues were successful at providing the foundations for order in the nineteenth century because even when these virtues were not practised their desirability was widely recognised by individuals and institutions alike. They thereby exercised a powerful constraint upon people's moral behaviour through the operation of shame and guilt. In contrast, modern values are highly relativistic, and consequently exercise little or no normative force over the whole of society. The virtues of self-reliance, duty to others and patriotism demand more of the individual than do mere 'values', which have no basis in tradition, religion, or social institutions. If one tires of one set of values, another set of equal validity can easily be selected.

Himmelfarb places much of the blame for the shift from rooted virtues to groundless values on the permissiveness of liberal society, particularly since the 1960s. Codes of sexual behaviour, which protected women, and constrained the urges of men, are flouted in the name of individual liberty. The consequence of such moral recklessness is, for Himmelfarb, a huge increase in illegitimate births, divorce, welfare dependency and family breakdown, which together are undermining social order. However, Himmelfarb's arguments are contradictory. While she identifies the dangers of excessive individuality, she also points to the dangers of collectivist values that have, in the twentieth century, underpinned social policy and which have, in contrast to the Victorian era, broken the link between morality and welfare (Himmelfarb, 1995: 244). Himmelfarb (1995: 261) insists that 'we have become accustomed to the transference of responsibility from the individual to society'. The logic of Himmelfarb's position is not only to place greater responsibility upon individuals and reduce the interference of the state in civil society, but also to ground these individual responsibilities in a set of moral virtues promoted through state legislation, such as protection of the traditional family through advantageous tax policies for example (Himmelfarb, 1995: 248).

Although Himmelfarb provides some interesting discussion of the nature of Victorian society, the thrust of her thesis is the need to provide a theoretical and historical case for the restoration of a moral civil society based on the traditional virtues of family life, charity, respectability, self-restraint and hard work. However, her case is unconvincing. Her depiction of Victorian society is highly romanticised. She ignores the fact that the 'morality' of Victorian Britain was founded upon the immoral practices of slavery, colonialism and empire. The imposition by Britain of foreign norms, at odds with those found in colonies such as India and Africa, points to the authoritarian core of Victorian virtues, as well as to the hypocrisy of the celebration of a morality rooted in tradition at home, while defending the suppression of other traditions throughout the empire. The widespread acceptance of Victorian virtues within societies like Britain is also contested. Abercrombie et al. (1980: 111) have rejected the notion that the working class absorbed the dominant Victorian virtues to any great extent. They argue that 'the working class in the mid-Victorian era had a distinct, autonomous culture' that contained both elements of political radicalism, at odds with liberal and conservative values, and large deviations from the Victorian virtues of chastity and sobriety in terms of lifestyle patterns.

Even if one were to accept Himmelfarb's account of the hegemonic influence of Victorian virtues in the nineteenth century, rapid social changes in gender roles, education and work preclude the kind of cultural restorationism Himmelfarb advocates to cure contemporary problems. Himmelfarb sees in Victorian society a subtle balance between elements of tradition, which exist in harmony with the positive aspects of liberal society, and entail the need for a 'moral citizenry' (Himmelfarb, 1995: 51). Interestingly this is very close to Almond and Verba's (1963) definition of civic culture as a combination of modernity with tradition. Both Himmelfarb's and Almond and Verba's arguments underestimate the disruptive effects of modernity on traditional allegiances. The liberalisation of the economy and extension of personal freedoms is always in tension with traditional influences. Therefore the balance between tradition and modernity identified by Himmelfarb and the civic culture thesis was at best temporary. Tester (1997) has argued a similar point in his critique of the de-moralisation thesis. The problem for Himmelfarb, Tester contends, is that she equates morality with the notion of civilisation in Victorian society, which was in fact driven by abstract, mechanistic and rational logic. Such rationalism involves the denial of the very emotion that must lie at the heart of moral virtues. Himmelfarb, argues Tester, therefore fails to identify the inherent tension between morality and the civilisation that modernity creates.

Himmelfarb's thesis, like many arguments of the New Right, is contradictory. She wishes to defend the market freedoms of liberalism, while at same time ignoring the impact these freedoms have on traditions and communities. As Gray (1997: 129) argues, many of the trends Himmelfarb rails against, such as changing family structures, 'arise from time-honoured beliefs and long-standing trends in modern Western societies'. Moreover, the kind of virtues Himmelfarb wishes to see promoted have no basis for support in societies that have instead extended the liberal traditions of personal liberty and individual rights, which are themselves rooted firmly in the Victorian era, to their logical conclusions. These liberal traditions entail defending the rights of homosexuals and women's sexual freedom, which are at odds with Himmelfarb's conservative social philosophy.

Theories of the Underclass

According to underclass theories, the degeneration of social values identified by Himmelfarb is focused particularly upon a section of society which is said to be both materially and culturally cut off from the mainstream of the community. It is common within the literature on the underclass to differentiate between these two aspects. Thus leftist interpretations stress the structural factors of long-term unemployment and poverty in accounting for the underclass. Right-wing interpretations emphasise anti-social patterns of behaviour and a lack of morality as the key to understanding why some 'feckless' individuals stand outside the dominant values of society. However, even so-called structural theories have often referred to the different standards of behaviour exhibited by members of the underclass, and the term is imbued with a moralistic judgement. Some structural theorists have belatedly recognised this problem and have therefore dropped the term from their research agendas. For example, Wilson (1987), who was one of the first social scientists to refer to an underclass in analysing the conditions of America's urban poor, has recently used the term 'ghetto poor' in its place, because of the negative connotations of the term underclass (Morris, 1995: 58).

The best-known right-wing account of the underclass is associated with Charles Murray (1996), who through a series of books and articles has done much to popularise the term. Murray uses the concept in a negative way, which has made writers like Wilson so wary of its use. Murray finds in the underclass the worst excesses of moral breakdown in American and British society, which has its roots in the welfare state. For Murray, the state has allowed members of society to throw off their responsibilities to themselves and their families, and to rely instead upon handouts, which are unconnected to the individual's behaviour. The result can be detected in high levels of illegitimacy (where childbirth becomes the means to a higher welfare cheque), voluntary unemployment and criminality. These outcomes are interconnected, as illegitimacy encourages family breakdown, cutting men off from the civilising effects of marriage. These men lose the motivation to work and drift into drunkenness, drug addiction and criminal activity. In turn, family breakdown leads to delinquent children because children born into unstable and single parent families lack a positive male role-model and therefore become equally criminally minded. For Murray, members of the underclass choose their membership of this class through their own 'deplorable' actions.

The impact of the underclass debate on public policy in Britain and the USA has been considerable. In the USA, and more recently Britain, the threat of a criminal and state dependent underclass has been behind such policies as the development of workfare and 'zero-tolerance' policing. The underclass has come to be seen as a moral cancer that needs to be subjected to radical treatment if it is not to endanger the wider moral order. If such language seems colourful, a reading of Murray's work will illustrate that it is just such language that has been employed in discussions of the underclass. For instance, Murray (1996: 42) asks 'how contagious is this disease?' The underclass is referred to as a virus that may infect other neighbourhoods, if a cure is not found. Such 'medical' terminology runs throughout Murray's arguments and emphasises the judgmental tone of much of the debate surrounding the underclass.

The problem, however, is that such a 'class' has never been satisfactorily defined. Even more sober commentators than Murray, such as Wilson, have tended to include a startlingly wide range of different social groups in attempting a definition:

> Included in this group are individuals who lack training or skills and either experience long-term unemployment or are not members of the labour force, individuals who are engaged in street crime and other forms of aberrant behaviour, and families that experience long-term spells of poverty and/or welfare dependency. (Wilson, 1987: 8)

Despite standing on the structural side of the underclass debate, Wilson's definition, like many definitions of the underclass, mixes up so many different categories of people, some defined in terms of their relationship to the labour market, and others in terms of their 'aberrant behaviour', that the status of the 'underclass' as a useful sociological concept rests on decidedly shaky ground.

The attraction of an underclass approach may lie in the fact that it is an attempt to capture the all-pervasive nature of poverty, encompassing its emotional as well as material effects. Undoubtedly it is important to recognise how several factors such as poor housing, exclusion from work and a lack of access to the cultural heritage of society compound each other. However, the imprecision of the term underclass obscures rather than illuminates the roots of social exclusion. The concept implies a level of separation from the experiences of the rest of society which evidence has yet to substantiate. Morris (1995: 74), in surveying the evidence of a dependency culture, concludes, 'there is no direct evidence of a distinctive culture of the underclass'. Marshall et al. (1996: 40) are also unable to find any empirical support for the underclass thesis in terms of attitudes to work and social marginalisation.

The popularity of the underclass concept can in part be explained by the ideological dominance of neo-liberal discourses since the 1980s concerning poverty and the problem of social order. These have centred upon the morality of individuals, rather than seeing threats to social order as resulting from the failure of neo-liberal economic policy. The negative connotation of the term underclass, with its implication of a parasitic group of sub-human, depraved individuals, who inhabit an underworld of drunkenness and criminality, fits well with the view that there is a division between the deserving and undeserving poor. This suggests policies of targeting benefits at the 'truly needy' would be most successful in tackling poverty. The erosion of universal social rights can in this way be legitimised by the usage of the underclass discourse.

More socially liberal thinkers who have made use of the term have also failed to root the problems of structural unemployment firmly in the political and economic crises that afflicted liberal democracy in the 1970s. These problems highlighted the limitations of the democratic elitist model, which dominated the politics of liberal democracies following the Second World War, and bureaucratic state-centred wel-fare provision. Both systems divorce active participation and individual responsibilities from the rights citizens receive, and this problem supports the main argument of this book that there is a real need to rethink the state–civil society relationship (see Chapter 9).

The Culture of Contentment?

The culture of contentment thesis, associated with the liberal econo-mist Galbraith (1992), accepts the existence of an underclass. For Galbraith, the underclass is a functional necessity for the operation of a successful economy. In particular, a largely immigrant underclass performs the repetitive tasks associated with insecure unskilled labour. This helps maintain the wealthy conditions of the 'contented majority' (Galbraith, 1992: 15). However, the main source for the moral vacuum within liberal democracy for Galbraith is not the anti-social attitudes of those at the bottom of the class structure. It can instead be attributed to a lack of moral concern within the affluent social groups for the plight of the rest of society.

Writers such as Therborn (1989) and Hutton (1996) have advanced similar ideas to those of Galbraith. For Therborn (1989: 111) the abandonment of full employment policies in many liberal democracies since the 1970s has led to the 'Brazilianisation of advanced capitalism'. By this Therborn means that liberal democratic societies are increas-ingly divided into three groups: the first group are those who are either permanently unemployed or on the fringes of a highly unstable job market; the second group are those who are 'stably employed, or with a stable likelihood of re-employment'; the third group are the ruling class whose position is increasingly legitimised by government policies that seek to secure the interests of those already employed, thereby marginalising the long-term unemployed. Hutton (1996: Ch. 8) has described how the interests of those who enjoy a reasonable living has become the basis for a divide and rule strategy by politicians seeking re-election. Those who are economically excluded are also witnessing a deterioration of the effectiveness of their political rights, as politicians seek to serve only the contented majority. This becomes a vicious circle, as the poor increasingly fail to vote thereby increasing the incentive for politicians to ignore their interests (Galbraith, 1992: 40).

Although these developments are partly a product of a growing affluence for the majority of citizens, the effects of these divisions are moral, as well as material. Selfishness has become 'the controlling mood of the contented majority' (Galbraith, 1992: 17). This majority seek to justify their lack of concern for their less fortunate fellow citizens by blaming the poor for their own problems:

> In what is the accepted and, indeed, only acceptable view, the underclass is deemed the source of its own succor and well-being; in the extreme view, it requires the spur of its own poverty, and it will be damaged by any social assistance and support. None of this is, of course, quite believed; it serves, nonetheless, to justify the comfortable position and policy. (Galbraith, 1992: 40–1)

Like the underclass thesis explored above, the notion of a culture of contentment is an oversimplification. It overestimates the extent to which any large group of citizens can, in the context of the increasingly flexible and uncertain nature of Western labour markets, feel truly secure in their position. Miliband (1994: 134) contends that there may be only a contented minority. For in the USA very low voter turnout fails to substantiate the view that politicians are effectively mobilising a majority of contented citizens. In Britain, it was the peculiarities of the first-past-the-post system of voting that accounted for the existence of the Thatcherite governments in the 1980s and 1990s: Thatcher and Major never attracted more than 45 per cent of the voting electorate in support of their divisive policies.

Giddens (1994: 141–2) also rejects Galbraith's thesis and instead has referred to a 'culture of anxiety', which is the dominant reaction of all classes to the increased risks of late modernity. It can be argued that Galbraith, as a social liberal, fails to comprehend the problems of the state model of welfare that has been unsuccessful in empowering citizens and which in many aspects has become delegitimised, not just amongst a contented majority, but across the whole social spectrum. As Hirst (1994: 164) contends, the challenge for supporters of the welfare state like Galbraith is to 'come up with a clear new strategy that encompasses reforms to both funding and service delivery' rather than relying upon 'schoolteacherly social democratic exhortation to be altruistic and pay-up'.

Political Culture and Governance

Any system of governance, whether it be a small stateless community or a large state, is founded not just upon a set of political arrangements, but also upon a conception of social order and the place of each individual within that order. For this reason, we can reject the view that governance can be truly stable where there is no agreement on the basic values that underpin political behaviour. Writers like Almond and Verba are therefore right to identify the feeling people have towards their political system as an important aspect of a successful polity. Such questions have often been underplayed by theorists who have concentrated upon purely material factors for explaining the obedience and obligation individuals display towards their political communities.

However, a problem with many of the theories of political culture I have examined in this chapter is that too much emphasis is given to cultural factors in explaining the success or failure of a particular system of governance. The main weakness with Bell's, Himmelfarb's and Murray's explanations for the crisis of civil society is that they treat individual morality as an independent variable, which is then used to explain the disintegration of social order. The problems of liberal democracy are seen to lie, not in its faulty institutions, but in the decline of its supportive cultural system, which is at once conservative and individualistic. This last contradictory point is crucial in understanding the flaws of the neo-liberal approach towards governance which such writers explicitly or implicitly adopt. The point is that one cannot support unfettered market relations and then expect these relations to have no impact upon the values and institutions of civil society. The changing needs of a dynamic market have had huge effects on male and female employment and family structures and have also encouraged cultural individualism (Lash and Urry, 1987).

However, such writers as Bell, Himmelfarb and Murray ignore the implications of such economic and social changes and instead place the blame for the decline in civic culture upon the individualism of the 1960s or the collectivist values of the welfare state. In so doing, they display a very static view of gender relations and the nature of masculinity. Thus when Murray decries the decline of the male role within the family he fails to link such changes to wider structural and value changes that have their roots in the dynamic nature of capitalism and liberal notions of equal rights, which have transformed gender relations and undermined an unquestioning deference to traditional social and political institutions.

An alternative interpretation of shifts in the 'civic culture' of liberal democracies celebrates the very changes that the neo-liberals and conservatives condemn. Thus for some post-modernists, the breakdown of social hierarchy, the plurality of family structures and the dilution of deference are all symptoms of healthy diversity rather than moral decline (Lyotard, 1984). Under post-modern conditions, women and minority groups who do not wish to conform to the conservative culture desired by the right, are increasingly freed from the logic of such hierarchical assumptions that seek to keep them in their 'proper place'.

Clearly a return to a traditionalist and conservative civic culture, as advocated by people like Bell, is impossible given the irreversible social changes that are to a certain extent correctly identified by post-modernists. A key weakness of the kind of supportive cultural system identified by Himmelfarb in her celebration of Victorian virtues, or by Almond and Verba in their defence of a deferential political culture, is that they enshrine a gendered and elitist view of the state that is no longer tenable. However, the problem for post-modernists is that social diversity can easily become mutated into dangerous fragmentation when there exists within society no clear agreement or support for at least the procedural values that legitimise governance.

It would seem that the answer to these problems is to be found in the promotion of democratic structures that break down the divide between state and civil society and engender support for democratic principles. This does not imply cultural uniformity, but neither can successful governance be built upon a moral vacuum that provides no cultural basis for any system of politics. It could be argued that although values do form an important context of governance, the key factor in gauging the stability of a system of governance is the effectiveness of its political mechanisms, and the level to which individuals are able to utilise their citizenship and participate democratically. It is a lack of effective linkages between citizens in civil society and the state that is crucial in explaining apathy and alienation, rather than vague notions of cultural crisis or moral decline.

Conclusion

This chapter has acknowledged the importance of political culture to any system of governance. Political culture is, partly, the product of the concentration of communicative power in the state and within certain institutions of civil society (such as media organisations) which allows political and economic elites to shape the political agenda, and therefore political values, to some degree. Almond and Verba are therefore right to argue that attitudes to political and social behaviour are an important ingredient in the success of any political system. However, the civic culture that Almond and Verba defend is founded upon an elitist view of the state, which is increasingly at odds with the expectations of an ever more educated and informed civil society. Moreover, Almond and Verba's neglect of the structures of power which underpin civil society, such as class and gender, lead them to overstate the levels of cultural support that ever existed for liberal democracy.

For the conservative and neo-liberal critics explored in this chapter, however, the decay of civic culture is real enough, and is to be explained by moral decline and a weakening of political authority. The solution is to firm up the coercive and authoritarian aspects of the state and civil society. But such an interpretation is, it has been argued, wide of the mark.

What is clear, as post-modernists have argued, is that civil society now consists of an ever-more diverse and critical population. There can be no return to a romanticised and mythological past of shared culture values. However, widespread alienation with current systems of governance, which theories of the underclass and culture of contentment inadvertently highlight, is a problem that must be tackled. Therefore, the relationship between state and civil society must be rethought and more opportunities for participation created to accommodate new demands and expectations. The challenge for theorists and practitioners alike is to re-construct citizenship and participation, which link civil society to political community, in ways that take account of recent social change. The nature of citizenship and political participation are the subjects of the next two chapters.

7

Citizenship

When analysing civil society's relationship to the state, an under-standing of citizenship is crucial. This is because it is this status which determines who is a legitimate member of a particular state. Citizenship tells us who owes duties to the state and enjoys protection of their rights. It also provides a legal framework for individuals' associations within civil society. However, citizenship is not purely a legal status, since considerable economic benefits often accrue from its possession. These benefits include public health care, education and social security, which, when taken together, are normally referred to as social citizen-ship. Citizenship may also provide a sense of common identity to all those who possess it. Thus in some theoretical formulations citizenship is said to function as a kind of civil 'religion' that unites civil society and binds individuals to the state.

Like political culture, then, citizenship is an important concept which mediates the relationship between civil society and the state. How citizens understand and exercise their rights and responsibilities is a crucial factor in determining the health and stability of any system of governance. Furthermore, in analysing the shifting meaning of citizen-ship we can learn much about the instability of the state–civil society relationship.

This chapter will begin by exploring how political sociologists have understood the nature and development of citizenship. The domi-nant liberal model of citizenship, as expressed most famously by T. H. Marshall, has been criticised for its evolutionary account of citizen-ship, and for failing to analyse citizenship in the context of shifts in civil society's relationship to the state. Recently, however, the failure of citizens to exercise their responsibilities has been blamed upon liberalism's overemphasis upon rights, and communitarianism has become one of the most influential critiques of liberal citizenship. In the final section of the chapter it will be argued that the commu-nitarian critique is itself flawed in its understanding of the impact social change has had upon citizenship. In fact, the problem of citizenship cannot be divorced from the tensions of the state–civil society relationship.

Theorising the Development of Citizenship

According to one famous definition, citizenship denotes all those who are 'full members of the community' (Marshall and Bottomore, 1992: 18). Marshall's conception of citizenship implies a commitment to a shared set of values. He also defines this membership in terms of the possession of three kinds of rights: civil, political and social. Each of these Marshall sees as complementary. Indeed, Marshall describes how historically in Britain each type of right built upon entitlements already gained. Basic civil rights, such as free speech, justice, worship and property ownership, preceded the growth of political rights, such as the right to vote and stand for office. The former was developed in the eighteenth century and the latter associated with the Great Reform Acts of the nineteenth century, which granted political rights to the male working class. Social rights were extended in the twentieth century as political rights enabled the economically vulnerable to press the state for social protection. However, how can the inequality of a capitalist civil society be reconciled with the ethos of equality associated with citizenship of the state?

The inherent difficulties of building a meaningful concept of citizenship upon the contradictory relationship between state and civil society was first identified by Marx in 'On the Jewish Question' (1994). For Marx, the state reflects the class divisions of civil society. The state exists to preserve those divisions, so that its associated citizenship must at best be a partial status. Although Marx welcomed the extension of voting rights to the masses as a potential platform on which to build the working class movement, the logic of his theory of capitalism led him to conclude that, without revolutionary change, the inequalities of civil society would always serve to dilute the impact of citizenship. Individuals would remain alienated from themselves and their community, because for the greater part of their life they were workers and not citizens. Their rights did not extend into the factory or office and they left unaltered the basic inequalities of control, wealth and security inherent in a capitalist civil society.

Marshall, however, wrote some hundred years after Marx. He was thus able to witness a tremendous growth in the functions of the state. From the late nineteenth century onwards, the citizen began to gain important social as well as civil and political rights. For Marshall, these social rights greatly modified the impact of inequalities in civil society.

Provision of extensive public education meant that inequalities were legitimised by increased opportunities for individual advancement. Social security and the public health services, which developed in the post-war period in various forms throughout Europe, meant that those inequalities that persisted were increasingly confined to the narrow field of consumer goods. Poverty was thus minimised, and the class tension that threatened capitalism in earlier historical periods subdued.

With the rise to prominence of neo-liberalism in the late 1970s, many of Marshall's assumptions have been questioned. The policies of neo-liberal governments, particularly in the USA and Britain, aimed to roll back the frontiers of the welfare state. Extensive social rights, it was contended, were partly responsible for the decline in profitability of capitalist enterprise in the 1970s, and needed to be diluted if this decline was to be reversed. Social rights were seen as placing impossible demands upon the state which was increasingly forced to interfere in civil society. This interference took the form of higher taxes upon individuals and businesses and greater regulation of the private sector, thereby constraining the entrepreneurial spirit necessary to the capitalist system. In addition, the provision of social rights created a dependency culture amongst the working class, destroying self-reliance and undermining the work ethic.

The rise of neo-liberalism, with its emphasis upon diluting social citizenship, clearly called into question Marshall's optimistic theory that, with the development of social rights, the inequities of capitalism had become civilised and therefore stabilised. The key problem with Marshall's theory was his failure to consider how shifts in civil society's relationship with the state, which result from social change, impact upon the meaning of citizenship. What is required is a more sophisticated theory as to why citizenship has developed in the way that it has. Two such theories have been advanced by Michael Mann and Bryan Turner.

Michael Mann: Citizenship as Ruling Class Strategy

The key to understanding modern citizenship for Mann (1996) is its use as an instrument by the ruling class to control the potentially disruptive impact of, first, the rise of the bourgeoisie and, subsequently, the development of the working class. The extension or dilution of citizenship over time is therefore primarily determined by the actions of the ruling class, who control the state and who are defined by Mann as 'a combination of the dominant economic class and the political and military rulers' (Mann, 1996: 127). How the ruling class within each country manages citizenship is linked to particular historical, cultural and political circumstances. Because these vary greatly from one state to the next, so too will the ruling-class strategy adopted. This means that the nature of citizenship is contingent and never universal.

Following this central thesis, which may be described as a top-down-theory of citizenship, Mann explores several historical examples where the development of citizenship differed markedly from the model outlined by Marshall. Mann refers to four types of political regime, each of which managed the impact of modernity differently. These regimes are: constitutional, absolutist, contested and merged (Mann, 1996: 129). In my discussion I shall concentrate on the first two, which illustrate the essence of Mann's position.

The constitutional tradition in the USA and Britain ensured that by 1800 'civil citizenship was well developed' (Mann, 1996: 128). However, citizenship developed differently in the two states from this point on-wards, largely because of the divergent strategies adopted by the ruling class towards the emerging proletariat. Because of the revolutionary overthrow of British rule in the USA, it became impossible to deny political rights to white adult males who had participated in the revolu-tion. Thus, in the USA, the workers were granted voting rights before a powerful labour movement could develop. This meant that a large section of the working population was incorporated into the nation-state. Such a relatively privileged status, coupled with America's economic prosperity, precluded agitation for the extension of citizenship to the social realm. In Britain, however, the ruling class was forced to be more reformist, as the working class became politicised through a more protracted struggle for political recognition. The working class was able to form powerful political associations within civil society, such as the Trades Union Congress and the Labour Party, which placed considerable pressure upon the state to extend rights. Consequently, Britain has developed extensive social rights and an ideologically divided political structure.

In contrast to the liberal regimes of the USA and Britain, the passage of citizenship rights in absolutist states such as Germany, Japan and Russia was very different. In Germany, for example, the largely agri-culturally based ruling class were willing to cede civil rights to the bourgeoisie but denied them meaningful political rights. Concessions were also made in the social sphere, where paternalistic welfare rights were granted to undermine potential working-class rebellion. However, the extension of certain limited citizenship rights was just one aspect of a divide and rule strategy that involved striking a balance between negotiation and repression. Citizenship was merely one of a set of trade-offs which the ruling class made with various sections of civil society to maintain their rule.

The comparative analysis employed by Mann illustrates the importance of exploring citizenship in the context of particular historical examples of the state–civil society relationship. His theory shows that citizenship does not necessarily develop uniformly. What is more, Mann denies that the liberal approach of Britain was necessarily superior in maintaining the ruling class in power. He argues that were it not for external factors, in particular defeat in war, the authoritarian strategy of countries like Germany could have 'survived into advanced, post-industrial society, providing a distinctive, corporately organised, arbitrary combination of partial civil, political and social citizenship' (Mann, 1996: 139–40).

Bryan Turner: Citizenship Theory beyond Marshall and Mann

Like Mann, Turner (1994) has consciously attempted to transcend Marshall's theory by adopting a comparative approach to citizenship. For Turner, while Mann's theory is a considerable advance on Marshall's, it is also open to criticism. First, Mann ignores the role of ethnic difference, which is of particular importance in analysing citizenship in the 'new world' where indigenous populations such as aboriginal communities in Australia were the casualties of the 'development' of modern citizenship. Second, Turner points to the importance of religion in shaping citizenship. Turner argues that particular forms of Protestantism helped create a 'passive' citizenship in some countries, where the state and politics were regarded as necessary evils rather than positive goods. This meant that the important aspects of life took place within the private sphere of human relations. Third, because Mann works implicitly within a Marxist framework, he over-concentrates upon citizenship as a ruling-class strategy and therefore underestimates the importance the struggles of social movements within civil society have had in shaping citizenship.

Turner builds upon his critique of Mann to devise a fresh understanding of citizenship. First, Turner points to the possibility, in some instances, of the creation of citizenship from below as well as from above: citizenship can be a consequence of the actions of associations within civil society, as well as a state-led strategy of social control. Secondly, he focuses upon the difference of emphasis placed upon the public and private spheres. In countries which experienced modern revolutions, like France and the USA, citizenship was largely the product of struggle instigated by discontented sections of civil society. In contrast, citizenship in England was more peacefully obtained and resulted largely from political compromise between rival elites. The 1688 settlement reformed, but retained, the important traditional institutions of the monarchy, House of Lords and Church of England. These enshrined a deferential and passive subject status, in contrast to the model of active citizenship within revolutionary France. In Germany, as in England, citizenship was largely instigated from above, but in this case by an authoritarian state.

Each of Turner's examples have a different understanding of the public–private divide, which further influenced the national character of citizenship. Active citizenship in France implied a suspicion of a separate private life. Thus in the interests of the general will the state was justified in interfering in the affairs of civil society. In the USA, the political culture was more individualistic and therefore wary of an extensive public sphere: for Americans, 'the political is morally suspect' (Turner, 1994: 218). Although in England there was an ethos of public service, this was combined with a heavy emphasis upon the 'little platoons' of civil society as mediators between the individual and the state. Such associations, coupled with the common-law tradition of prescriptive rights, prevented excessive interference in the private sphere by the state. In the case of Germany, with its limited access to political institutions, stress was placed upon the attainment of personal satisfaction within the context of the family. Table 7.1 summarises some aspects of Turner's theory of citizenship.

Table 7.1 Turner's Typology of Citizenship

Country	Development of citizenship	Attitudes to public and private spheres
France	Citizenship advanced by revolution from below	Public sphere privileged over private
America	Citizenship constituted by revolution from below	Citizens' activism tempered by suspicion of politics and defence of individualism
England	'Glorious Revolution' constituted subject–citizen status and deferential service to the Crown and parliament	Passivity in public sphere and stress upon autonomous associations in civil society
Germany	Extension of citizenship as one aspect of state-led strategy of modernisation	Minimal citizen input in public sphere; sanctuary in private world

Source: Turner (1994: 218)

A Critical Assessment of Marshall's legacy

Both Mann's and Turner's theories are useful additions to Marshall's analysis. In particular, both identify rights as contingent upon social change and place citizenship firmly in the context of the dynamic relationship that exists between civil society and the state. This marks an important step forward from Marshall's overly descriptive account, which fails to explain why citizenship expands and contracts over time. In adopting a comparative analysis, Mann and Turner also highlight the importance of exploring such variables as divergent political cultures, class strategies and geo-political factors, all of which point to a lack of a single developmental path towards a rounded citizenship status. A number of problems with Mann's and Turner's theories can be identified, however.

Turner is surely right to criticise Mann for his overemphasis upon class factors at the expense of other social divisions that have impacted upon citizenship. Mann underplays the role of ideology in shaping the actions of the ruling class and giving direction to those social movements which struggle for citizenship. Ideologies may be based on ethnicity and nationality as well as class. Such identities help to determine individuals' access to both formal citizenship as a legal status and to the substantive rights that, in practice, an individual can enjoy in what may be a racist society. A good example of this is the lack of substantive voting rights enjoyed by African Americans in the USA prior to the civil rights legislation of the 1960s. Although blacks had formally enjoyed political citizenship years before, they were prevented from effectively exercising this right in many southern states because of racist violence. Mann, however, fails to consider such issues in his analysis.

Despite his criticism of Mann's neglect of cleavages other than class, Turner himself fails to incorporate an analysis of such crucial social divisions as gender firmly into his theory. Turner, like Mann and Marshall, overlooks the fact that citizenship is a gendered concept. This is particularly problematic for Turner's treatment of the public–private divide in the various historical examples he discusses. Although much of the originality of Turner's argument rests upon this distinction, he makes no reference to the vast feminist literature on the inequalities that are perpetuated by a differentiation between the public realm as political and the private sphere as a 'haven from a heartless world'. The private sphere has traditionally been seen as a place where male citizens can rest and be comforted by their spouses, whose own opportunities for active citizenship are constrained by their domestic role as carers. These responsibilities are often enshrined in welfare legislation that discriminates against women. As Pateman has persuasively argued (1988), the supposedly voluntary contract between citizens, which according to liberal theory forms the basis of citizenship, is premised upon a pre-existing sexual contract where women are confined to the private sphere. Women's role has been to reproduce and rear future citizens, and to provide unpaid care to the wider community. The state is the domain of males, and the fact that citizenship is a gendered status reflects how structures of power within civil society shape the character of the state.

Another problem that Mann and Turner share with Marshall is the unsatisfactory terminology they employ in their definitions of citizenship rights. The problem here is that in the context of the tensions of the state–civil society relationship, the three types of rights discussed by Marshall are far from complementary. Each type of right has diverse functions and has a different relationship with the state. To take Marshall's model:

1. Civil rights are rights held by members of civil society against the state
2. Political rights denote the exercise of a degree of control over the state
3. Social rights are claims from the state.

Marshall identifies a potential tension between these sets of rights. However, as his theory of the state is implicitly classically pluralist, and due to his optimism concerning the longevity of social citizenship, he believes that ultimately these tensions could be managed. In his later writings, he describes the uneasy but workable relationship of welfare-democracy-capitalism as the 'hyphenated' society, thus unwittingly identifying the contested and uncertain status of citizenship in liberal democracies (Marshall, 1981).

Several writers have discussed the potential conflict between civil rights, which are essential to capitalism, and social rights, which, because they are paid for by taxation, are potentially damaging to the capitalist profit motive. Hay (1996: 76) has even gone so far as to suggest that 'civil and social rights express fundamentally antithetical principles of social organisation'. Alternatively, Frazer and Gordon (1994: 94) argue that civil rights are not 'inherently antithetical to social rights'. The key to solving this dispute lies in the definition of civil rights employed. If we define civil rights as including rights to free speech, justice and association, which are essential preconditions for the voluntary interactions of civil society, then what writers like Marshall and Mann describe as the development of civil rights is a mistaken description. Take, for example, Mann's account of German citizenship under the absolutist state. Mann (1996: 133) argues that the 'German absolutists were willing to concede on civil citizenship'. However, such concessions did not include basic rights essential to the development of civil society such as 'freedoms of the press, speech or assembly' (Mann, 1996: 134). Mann skirts around this by defining these last rights as aspects of political citizenship. However, it is difficult to see how one can speak meaningfully of civil rights if these crucial freedoms are excluded from the category.

The need to clarify our conceptions of civil rights becomes even clearer if we again consider Hay's argument that they are incommensurable with social rights. The problem here is that Hay wishes to argue, as part of a general critique of Thatcherism, that the Thatcherites sought to 'reassert civil over social rights' (Hay, 1996: 76). This, however, fails to explain the simultaneous attack upon basic civil rights by the Thatcherites, which undermined civil freedoms as basic as the right to silence when in police custody (Faulks, 1998: 163–70). It is also unclear exactly whose civil rights are enhanced by such a project.

The logic of my argument suggests that the kind of rights described as civil by Marshall and many of the theorists who have adopted his terminology would best be reclassified as market rights (Faulks, 1998: 42–3). This term more accurately captures the ideological import of these rights. Rights to accumulate property and have that property protected by the state underpinned the development of capitalism, which is inherently class based and gendered. Consequently, women and workers were systematically excluded from exercising many basic civil rights. Instead they were forced by a combination of the imperatives of the economy and the coercive arm of the state to play their part in the development of the market, which in reality was, in all senses of the word, decidedly unfree. It is important to stress that market rights, unlike civil rights, also imply the right to fail: in a capitalist society the costs of the failure to manipulate economic forces to one's advantage have to be borne primarily by the individual, rather than collectively.

This argument brings us to a final criticism of Mann's and Turner's adaptations of Marshall's theory. Neither thinker gives sufficient consideration to economic factors in the shaping of citizenship. Mann, in stressing the importance of geo-political factors, and Turner, with his emphasis upon activism versus passivity and the public versus private, miss the centrality of shifts in economic fortune as a key factor in the extension or narrowing of citizenship rights. This is not to advance an economic reductionist theory of citizenship. Rather it is to argue that, in times of economic recession, market rights are likely to be asserted at the expense of tax-based social rights. This is because a successful state strategy is premised upon economic performance. A reduction in social rights is more likely if they exist purely as claims from the state and are therefore bureaucratically administered and largely unconnected to political activism or individuals' responsibilities. For these reasons, the failure of social rights to empower individuals has weakened support for them politically, particularly in the individualistic political cultures of the USA and Britain. As Marshall contends, the development of political rights for workers meant that the potential existed to exert some control over the polity and to argue for the extension of social rights. However, in the late twentieth century, as the labour movement has become more fragmented and economic opportunity for some has been extended, the defence of social rights for those who remain poor has become problematic.

Citizenship then cannot be understood outside of the state–civil society relationship. The contradictions and tensions of this relationship will vary between countries, but the key point is that citizenship is never a fixed status. Its fortunes fluctuate according to social change. I would argue that citizenship is likely to be transformed in the context of various crises faced by the states system and the capitalist economy. The instabilities of both mean that states are often forced to shift the parameters of citizenship. Thus, a military crisis may precipitate the restriction of certain civil rights, for example, through the internment of residents considered a threat to the state. As history has shown, however, rights have often been extended following warfare, as individuals who played a part in the war effort are rewarded with extended rights. The development of women's suffrage can, in part, be explained by this, as can the development of the welfare state after the Second World War. An economic crisis, for example the decline of profitability in the 1970s, is likely to lead to the rolling back of expensive social provision. In the future, citizenship rights may have to be curtailed and individual obligations extended in the face of the various ecological crises which loom on the horizon.

However, an alternative and highly influential explanation for the apparent decline of citizenship has recently been advanced by communitarianism. For these theorists, the problem of citizenship lies with the failure of liberal conceptions of citizenship to generate allegiances to the wider community. Thus the key to understanding the nature of citizenship in modern society lies in the political and moral crises of liberalism. In the next section we shall explore this challenge.

The Limits of Liberal Citizenship

In the introduction to this chapter, it was noted that citizenship entails a set of rights and obligations and a sense of identity within civil society. It is accepted by advocates and critics alike that liberals place primary importance upon the protection of individual rights as the foundation of citizenship. Thus Marshall's work is typical of the liberal tradition in its relative neglect of citizens' obligations. This neglect has prompted the development of what has become known as communitarianism. Because of an imbalance between rights and obligations, it is argued that many Western countries are suffering from an identity crisis, as the glue that holds the fabric of civil society together is weakened because of an overemphasis upon rights. The most well-known account of communitarianism has been developed by Amitai Etzioni in his two best selling books *The Spirit of Community* (1995) and *The New Golden Rule* (1997). In this section, we shall investigate the central tenets of the communitarian theory of citizenship, through a critical analysis of the work of Etzioni.

Etzioni: Revitalising Citizenship and Civil Society

The work of Etzioni, like that of all communitarians, is built upon a critique of liberalism. The problem with liberalism is that citizenship is conceived in primarily defensive and therefore negative terms. Citizenship exists to protect the individual from the political community, which is at best a necessary evil. Liberals are therefore suspicious of overburdening the citizen with too many responsibilities to the state for fear that this may undermine the freedoms of civil society. Liberalism starts with the assumption that we are individuals first and members of society second, and it is this which creates a tension between citizens' rights and responsibilities. This assumption has (communitarians argue) undermined the social foundations on which liberty rests. Writers like Etzioni identify several dangers emerging from the dominance of liberal citizenship in Western societies:

1. Liberalism fails to generate a convincing theory of political obligation. Given the assumptions of liberalism it is unclear why individuals should feel a sense of loyalty or duty to the community.
2. In stressing rights, while largely ignoring responsibilities, the state has become overburdened with claims from a multitude of minority interests. This has undermined the legitimacy of the state, which cannot possibly meet all such demands successfully.
3. By failing to generate a sense of responsibility to the wider community, liberal democracy has created a moral vacuum where individuals pursue their interests at the expense of the shared values and associations of civil society that are necessary to bind communities together.
4. As a result of flaws 1–3, individuals are increasingly alienated and

dysfunctional in both their public and private lives. They feel little affinity with their fellow citizens, and look to the state rather than to themselves to solve their problems and furnish their needs. This has led to the breakdown of civil society, of family and community ties, resulting in the growth of anti-social behaviour, including public disorder, crime and drug abuse.

Etzioni's work aims to find ways to rebuild a sense of citizenship and civil society to reverse these damaging developments. In identifying these trends, communitarianism shares some criticisms of liberalism with Marxism. Both theories start with the assumption that human beings are not egoistical loners, but are social animals. Both identify the alienation that results from putting liberal theories of citizenship into practice. However, writers like Etzioni are closer to conservatives in their emphasis upon morality and in their rejection of economistic explanations for the problems experienced by liberal democracies. Although Etzioni does accept that vast material inequalities may be detrimental to the performance of civic responsibility, he places much more emphasis than Marxists upon individual responsibility. For Etzioni, the basis for social order is individuals volunteering to perform their 'moral commitments and social responsibilities' (1995: 30). He does not seek the destruction of liberal society and its replacement by communism, but looks instead to reinvigorate and augment existing or dormant social practices.

The starting place for reforming liberal society must first be to ensure the development of suitable 'basic personality traits' in each individual, so that base impulses can be held in check and individuals can learn self-restraint. Second, societies require an adherence to a common set of standards that promote responsibilities and tolerance to others. To promote these two preconditions to citizenship, Etzioni suggests pursuing policies, such as economic sanctions to discourage divorce, which protect and facilitate family life, for it is here that the development of the citizen begins. Indeed Etzioni appears to place most of the blame for the deterioration of civil society upon what he calls the 'parenting deficit'. Thus he argues that: 'Gang warfare in the streets, massive drug abuse, a poorly committed work force, and a strong sense of entitlement and weak sense of responsibility are, to a large extent, the product of poor parenting' (Etzioni, 1995: 69).

Regarding civil society, Etzioni suggests that government should withdraw from the sphere of voluntary interaction, playing instead a facilitating role for citizens' associations to generate for themselves a sense of empowerment and community responsibility. However, the plurality and autonomy of civil society must be framed by a set of core values that prohibit extreme behaviour, such as the burning of books or religious intolerance, and Etzioni defends the American constitution as providing suitable principles for governing the political community.

In *The New Golden Rule*, Etzioni attempts to develop a philosophical underpinning for his communitarian policy prescriptions. Etzioni contends that a successful social order must be based upon both morality and voluntarism, thus answering those critics who point to the potential authoritarianism of communitarian thought. The crucial question for Etzioni is: how can one generate support from individuals for a system that will necessarily entail more responsibilities? The answer to this question, Etzioni insists, is to demonstrate that individual autonomy and social order are complementary, rather than opposed. Thus Etzioni argues that communitarianism differs from conservatism in its defence of individual autonomy as a primary rather than secondary value, and in its stress upon the 'moral voice', rather than the sanction of law, as the basis for individual responsibility. The moral voice is, for Etzioni, an inherent human sense of right and wrong, which only a few dysfunctional 'sociopaths' lack. The sign of good society is the extent to which it relies 'more heavily on the moral voice than coercion' (Etzioni, 1997: 120). However, Etzioni's conception of autonomy also differs from liberal conceptions in its stress upon the importance of community in providing the necessary conditions for its existence.

Etzioni therefore advances a theory of equilibrium between autonomy and order. The levels of autonomy and order will differ across societies, but importantly 'the tensed relations between the two formulations cannot be overcome' (Etzioni, 1997: 45). Democracy, by itself, cannot create the necessary balance between these two elements of the good society. This is because modern pluralistic societies like the USA are not, and cannot be, based upon rational decision making alone. Instead communities rest upon moral, rather than logical judgements. What binds autonomy and order together is a set of common norms, not a series of democratic deliberations and rational decisions.

What is required to reform the liberal (dis)order are moral rather than political dialogues. An emphasis upon rights is a barrier to such dialogues, because rights allow no compromise: in the liberal tradition they are seen as absolute and inalienable. Etzioni therefore calls for a moratorium on the creation of new rights, and stresses that core norms must rest instead upon the promotion of individual responsibilities. The content of these values will not be universal. Etzioni recognises the importance of dialogues across societies, to ensure that a society does not remain morally closed and potentially intolerant and suspicious of other moral communities (Etzioni, 1997: 237).

The urgent need to reinvigorate civil society through an active conception of citizenship, where rights and responsibilities are in balance, is at the heart of all communitarian theories of citizenship. Etzioni's work is a particularly clear and developed example of this theory. However, communitarian citizenship is conceptually flawed and it is therefore debatable whether it provides a coherent alternative to the liberal model advanced by writers such as Marshall.

A Critical Assessment of Etzioni's Communitarianism

Communitarians have had considerable influence in the 1990s amongst those on the centre-left of the political spectrum. For example, Etzioni's work has been an inspiration to Bill Clinton's Democratic Party in the USA and Tony Blair's New Labour Party in Britain. This is because communitarian ideas provide a diagnosis of the problems of liberal democracy that does not rely on a politically unpopular class analysis. It also accords with a common-sense impression that the root of society's problems lies in an over-reliance upon the state and the need for citizens to be as ready to accept responsibilities as they are to claim rights. Thus, ironically, communitarianism provides a critique of neo-liberalism that leaves the bulk of neo-liberal policies unchanged. This fits well with the new 'realism' of centre-left politics, which calls for piecemeal, rather than radical reform, and which largely accepts the logic of free-market economics, while seeking to manage more effectively its side effects. The first criticism of communitarianism I wish to make flows from this observation.

Etzioni fails to offer a convincing explanation for why a decline in civil society has occurred. His diagnosis of the problems faced by liberal societies is simplistic. First, when he places the blame on the decline of marriage and the family, his explanations are cultural rather than economic or political, being rooted, he argues, in the permissiveness of modern society. He therefore fails to place such developments in the context of the economic crisis of the 1970s and the response of capital in the form of the promotion of job flexibility and deregulation. Although he is aware of these developments, and suggests the need for the protection of some welfare provision, and the regulation of parts of the economy, he fails to comprehend fully the impact such changes have had upon the basis of family and community life. Structural unemployment, part-time and temporary jobs, which are extremely insecure, and the destruction of many traditional work-based communities that result from neo-liberal policies have had a massive impact upon the social fabric. Etzioni fails to deal with these economic changes and suggests a separate volume would be needed to tackle them

(Etzioni, 1997: 28). However, given their importance in explaining the decline of community, such an oversight seems unjustified. Second, Etzioni sees the assertion of rights over duties as generating a sense of irresponsibility and undermining civic virtues. However, he is over-optimistic about the extent to which substantive rights are enjoyed by many citizens in liberal democracies. His faith in the American con-stitution belies its failure to guarantee many citizens' rights. The moratorium he suggests on the creation of new rights would ensure the continuing exclusion of some minorities from the community. For example, as he acknowledges, homosexuality is effectively illegal in many states in the USA (Etzioni, 1997: 69). Etzioni also overlooks the fact that the struggle for rights empowers individuals and groups through their battle for recognition. The constant reappraisal of the extent and nature of rights, including demonstrations and protest, can be seen as a sign of a healthy civil society and an expression of citizens' responsibilities, rather than a threat to social order.

Etzioni's attempt to reconcile the values of autonomy and order is also unsuccessful. Ironically, by arguing that the two values are in-evitably contradictory his theory seems closer to liberal assumptions than he is willing to concede. Indeed, at times, his position seems to be an uneasy combination of conservatism and liberalism. He argues that humans are 'born basically savage' (in itself a highly problematic term), implying that like conservatives he sees humans as naturally flawed, but at the same time such a view is consistent with the liberal argument that human nature can be abstracted from the social arrangements that shape it (Etzioni, 1997: 165). A truly relational and social understand-ing of human nature would see no inevitable contradiction between autonomy and order. Etzioni sees a tension between the two concepts because of his abstract conception of community, and he shares this problem with writers like Hegel and T. H. Green. Their celebration of the state as the embodiment of the ethical community is ultimately metaphysical and unattainable because they ignore the social realities of gender, class and ethnicity that render the unity of civil society problematic. Without a theory of the state and civil society that recognises these divisions, communitarians can offer no more than a wish list of desirable social behaviour. The fact that Etzioni (1997: 71–3) groups together such diverse phenomena as date rape and the creation of sweat shops by unethical multinational corporations as examples of a trend towards 'social anarchy' again suggests a lack of theoretical clarity.

Because Etzioni fails to generate a theory of the state–civil society relationship, he, like Marshall, fails to recognise the contingent nature of citizens' rights and the real impediments that exist to the exercise of responsibilities. He overlooks the fact that both the state and the market are stratified entities: they are organised in ways which reflect and reinforce structures of power. Thus the state is a gendered institution and privileges some ethnic identities over others, while the market generally rewards those who are already favourably placed in society. These two sets of inequalities compound each other, creating the impression that some groups are more industrious than others, thereby reinforcing and justifying the positions of the powerful.

Finally, Etzioni fails to place his discussion of citizenship and civil society in the context of globalisation. Where this issue is raised, he is concerned only with the internal impact upon the community under discussion (Etzioni, 1997: 80–4). Communitarianism has therefore been criticised for being obsessed with local problems, when many of the challenges to individuals' rights and security are global in nature. What might therefore be required is a greater emphasis on global citizenship obligations that transcend the needs of the immediate community. Etzioni (1995: 119) argues that to give impetus to the rebuilding of civil society, the USA 'will have to work its way to a stronger, growing, more competitive economy'. However, it may be that in a highly unequal world economy, prosperity for one country means indirectly undermining the wealth of others. A growing awareness of humanity's ecological responsibilities may also make such a policy self-defeating in the medium to long term. Against this background of global inequality and impending ecological crisis, Etzioni's (1997: 241) claim that 'global values cannot serve as a satisfactory frame for societal values' is likely to become increasingly untenable for developed as well as developing countries.

Conclusion

In this chapter, I have argued that contrary to optimistic liberal accounts of the development and sustainability of citizenship, the nature of the rights and responsibilities which underpin civil society are in fact contingent. It is more accurate to understand citizenship as expanding or contracting as a result of a combination of factors, both internal and external to individual states. Warfare, shifts in the international economy and ecological threats are all likely to alter the balance of power between the state and civil society upon which the content of citizenship depends. Rights are never absolute, never inalienable and always contested. The same is true of the relationship between rights and responsibilities.

Communitarians like Etzioni share with many conservatives and socialists the sense that liberal citizenship has failed to instil a proper sense of personal obligation and social duty amongst the citizens of liberal democracies. Although a sense of moral commitment to the wider community is, as communitarians argue, important to the performance of citizenship, writers such as Etzioni fail to address properly the barriers that exist to the performance of obligations. Poverty, a lack of cultural capital and access to the information necessary to the exercise of citizenship should all be considered in accounting for the failure of some to discharge their obligations. Moreover, to privilege one side of the citizenship equation, as liberals do with rights, and communitarians do with responsibilities, is to miss their mutual dependence upon each other. What is crucial to the practice of citizenship is the context in which these rights and obligations are exercised.

Because of the dominance of democratic elitist models of participation and the inequities of market-led civil societies in liberal democracies, however, many citizens have been effectively excluded from making a full contribution to the institutions of the state and civil society. Effective citizenship cannot be passive: it demands political participation by all, to the best of their ability. However, this raises the question of how successful the mechanisms of liberal democracies are in facilitating this participation. This question will be addressed in the next chapter.

8

Political Participation

In his famous account of democracy in nineteenth-century America, de Tocqueville (1945) correctly identified the tendency of the state to centralise power, and consequently underlined the need for alternative civil and political associations to counterbalance and control this power if liberty was to be maintained. A willingness on behalf of citizens to participate fully in the governance of their own lives is central to a thriving civil society. Such participation is an expression of citizenship, and is crucial to engendering a shared political culture. In this chapter therefore, my analysis of the impact of recent social change upon civil society will be continued by an examination of the state of political participation in liberal democracies.

A working definition of political participation may read something like this: political participation is the active engagement by individuals and groups with the governmental processes that affect their lives. This encompasses both involvement in decision making and acts of opposition. Crucially, political participation is an active process: one may be a member of a party or pressure group, but play no active role in the organisation. Acts of active engagement include conventional political participation, such as voting, standing for office, campaigning for a political party or contributing to the management of a community housing co-operative, and unconventional acts, which may be seen as legitimate, such as signing a petition or attending a peaceful demonstration, or illegal, such as violent protest or refusing to pay taxes.

I shall first review the main theories of participation: democratic elitism, rational choice and participatory theory. In the second part of the chapter, the changing nature of participation in liberal democracies will be discussed. In the light of strong evidence that citizens are increasingly disenchanted with their political systems, the third section will be an examination of how political participation might be enhanced. I shall explore how citizens might develop political competence through the use of information and communication technology (ICT), and innovations such as citizens' juries. My conclusion is that only through a more developed participatory and democratic system of governance can the problems of the state–civil society relationship begin to be overcome.

Theories of Political Participation

Democratic elitists such as Schumpeter (1942) are primarily concerned with the problem of sustaining political stability; democracy is of secondary importance to this primary goal. Schumpeter argues that enlightened leadership, sanctioned by minimal acts of participation by the masses, is the best way to maintain order, and it is democratic elitism which has become institutionalised in representative systems of government in the post-war period. The defence of this minimalist approach to participation rests upon a view of what is desirable and practical.

Since the masses are generally ignorant and apathetic, extensive participation by them (it is argued) will necessarily undermine stability. An over-active citizenry is likely to make ill-considered, short-termist and generally poor policy decisions. They are liable to be manipulated by ideologues bent upon the overthrow of the system, and are prone to shift dangerously between periods of apathy and manic activism. Either way, prudent government will be impossible. It is desirable, therefore, for policy making to be left to those who are intellectually suited to the task, and who make politics their chosen career. A responsible elite can then neutralise the worst excesses of the masses through subtle manipulation. For, as one democratic elitist asserts, the art of governing is concerned with 'giving the people not what they want but what they will learn to want' (Lippman, cited in Thompson, 1970: 23).

It is implicit in Schumpeter's argument that the masses lack the independence of mind to govern themselves. For Schumpeter, this lack of autonomy seems to be immutable. It is difficult for democratic elitists to argue otherwise, for to acknowledge that greater participation leads to increased competence to govern would be to concede ground to advocates of participatory democracy.

Even if more extensive political participation was deemed desirable, it is argued that the practicalities of institutionalising it are intractable. Thus direct democracy, as practised in ancient Athens during the fifth and fourth century BC, where citizens voted directly on all important decisions and many government posts were filled by lot, is impossible where citizens number millions rather than thousands. The practicalities of making effective decisions in complex and large states, as much as normative considerations, make democratic elitism the only credible theory of participation (Sartori, 1987).

A minimalist view of political participation also logically follows from the assumptions of rational choice theory. According to Olson (1971) and Downs (1957) a lack of willingness to participate by the majority is a sign not of their ignorance but of their rationality. The question the rational individual will always ask themselves when considering whether to participate is this: 'What will I gain from this act of participation that I would not gain if I fail to act?' In a society of millions, the answer will almost always be: 'Nothing'. This is the 'free rider' scenario where non-participation is the most rational option. This leads Olson (1971: 2) to the conclusion that 'rational, self-interested individuals will not act to achieve their common or group interests'. The implication of this is that political movements will be led by those who personally gain from their involvement. Thus, for political elites, participation is rational because it gives them power and prestige. The mobilisation of other participants will depend upon convincing them that they will directly benefit from participating, and that any gains will outweigh the costs. This means that some kinds of participation are more likely to be widespread than others. For example, individuals will be more easily persuaded to vote in an election, a relatively cost-free exercise, than to spend hours canvassing for a political party. Consequently, a limited representative democracy emerges as the most suitable political system for liberal societies. This results from the pursuit of rational self-interest, rather than any necessary distinction between a rational elite and an ignorant mass.

Both democratic elitism and rational choice are instrumentalist theories of participation: political participation is a means to achieve a more important end. In the case of the elite theorists, it should extend no wider than is necessary to maintain political authority. For the advocates of rational choice, it is one tool used by individuals to further their interests. In contrast, participatory theories of democracy see political involvement as developmental: participation is more than a method for governing; it serves the wider purposes of cementing civil society together and educating citizens in the art of governance. Participatory theorists start with two guiding principles. Democratic systems of governance must:

1. Maximise the instances and intensity of participation by all members of civil society.
2. Increase the areas of social life where democratic principles apply.

For Barber (1984), the majority of individuals in liberal democracies are passive recipients of elite decisions, rather than citizens who actively shape politics. This is a dangerous state of affairs, because, as de Tocqueville insisted, participation is a necessary precondition for our freedom. Not only is political activism of benefit to the participants themselves, it is also a more secure basis for the stability sought by elitists. Instrumentalist theories can only lead to what Barber terms 'thin democracy'; where democratic values are 'prudential and thus provisional, optional, and conditional – means to exclusively individualistic and private ends . . . A democracy that can be defended only by mordant scepticism may find it difficult to combat the zealotry of non-democrats' (Barber, 1984: 4).

Barber offers instead a vision of 'strong democracy' where 'politics is something done by, not to, citizens' (Barber, 1984: 132–3). This means strengthening local government and extending democratic practice into the institutions of civil society, as well as increasing opportunities for the use of national referendums and citizen-led policy initiatives (Barber, 1984: Ch. 10). In a strong democracy, participation is not merely the defence of an entrenched interest, but instead is a deliberative and public process that does not lay claim to any truth above what can be agreed consensually by its citizens. By extending the responsibility for decisions to everyone, democracy is more successfully defended against its opponents because every citizen would have a stake in its survival. It would develop individuals' political competence, thereby increasing the quality of decisions made. It would also foster amongst citizens a sense of empathy for those with different interests, thus enhancing a shared political culture. Conflicts between social groups would be resolved openly, rather than by secretive elites representing only the most powerful groups within civil society.

An Assessment of Theories of Participation

The problem for rational choice theory is this: if individual self interest is the only basis for political action, how can we explain the considerable time and effort citizens put into their membership of voluntary political associations?

Rational choice has its roots in economic models of market exchange, where goods and services are supposedly made and bought by rational producers and consumers. This model cannot easily be applied to the world of politics, where altruism, ideology, social networks and a sense of citizenship all play a part in shaping people's behaviour. Similarly, the problem of the 'free rider' is acute only if we accept the abstract individualism on which it is based. After all, it may be quite 'rational' to choose to throw your waste onto a nearby railway line rather than drive five miles to the nearest community dump. But if all individuals in society were to act in this way, the conditions that allowed for such a selfish act in the first place would soon disappear. Similarly, without individuals taking their citizenship obligations seriously, the basis for our freedom within the political community will be eroded. It may therefore be wholly rational to participate in politics. Indeed this is implied in Aristotle's notion that humans are by nature 'political animals'. Politics is an expression of humanity's capacity for rationality. We need not therefore deny the importance of rational decision making to political participation: a prudent voter will wish to assess the candidates rationally before they cast their vote, for example. As Green and Shapiro (1994: 204) argue, however, the challenge for rational choice theory is to ask how notions of rationality interact with other motivational forces.

Rationality as a factor in politics is, for democratic elitists, only significant for those who govern. The emotional nature of the masses means that they can be trusted to do little more than give their consent periodically to one or other of a set of competing programmes drawn up by elites. However, if this is the case, why allow the masses to even choose who governs? The argument against direct democracy is logically an argument against any kind of democracy. Because of this, the commitment of elitists to democracy is weak: even representative democracy is conceded only on the grounds of expediency. This allows for the possibility that democracy could be dispensed with altogether, if another way could be found to pacify the masses' demands.

The concession of a limited form of democracy on opportunist grounds by the elitists gives force to the argument that democracy is an unfinished project. Its very development reflects the desire by the 'masses' to have a hand in governing their own lives. This is a real difficulty for elitists, because their arguments rest not only upon an unproven distinction between a competent elite and an unreliable mass, but also upon what is deemed practical in the real world. This view is succinctly stated by Etzioni-Halevy (1993: 75): 'Important as public participation is for democracy, and beautiful as the theories that call for such participation may be, the problem is that they have little to say on how Western democracy actually works'. Arguments like this have been made prior to every extension of participation rights to workers, women and minorities. However, statements that we have achieved all we can politically are quickly made to look complacent by an ongoing process of democratisation.

My analysis of instrumentalist theories of participation suggests that a developmental theory of democracy is a more compelling one. Political participation is seen as a good in itself; something that all individuals can play a part in and through which they develop not only their own political competence, but also forge the links that form civil society. Many of the normative arguments against participatory democracy are also arguments against democracy itself and can be discounted if we believe that some form of democracy is desirable. It may also be possible to overcome the practical objections to direct democracy through the innovations of ICT and new methods of citizen involvement. Before I investigate how participation may be enhanced, I shall first analyse some recent trends in political participation.

Political Participation in Liberal Democracies

In an authoritative survey of the impact of recent social change upon political participation, Russell Dalton (1996) identifies several interesting trends. These can be summarised as follows:

1. an increasingly informed and critical citizenry
2. a decline of trust in the effectiveness of political elites and institutions
3. a decline in loyalty to traditional political parties
4. a drop in turnout rates in elections
5. an increase in unconventional political participation.

Before I analyse these developments in more detail, it is important to remember that I am concerned here with mapping general trends and not every country conforms to them all. For example, there is some evidence to suggest that voter turnout is affected by the level of choice offered to the electorate (Dalton, 1996: 44). Thus low voting turnouts in the USA may partly reflect a lack of meaningful political choice for voters, as the Republicans and Democrats have often been referred to as 'the two wings of the property party'. Similarly, the levels of satisfaction in government may be greater in those 'consensual' systems, where mechanisms, such as proportional representation, force parties to compromise. Nonetheless, despite these qualifying remarks, the weight of evidence supports the general conclusions drawn by Dalton (see Verba et al., 1995; Parry et al., 1991; Klingemann and Fuchs, 1995). Readers should consult these sources for details of the exhaustive data that support the few examples that space permits me to include here.

A More Informed Citizenry

The two most important factors raising citizens' awareness seem to be, first, an increase in educational achievement and in particular a rise in the numbers of people attending higher education and second, a much greater availability of information supplied by the mass media, and in particular by television. In the 1930s higher education was a privilege enjoyed by a small minority. Following the end of the Second World War, the extension of this privilege has been dramatic. University enrolments between 1950 and 1975 grew by 347 per cent in the USA, 472 per cent in Britain and 586 per cent in France (Dalton, 1996: 25). Since 1975 these numbers have increased at least steadily, with Britain experiencing particularly impressive growth in higher education since the late 1980s.

Television also has a tremendous influence on political awareness: Dalton (1996: 24) found that, in 1992, 69 per cent of people in the USA cited television as their most important source of information on politics. In Britain in 1990, 21 per cent of total viewing time was devoted to news programmes. Add to this documentaries and drama with a large political content, and a high percentage of the hours people spend watching television is devoted to programmes containing a large political element (Budge, 1996: 19–20). Many people also have access to electronic sources of information such as the internet and CD-ROM data bases, as well as to a vast and growing array of specialised journals and newspapers.

The mass media now plays a more prominent role in forming political attitudes. This is because of what Beck (1997: 94–7) calls a process of individualisation, whereby citizens rely less upon associations within civil society like the church or trade unions to help shape their political attitudes. Individualisation is linked to wider processes of social change. These include greater affluence for the majority of citizens, the decline of working-class organisations, the relative shift from manufacturing to service sector work, and the development of post-material and secular attitudes (Inglehart, 1990; Lash and Urry, 1987).

These developments do not necessarily translate into greater interest in politics for all citizens. Although citizens' general knowledge and critical skills have undoubtedly been enhanced, many still lack an understanding of the specific details of conventional politics (Bennet, 1997). A particularly worrying trend is the lack of interest in politics amongst the young. Young people have always exhibited less political interest than older citizens. However, the extent of their disinterest is growing. A survey of 250,000 American college students by the University of California in 1998 found that only 27 per cent felt it was important to keep up with political affairs; this compared to 58 per cent in 1966 (*Guardian*, 1998a). In Britain, in 1997 the British Cohort Survey found that of 9,000 people born in 1970, 60 per cent of men and 75 per cent of women had 'no interest' or were 'not very interested' in politics.

This marked a considerable increase in political apathy compared to similar surveys conducted six years before (*Sunday Times*, 1997).

As we shall see, however, citizens are committed to democracy and are ever more willing to involve themselves in unconventional forms of participation. This apparent contradiction can be explained by the public's association of politics with discredited politicians and elite systems of democracy.

Declining Political Trust

The faith people have in their politicians, and in the way that democracy functions in their country, is decreasing and the willingness of citizens to cast a critical eye upon their political institutions is growing. Again, the media plays a big part in this. The intensity of concentration by the media upon the weaknesses of politicians, in their private as well as public lives, has certainly contributed to the mistrust politicians seem to attract. An unprecedented number of high-profile scandals in the 1990s has helped to expose the human frailties of politicians. In the USA, President Clinton's colourful sexual past dominated the mass media in 1998, and helped discredit the office that he held in the eyes of some citizens. More significantly, one of the key factors in explaining the Conservative Party's defeat in the 1997 General Election in Britain was political sleaze and corruption. This ranged from MPs accepting cash to ask questions in the House of Commons to Government ministers withholding information from the House on the issue of selling arms to Iraq (Pienaar, 1997:187–95).

The public's distaste for such improprieties is symptomatic of a deeper sense of political dissatisfaction. The European Union's Eurobarometer provides a thorough guide to political attitudes in its member states. Its figures indicate that since 1976 satisfaction with the workings of democracy in Western Europe has declined considerably (Fuchs and Klingemann, 1995: 440). In the spring of 1997, 41 per cent of citizens said they could not rely upon their national parliament, and 45 per cent felt their government to be unreliable (Commission of the European Communities, 1997: 43). In the USA, those citizens expressing a great confidence in Congress fell from 42 per cent in 1966 to 8 per cent in 1993 (Dalton, 1996: 268). Recent evidence from Britain suggests that 63 per cent of the population think the system of government could be improved 'quite a lot' or a 'great deal' (Curtice and Jowell, 1997: 91).

Despite these discontents, the citizens of liberal democracies place a high value on democratic norms. There is also very little support for violence as a legitimate act of participation. However, there appears to have been a shift away from collective to individualistic democratic values. These individualistic values include support for individual liberty over equality, limited government over interventionist government, and a defence of plurality over notions of the common good (Thomassen, 1995: 384–6). As Kaase and Newton (1995: 155) observe, this evidence supports Beck's thesis of individualisation discussed above.

Declining Loyalty to Political Parties

Political parties have been the most important political mediators between the state and civil society. They have been the main actors in mobilising citizens' participation, often by adopting political programmes that represent a broad sectional interest such as those based upon religion or class. With the proliferation of new political issues, and the fragmentation of collective social identities, it is increasingly difficult for parties to play this role. As Hirst and Khilnani (1996: 3) note, the foundations of party support are now 'shallower and less stable'. Given the growing competence of citizens, 'it is only to be expected that citizens will take a more sceptical view of political actors as a whole, and thus of political parties' (Kaase and Newton, 1995: 432).

The available evidence supports the claim that citizens are becoming less loyal to political parties (Schmitt and Holmberg, 1995). Many political parties have experienced a decline in membership and in the numbers of individuals willing to take an active role in party business. A good example of such decline is the British Conservative Party. In electoral terms, the Conservatives have been one of the most successful parties ever, and one that has enjoyed traditionally high membership levels: in the post-war period, membership reached a high of two and three-quarter million. By the 1990s this fell to around 750,000 members. The number of full-time local conservative agents, who play a crucial role in managing election campaigns, fell from 421 in 1966 to 234 by 1993 (Whiteley et al., 1994: 24–8). A similar picture can be found in the USA, and in Western Europe amongst parties across the political spectrum (McKay, 1997: 100–8; Widfeldt, 1995: 134–75).

Electorates are also becoming more influenced by current political issues in casting their vote, rather than voting out of a sense of loyalty to a particular party. Consequently, voting patterns are more volatile. Parties have responded by attempting to utilise the mass media more effectively. The use of the techniques of political communications, such as hiring advertising agencies and employing special media advisors, has become increasingly important to parties as they seek to augment their shrinking band of traditional loyalists with appeals to as many diverse social groups as possible. However, the impact on democracy of campaigns that increasingly resemble mass public-relations exercises is unclear. Such tactics by political parties, though understandable, have helped to increase the dominance of the mass media, which by trivialising and personalising politics may well have helped to alienate the public from conventional politics. Beck (1997: 144) diagnoses succinctly the problems facing political parties in their search for stable support:

> Who votes in what way for a given issue and candidate no longer follows any predictable and easily consulted pattern. Individualization destabilizes the system of mass parties from the inside, because it deprives party commitments of tradition, making them dependent on decision-making or, seen from the party perspective, dependent upon construction. Considering the fragmentation of interests, opinions and issues, this is like trying to herd a sack of fleas.

Falling Electoral Turnout

In an analysis of voting trends in the USA and Western Europe from the 1950s to the 1990s, Dalton (1996: 44) concludes that 'voting participation is generally decreasing across national boundaries'. It should be noted that some country's turnout rates are still reasonably healthy, and in certain others the trend downwards is by no means a dramatic one. This is perhaps not surprising given that the act of voting costs the citizen little. Nonetheless, Lijphart agrees with Dalton's assessment that the general trend of voting is downwards. Lijphart argues turnout rates are strikingly low if they are measured as a percentage of the voting age population rather than as a percentage of those registered to vote (Lijphart, 1997: 5). Low turnouts are a worrying sign of a lack of engagement with conventional politics, particularly as general levels of political competence are rising. In the USA since the 1960s the decline in turnout rates in Presidential and House elections has been particularly marked: in 1964 they stood at 61.9 per cent; by 1996 the figure was 48.8 per cent (McKay, 1997: 119).

Voting turnout is shaped by socio-economic position. Wealthier and more educated citizens are more likely to vote than the poor and badly educated (Lijphart, 1997: 2–5). Ethnic minorities within liberal democracies are also less likely to participate in elections. The danger is that politicians will be tempted to ignore the interests of the already marginalised elements of society who may react by turning to violence, disorder or to anti-party organisations. In their search for a broad coalition of support, parties are converging towards the political centre to capture as many middle-class votes as possible. Issues of poverty and exclusion are being pushed to the political margins. As income inequalities between rich and poor are growing in some industrial countries, this is a worrying trend.

An Increase in Unconventional Participation

At a time when support for conventional acts of participation is waning, involvement in unconventional participation is increasing rapidly. Direct action by citizens is a growing feature of civil society. The World Values Survey in 1990–1 found that around a quarter of the population in West Germany, the USA and Britain had 'engaged in a challenging act' such as a demonstration, a boycott, an unofficial strike or occupying a building (Dalton, 1996: 74). Membership of campaign organisations such as environmental or women's groups now outnumber membership of political parties in many countries (Dalton, 1996: 54). However, interpretations of the significance of these phenomena differ.

Advocates of the new social movements thesis suggest a shift from the old politics of parties, parliaments and elites to a new age of spontaneous participation by informal groups pursuing ethical and post-material concerns such as peace, ecology and animal rights. Sub-politics is becoming increasingly important as a site of political innovation and a chance for an individualised citizenry to pursue divergent interests that cannot easily be articulated by centralised party structures (Beck, 1997).

Other commentators are more cautious than Beck in concluding that traditional forms of participation are becoming redundant. Kaase and Newton (1995: 12–13) argue that the old system of politics is suitably adaptable to meet these new challenges creatively: 'the new political agenda has not replaced the old one, but has merged with it in a symbiotic fashion'. Rather than bypassing traditional politics, this new politics has helped to put on the agenda issues such as environmental protection, which parties have responded to by 'greening' their party programmes. NSMs are no more certain to gain the long-term support of such citizens than are political parties. It is more likely that traditional political organisations are in a transitional phase, as they seek to incorporate new social issues (Kaase and Newton, 1995: 96).

Koopmans (1996) suggests that in some countries where NSMs have been particularly strong and traditional allegiances have declined, such as Holland and Germany, unconventional participation has actually decreased. This is partly because in the first half of the twentieth century the labour movement engaged in more dramatic unconventional activity (such as wildcat strikes) than is witnessed today. It is also partly because NSMs are increasingly becoming incorporated into traditional political structures and in many cases are better described as pressure groups. They often possess budgets of several millions of dollars, have professional staff and mobilise their supporters only on rare occasions (Koopmans, 1996: 35–6). As such, NSMs are vulnerable to the criticisms often levelled at pressure groups, namely that they distort democracy by pressing well-organised but minority interests, they represent only certain privileged socio-economic groups, and their impact is less to do with democratic expression and more to do with effective resource mobilisation. This argument is supported by Jordan and Maloney who in a study of campaign groups associated with promoting NSM values (such as Amnesty and Friends of the Earth) found that these organisations are themselves hierarchical and offer little opportunity for participation by ordinary members, other than low-intensity acts such as the payment of a donation (Jordan and Maloney, 1997: 188).

Summary

From the evidence surveyed above, I conclude that political participation in liberal democracies is in a period of transition. A generally more educated and informed electorate is increasingly sceptical of the ability of elites and existing political institutions to meet their expectations. This is illustrated by the growing mistrust of traditional forms of participation. When citizens do vote, they are more volatile in their voting patterns and are becoming increasingly concerned with post-material as well as material issues.

   Citizens are also more likely to take part in a wide range of alternative forms of participation to express their opinions, many of which conform to the issues promoted by NSMs. Although the diversity of unconventional political acts has increased, as Koopmans (1996) reminds us, it is important to remember that unconventional politics has always been a feature of politics and NSM activity is generally less violent than political protest in the past. NSMs cannot in any case perpetually stand outside of traditional power structures and are likely in time to become indistinguishable from pressure groups. It is therefore questionable whether NSMs can in the long term provide a suitable vehicle for the commitment citizens show to individualistic democratic values. It is unlikely that they can replace parties as the main link between state and civil society, and therefore political parties remain indispensable to the exercise of political participation. They will continue to provide a focal point for voters and to play a major role in shaping the content of political debate. The evidence does suggest there are good reasons though for thinking that parties will have to adapt considerably to meet the challenges posed by an electorate that is becoming unwilling to be blindly led by political elites. Parties, if they are to govern effectively, will need to look for new methods of interacting creatively with ordinary citizens. In the next section consideration will be given to some ways in which this may be facilitated.

Enhancing Political Participation

Many of the changes necessary to enhance participation may involve removing institutional barriers to conventional forms of participation, or increasing the use of devices such as referendums that are already utilised to some extent. Institutional reforms might include measures to make participation easier and more worthwhile, such as: simple and more comprehensive systems of voter registration; greater use of postal votes (which may aid disabled citizens to participate); an extension of the time allowed for people to vote, with perhaps an election extending over three or four days; a more proportional system of voting that more accurately reflects the plurality of modern societies; and perhaps even compulsory voting in at least national elections (as is the case in Australia). The advantage of this last measure would be that it would help offset socio-economic inequalities in voting; it may encourage citizens to increase their awareness of politics; and it would also prevent parties from ignoring groups who in the past have failed to exercise their right to vote (Lijphart, 1997).

The use of referendums is on the increase in liberal democracy (Butler and Ranney, 1994). These offer citizens an opportunity to pass judgement on a contentious issue that may have divided party opinion. However, this device does not necessarily have to be party led. In Switzerland and some states in the USA, it is possible for citizens who gather a predetermined level of support through petitions to force a referendum on an aspect of government policy, or even to initiate a vote on an issue of their own choosing. The fear that this will lead to incoherent government is certainly not borne out by the Swiss experience, where since 1848 over 150 post-legislative referendums have resulted in less than 10 rejections of the original parliamentary decisions (Adonis and Mulgan, 1997: 235).

Of even greater potential significance for political participation are advances in ICT and the intensification of participation through innovations like citizens' juries.

The Democratic Impact of ICT

In an excellent study of direct democracy, Budge (1996) contends that ICT removes the barriers of size, time and space by allowing instantaneous and interactive forms of participation via e-mail, the internet, video conferencing, the digitisation of data, two-way computer and television links via cable technology and numerous other innovations (Bryan et al., 1998: 2–3). It is no longer necessary for citizens to meet face to face to discuss and decide policy. Participants can remain at home, listening and contributing to debates, before voting swiftly and efficiently using electronic rather than manual voting systems. The main positive implications of ICT for political participation can be summarised as follows (Bryan et al., 1998: 6–7):

1. ICT presents unprecedented opportunities to increase the diffusion of information in order to legitimate and enhance awareness of governmental decisions. For instance, ever increasing numbers of local government organisations are making use of web sites and e-mail to publicise their decisions and agendas.
2. Information can also pass more easily from citizens to government. The advantage of communicating easily and quickly, without the need to leave one's home, is of particular significance to the disabled or those with little spare time. ICT could make citizens' preferences more transparent to government organisations and help bridge the gap between state and civil society. Citizens could also shape the form of policies on an ongoing basis, rather than merely shifting their allegiance in elections by withdrawing their support from one party and transferring it to another.
3. New technologies increase the potential for the associations of civil society either to publicise themselves relatively cheaply, or to recruit new supporters, or to canvass the opinion of their members. The informality and spontaneity of much NSM activity could be enhanced through computer networking, thus aiding the organisation of protests, boycotts and petitions. The use of such opportunities by radical groups is illustrated by the proliferation of anarchist writings available on the internet.
4. The interactive qualities of ICT may release citizens from a passive dependence upon the mass media and contribute to open government. The storage capacities of computers means that the potential exists for citizens to access governmental papers in their entirety, rather than receiving edited versions

via distorting gatekeepers of information such as civil servants and journalists.

5. Social services may also be more effectively targeted at those most in need. ICT gives government the potential to 'model' the needs of those in receipt of benefits and to shape social policy accordingly. As Henman (1997: 335) argues, 'in the identification of poverty traps and the like, and the creation of statistics, computers help to give rise to newly defined social groups . . . Computers help to define these groups, to make them knowable, and therefore to assist their governance'.

There are a growing number of political organisations making use of the advantages of ICT to enhance their links with the public. For example, in 1994 the city government of Amsterdam set up its so-called Digital City, where citizens could either access government records and policy documents or interact with other citizens. It has generated great interest amongst the people of Amsterdam, with 100,000 'visits' to the Digital City within the first ten weeks of its existence (Francissen and Brants, 1998: 23). In Santa Monica in the USA the public electronic network, designed to enhance community action, has 4000 user logins per month. One citizens' action group set up through the network raised $150,000 to help the local homeless and persuaded government to make available lockers, showers and laundry facilities (Schuller, 1996). Such examples show the potential for ICT innovations to empower citizens and communities.

However, ICT is not a panacea for all the problems of political participation. It must be remembered that ICT does not operate in a political vacuum: political culture will shape its use. Also, it is by no means certain that all the implications of ICT will be positive ones for democratic practice.

First, there is the problem of regulating ICT. Access to ICT and the balance between the liberties of the user and the protection of privacy will all need to be resolved politically. I have noted already that political participation is linked to socio-economic position. As information becomes a more important power resource, ICT inequalities could further marginalise already excluded citizens unless ICT is brought more into public control and efforts are made to distribute the technology more widely.

Second, ICT increases opportunities for surveillance. Indeed, enhancing direct democracy may be the only way to guard against the centralisation of ICT by what Ravetz (1997) has called the 'information rich state' and by private corporations. The citizen as a consumer of services is faced with an ever-greater complexity of policy as a consequence of the computer modelling of social needs; while professional discretion at the point of delivery is reduced as decision making moves away from localities towards the organisational centre of the state or corporation. Ravetz gives the example of performance indicators that are increasingly popular as ways of holding public and private services to account. Because 'the model suppositions, input data and modelling are often unknown except by a few key people' the result is to 'dull participation' by ordinary citizens and to increase the surveillance capacities of the powerful (Ravetz, 1997). Only through strong regulatory bodies, which are not driven solely by market performance, can these effects be countered.

Third, some commentators have questioned the effects of ICT upon participation. Barber (1984: 54) has noted that a decline in face-to-face participation may sacrifice intimacy for immediacy. Schuller (1996: 136) argues that experiments such as the Santa Monica scheme have shown that the relative anonymity of ICT can lead to more confrontational interactions: citizens are more likely to lose their sense of restraint than would be the case in a public meeting. The art of deliberation might also be undermined by ICT, as the speed of technology may lead to rash and hasty decisions. In addition, encryption technologies that allow the user of ICT to remain anonymous enhances opportunities for the spreading of 'hate speak' by racist, misogynist or other pathological individuals or groups (Denning, 1997).

As McLean (1989: 173) contends, 'on balance, new technology is an ally, not an enemy, of democrats'. The opportunities exist to render obsolete the democratic elitist argument, that on practical grounds alone, direct democracy is unfeasible. However, we must beware of both over optimism and technological determinism. Technological advances in the past, from the railway to the telegraph, have been hailed as harbingers of greater democracy: Swabey, writing in 1939, thought that inventions such as the radio meant direct democracy had become 'realizable on an undreamt-of scale' (cited in Raab, 1997: 173).

Nonetheless, the sheer pace and complexity of developments in ICT suggest that it can play a key role in enhancing political participation in the near future. What is needed is an undogmatic and practical approach to ICT innovations. As Adonis and Mulgan (1997: 241) argue, what is required is an experimental approach to all aspects of ICT to ascertain what the effects, both positive and negative, might be upon democracy.

Citizens' Juries

One of the most interesting developments in political participation in recent times has been the use of citizens' juries by providers of public services such as in health care, or by local governments to advise on local planning issues. Citizens' juries have appeared in various forms in the USA, Germany and Britain. They involve the use of ordinary citizens, statistically representative of the population, to consider and make recommendations upon questions of public policy. In Britain in 1996 the Institute for Public Policy Research (IPPR) set up five such juries to study their implications for participation. These juries explored diverse and complex health issues including how the National Health Service (NHS) should be funded and what care should be provided for the terminally ill.

The IPPR found that as a participatory device citizens' juries have a number of strengths. As issues are discussed over several days, participation is intense and deliberative. Citizens' juries also make informed recommendations, as they are empowered to hear and question relevant experts. Jurors generally find the experience rewarding and the exercise increases the understanding citizens' have of policy issues (Coote and Lenaghan, 1997: 63). They give citizens a voice in how policy is shaped and are likely to improve exchanges of information between providers and users of services. For example, citizens are often unaware of why the NHS rations certain services. Without more active involvement, 'the public will assume all rationing decisions are about cutting services rather than the fair distribution of finite resources' (Coote and Lenaghan, 1997: 55).

There was no evidence in the IPPR pilot schemes to support the elite view that ordinary citizens are incapable of complex decision making and consensus building. Rather, the IPPR conclude that 'citizens are willing and able to share the complexities involved in decisions about health care provision' (Coote and Lenaghan, 1997: 55). The experience helped to foster a sense of confidence and community amongst the participants and their verdicts on the various issues were well considered.

More such experiments will be needed to measure the effects of citizens' juries. Nonetheless, the experience of them so far has been very positive and belies the view that elite decision making is necessarily superior. Citizens are just as likely to be able to come to an informed view on many issues as are members of Congress or Parliament. As Adonis and Mulgan (1997: 230) observe, 'in complex fields such as economics and law few of the politicians involved understand the complexities'. For this reason alone it would be foolish not to seek to utilise the diversity of skills that exist in civil society.

Other experiments in citizen participation support the view that ordinary citizens are capable of making intelligent decisions, and that active involvement has numerous advantages in terms of increasing self-confidence, a sense of citizenship and enhancing the legitimacy of policy making (Budge, 1996). For example, in Britain some local councils have experimented with community ownership schemes by transferring previously government-controlled housing into the hands of residents' associations. In a review of such schemes in Scotland, Clapham et al. (1996: 368) conclude that 'small, locally-based and resident-controlled housing organisations can provide an effective service, and crucially, can sustain this over a considerable period of time'. Tenants have considerably more faith in their own resident committees than in local councils, suggesting that direct participation in services increases a sense of community and empowerment which representative systems are less able to engender.

Workers' involvement in decision making at work is also increasing. Employers have lessened their hostility, as a growing body of evidence suggests that productivity, as well as participation, may be increased by the use of works' councils (Budge, 1996: 22; Archer, 1996: 93). In the face of diversifying consumer demand and international competition, it may be that corporations will need to apply notions of flexibility to decision making as well as to production. As the government seeks to tap the skills of its citizens, so the firm may draw upon 'workers' unused knowledge to improve the production process' (Archer, 1996: 91). If participatory methods of governance are to increase, powerful corporations cannot be allowed to swim against the tide. Unless the workplace is democratised too, measures to enhance participation elsewhere will ultimately be superficial exercises (Barber, 1984, Pateman, 1970).

Conclusion

Part III of this book has shown that recent social changes have had a significant impact upon civil society. A more diverse and critical citizenry has made the task of sustaining a shared political culture and a common citizenship increasingly difficult. Neither are the majority of citizens prepared to invest their trust in a distant and elitist state. A key question for political sociology therefore is this: how can the state and civil society be reconciled, and effective systems of governance constituted? As we shall see in Part IV, many contemporary political sociologists consider the democratisation of the state and civil society as the key to answering this question.

This is because at the heart of democratic theory is the notion that individuals are the best judges of their own interests. The increasing individualisation of civil society therefore demands democratic governance. As well as an expression of individual autonomy, however, democracy is necessarily relational. It involves compromise, tolerance of others, and accommodation between conflicting views. Democracy is therefore the best chance we have of reconciling the increased diversity of civil society. Democracy is also the most secure way of converting power into authority, because it entails citizens giving their consent to decisions made in their name. Democracy values in equal measure the contribution of all members of civil society. It therefore requires that wherever possible decisions should be taken by citizens themselves. These are the ideals of democratic governance. Theories that suggest that democracy is merely a method of government that best preserves the *status quo*, or is no more than the expression of narrow, predetermined interests, seem hollow and uninspired in comparison.

The evidence surveyed in this chapter suggests that on practical and normative grounds the democratic elitist perspective is in any case declining in its persuasive force. Citizens in liberal democracy, though believing strongly in the virtues of democracy, are becoming disenchanted with unaccountable governance. Following the collapse of communism, liberal democracies are reflecting upon their own political arrangements and finding them wanting. The personal conduct of politicians, coupled with their inability to cope with the complexities of decision making, belies the faith writers like Schumpeter have shown in elites. As Budge (1996: 190) contends,

> it is difficult to think of any major decisions of the last ten to twenty years which popular interventions might not have improved . . . Popular voting could have protected health and personal services better, safeguarded education and probably done more to protect the environment.

Technological advances may now provide the opportunity for aspects of participatory democracy to be realised. Much of the available evidence suggests not only that citizens are increasingly willing to involve themselves in politics, broadly defined, but also that participation is cumulative in its positive effects upon citizens' ability to participate. It is through such participation that the rights and responsibilities of citizenship can be reconciled. Without a pervading sense of active participation, citizenship becomes merely a passive status that fails to empower the individual. Only by decentralising decision-making processes can citizens have the opportunities to perform their responsibilities and make use of their rights (Pateman, 1970: 38).

However, we do not need to take the view that representative and direct forms of democracy are binary opposites. Even in direct forms of democracy, the institutions of civil society and particularly political parties will still mediate political debate. Any effective system of democracy is likely therefore to combine more citizen-centred involvement, such as citizens' juries and referendums, with more proportional, devolved and accountable representative bodies in the context of a constitution that defends basic rights and gives form to a variety of levels and types of political participation.

The discussions in Parts II and III lead to three initial conclusions. First, despite the challenges of globalisation, neo-liberalism and new social movements, the state has largely retained its ability to concentrate power and to assert its autonomy if it so wishes. The state–civil society relationship therefore continues to be the most appropriate focus for political sociology. Secondly, the state and civil society are nevertheless increasingly faced with the task of adapting themselves to demands for more active forms of political participation from their citizens. This will necessarily entail a rethinking of the relationship between civil society and the state. Thirdly, states will also encounter challenges from outside their jurisdiction. In order to cope with the intensification of global problems, participation may well move both downwards towards the associations of civil society and upwards towards more global forms of governance. In the final part of the book, then, we first explore in Chapter 9 how contemporary political sociologists have attempted to rethink the state–civil society relationship in the context of the social changes explored in Parts II and III. Secondly, in Chapter 10 the question arises whether globalisation, understood as the growth of global risks, requires the development of a global governance that reaches beyond the state.

Part IV

Rethinking Governance

9

Contemporary Theories of the State and Civil Society

Recent processes of social change have not only highlighted the continuing power of the state, they have also shown how problematic and contradictory the state's relationship to civil society really is. What is clear then is that if governance is to be enhanced, the ability of the state to concentrate power must be acknowledged and countered. In the light of this observation, how have political sociologists rethought the problem of governance? In the final part of the book this question is explored. In Chapter 10, we look at the prospects for extending governance beyond the state, while in this chapter, I examine some influential theories of how the state's relationship to civil society might be reconceptualised. This is by necessity a selective process, and not all will agree with the texts chosen for consideration. However, my choice is informed, not only by the undoubted importance of the chosen writers, but also by the desire to maintain continuity with the previous parts of this book. I am especially interested in analysing how contemporary political sociologists have modified the insights of classical political sociology, as discussed in Part I, in the context of the challenges to the state and civil society explored in Parts II and III.

In particular, one of the key questions of contemporary political sociology is the relevance of modernist ideologies in shaping future systems of governance. For Giddens and Beck, liberalism and socialism have become exhausted as the enlightenment project has run up against its own limits. They therefore seek to revive, albeit in greatly modified form, aspects of the conservative critique of these optimistic modernist theories. In contrast, Miliband and Wainwright have sought to rethink socialism and thereby preserve its essence as an emancipatory theory. It will, however, be argued that all of these thinkers, through their considerable adaptation of classical theories, have converged towards a radical pluralist position, which has at its heart the democratisation of the state and civil society. I conclude, therefore, with a discussion of this theoretical convergence, and the implications of this development for governance. In the final section of the chapter

Paul Hirst's theory of associative democracy will be introduced. It is a good example of radical pluralism and is one of the most interesting attempts to rethink the state–civil society relationship. However, before I proceed with this recasting of modernist arguments, I shall briefly consider the argument that the world in the late twentieth century is best described as post-modern, and therefore beyond the power of modernist logic to explain.

The Post-Modern Turn

Post-modernism presents a stimulating critique of all theoretical projects, including liberalism and socialism, that offer holistic accounts of human existence. Post-modernists are particularly scathing about metanarratives, which are theories that claim to be able to map the future direction of society by an analysis of the past and present condition of humanity (Lyotard, 1984). A good example of this would be Marxism, which sees capitalism as being pregnant with its communist successor, the 'father' of which is of course class conflict, embodied in the 'universal' class of the proletariat. Such ideas are, for post-modernists, delusions, and dangerous ones at that.

In place of the static individualism of liberalism, and the oppressive collectivism of Marxism, post-modernism stresses fragmentation, relativism and multiple, often contradictory, identities. To privilege one identity, one fragment, or one 'truth' is to oppress other equally valid positions. Therefore, metanarratives like Marxism can only ever be totalitarian and self-defeating. Linked to this denial of the notion of a universal subject is a radical view of power. Again, like identity, power is understood as multifaceted. As Foucault states, power is present in 'social institutions, in economic inequalities, in language, in the bodies themselves of each and every one of us' (Foucault, 1980: 87–90). Any system of knowledge, referred to as a discourse by post-modernists, inevitably involves the exercise of power. For example, a psychiatrist is in a position of power in relation to her patients because of her medical knowledge, expressed in a highly specialised language, of which her patients have perhaps little understanding. Due to the ever-present character of power in human relationships, attempts to locate the principal source of power, for example in the state, a class, or group of corporations, is futile.

Post-modernism has its strengths. It has been particularly attractive to some feminist thinkers who see in it a powerful critique of Marxism and liberalism, which appear superficially to be emancipatory, but rest upon concepts of justice, equality and fraternity that are distinctly gendered. In emphasising that power is exercised at a micro- as well as macro-level, the work of writers such as Foucault is sensitive to the feminist notion of the 'personal as political'. The concept of discourses of power operating through language is also useful in an analysis of sexist terminology that permeate and help to condition everyday interactions between men and women. However, despite these positive aspects of post-modernism, in terms of the central concerns of political sociology its contribution is limited. This is because post-modernists are strong on critique (of notions of universality and the limits of meta-narratives) but offer little in the way of a constructive alternative to the modernist positions they ridicule.

The problems of governance remain even in a post-modern world, and writers like Lyotard and Foucault offer no solution to them. If all life choices are equally valid, how can social order be maintained? If all attempts to reduce social divisions inevitably create different forms of inequality, how can the disparities of wealth and opportunity, which are very evident in modern society, be overcome? The problem with the post-modern approach to social institutions and power is its negativity: power is never conceived of in post-modernism as a potentially positive attribute, as understood in notions of empowerment for example. The point is that in any system of governance difficult choices have to be made between various institutional forms. Such choices necessarily involve normative judgements. Part of the purpose of social science is to make such judgements, based on empirical evidence and logic. With its denial of the tools of social science, post-modernist thought suggests two possible political positions. First, an extreme and nihilistic relativism that either returns to a pre-modern fatalism, or leads to a Nietzschian power struggle, where the strong triumph over the weak. Secondly, and ironically given the post-modern critique of liberalism, a radical libertarian perspective, where all that matters is the freedom to choose, not the nature or consequences of the choice itself. As far as the central questions of political sociology are concerned, the 'post-modern turn' leads inevitably to a dead end. The state is seen as merely one manifestation of the power relations that are all around us and therefore impossible to locate. Civil society is a market place in which we engage in a multitude of life-style experiences, with little apparent obligation to anyone, or anything, else.

Back to the Future: Restating Conservatism?

Both Giddens (1994) and Beck (1992, 1997) recognise the limitations of post-modernism in identifying the problems of governance faced by modern societies. For Giddens (1994: 10), post-modernism amounts to an unhelpful 'confession of impotence in the face of forces larger than ourselves'. Beck sees more potential in post-modernism than does Giddens. However, he shares the latter's preference for a notion of a recontextualised modernity, rather than the post-modernist assumption that the social change affecting modernity signals its end rather than its transformation to a new form. Both thinkers wish to disentangle the identification of modernity solely with notions of industrialism. Processes of globalisation and growing social awareness mean that modernity contains the seeds of its own renewal as well as its potential annihilation. As Beck (1997: 111) writes, 'many modernities are possible'. The similarities between Giddens's and Beck's theories are striking. I will argue that they are united by an approach that interestingly draws upon ideas central to philosophical conservatism.

Giddens: Beyond Left and Right

At the centre of Giddens's analysis in *Beyond Left and Right* (1994) of 'late modernity' is a radical view of globalisation. For Giddens, globalisation is not primarily a description of economic interdependence but instead refers to the interconnections between localised communities and global processes of modernity. The products of modern society, such as telecommunications, micro-computers and satellites, have allowed modernity to become self-conscious, and Giddens uses the term *social reflexivity* to refer to this process. Because of this growing global awareness, people increasingly evaluate even the most intimate aspects of their lives in terms of global change. Moreover, as the modern world reaches its limits, and reflects back upon itself, individuals and communities become increasingly aware of the risks and limitations of what Giddens calls the productionist logic of modernity. Indeed for Giddens the key problem we face is manufactured uncertainty, which consists of dangers of our own making, such as the threat of ecological collapse, a global epidemic of a 'man'-made virus, or a nuclear holocaust caused by war or accident: the 'achievements' of modernity in creating ever-more sophisticated technologies of annihilation and communication mean that we are simultaneously at greater risk of extinction and increasingly aware that this possibility exists.

The political consequences of the growth of manufactured uncertainty are profound, and Giddens cites the decline in support for traditional mechanisms of representation as evidence that late modernity requires a new form of governance (Giddens, 1994: 7). However, neither Marxism nor liberalism can provide a coherent programme of change, hence the need to move beyond the dogmas of left and right. Giddens is especially critical of the shift towards neo-liberalism by many right-wing parties. He identifies tensions in neo-liberals' promotion of, on the one hand, market forces which erode communities and tradition and, on the other hand, their 'dogmatic stress on traditional values' (Giddens, 1994: 43). Socialism, however, does not offer an alternative. With the collapse of communism, the left has been forced onto the ideological defensive, centred upon an outmoded vision of the welfare state (Giddens, 1994: 69).

Giddens argues that the problems of manufactured uncertainty instead demand a new politics centred upon life politics, generative politics and dialogic democracy. Life politics marks a shift from a politics concerned purely with 'life chances', associated with the struggle for freedom from material want or arbitrary power, towards a politics of 'lifestyles' informed by an awareness of how life choices impact on the whole planet. Individuals' lives are now more intimately connected to the risks generated by modernisation. However, in making sense of these threats, people can no longer successfully draw upon images of a return to nature or to traditional ways of living. This is because nature has been 'humanised', in the sense that technological developments have meant that humanity controls the destiny of the natural world, rather than nature being understood as an external threat to human existence. Modern society has also broken with the past. Traditional forms of behaviour can no longer be defended in a traditional way (Giddens, 1994: 48). What Giddens means here is that it is up to us to consciously decide what traditions we wish to utilise in order to recreate solidarity, which modernity has undermined.

The need to reappraise our relationship to nature and tradition lies at the heart of Giddens's use of conservative philosophy, which 'acquires a new relevance for political radicalism today' (Giddens, 1994: 10). Aspects of conservatism have a salience in a world that has run up against its own limitations, for the radical conservative an uncertain future requires a reappraisal of the past. Giddens therefore draws upon a number of themes found in the work of such conservative theorists as Burke and Oakeshott. These conservative themes include a scepticism about progress, an ethos of individual responsibility and the need to build solidarity at a local level, which helps to sustain the wider community and environment. Underpinning these themes is the notion of a contract between individuals who currently inhabit the present with those who are dead and those yet to be born. Such a contract, which transcends the narrow and egotistical contract of liberal theory, forms the basis for an ethic of stewardship of the environment and duty to other individuals.

The role of generative politics is to build institutions that nurture both personal autonomy and individual responsibility to oneself and to the wider society. A 'prime building block' for this is the creation of dialogic democracy where democracy is conceived not as the defence of sectional interest as in classical pluralist accounts but as a process that encourages 'active trust', tolerance and diversity, through collective discussions of the problems of governance. Such democracy cannot be confined to the institutions of liberal democracy (although Giddens sees these as having a continued importance), but is also extended into social movements and self-help groups; these 'little platoons' (to borrow a phrase from Burke) help to build self-confidence and mental health that are central to the success of life politics. However, some-what confusingly Giddens is adamant that the development of soli-darity cannot be fostered in a revitalised civil society. First, this is because the intensification of globalisation means it is impractical to revitalise a concept so closely bound up with the increasingly out-moded state. Secondly, if it was possible to enhance the autonomy of civil society, it may become a bedrock for fundamentalist assertions of a nationalistic and ethnic variety, which stand opposed to the principles of dialogic democracy (Giddens, 1994: 124–33).

Giddens acknowledges the threat large-scale inequalities of power pose to modern society. However, the welfare system as defended by socialism needs to be given a large dose of generative politics: it is no longer adequate to deal with problems as they arise. Instead, welfare must be rethought in terms of prevention and precaution. This applies to Third World poverty as much as it does to the unemployed or sick in the industrial world. Aid to the developing world, like welfare benefits in industrialised countries, has to be aimed at helping people find their own solutions to their plight. This necessarily entails a deconstruction of statist models of welfare, and instead involves a deliberative process between a wide range of welfare providers and the recipients of ben-efits, to tailor such help to maximise personal autonomy.

However, while Giddens favours a pluralist approach in the areas of the economy, politics and welfare, he does not fall into the relativist trap of post-modernism. On the contrary, at the heart of his argument is the fact that the threat of manufactured uncertainty is a basis for universality and solidarity. Through the growth of social reflexivity, modernity appears ever-more as a two edged sword that has delivered both great wealth and potential for many, while increasing risk for all of us. This requires us to radically rethink our understanding of govern-ance, and ironically forces us to reappraise the conservative critique of modernity and adapt its healthy scepticism to the conditions of the contemporary world.

Beck: Risk Society and the Reinvention of Politics

Beck shares Giddens's anxiety over the growing intensity of risk in late modernity. The key political question of our time is therefore this: 'How can the risks and hazards systematically produced as part of modernization be prevented, minimised, dramatised, or channelled?' (Beck, 1992: 19). The side effects of industrialisation and science have replaced class conflict as the new motors of history. In the face of these threats, advocates of modernist ideologies are 'like blind people discussing colours' (Beck, 1997: 137). Modernist categories like class and nation are irrelevant to the effects of risk. The struggle for equality is replaced by the maintenance of safety. As Beck contends, the side effects of our productionist ethos and the ill-conceived experiments of politically unaccountable scientists show no respect for 'man'-made boundaries, whether they be social or geographical. Global warming and the destruction of the ozone layer have their origin largely in the industrial world, which in the short term makes economic gains, but in the longer term such risks have a 'boomerang effect' that threatens rich as well as poor nations. Consequently, the 'grand coalition' between the state, business and science is increasingly challenged by a more reflexive and threatened population. For Beck, the state has lost credibility because it fails to protect its citizens from the risks that it has itself helped to create: 'the legal order no longer fosters social peace, because by tolerating the dangers it sanctions and legitimates a disadvantaging of people in general' (Beck, 1997: 129).

Although less explicitly than Giddens, Beck's analysis also draws upon aspects of conservative philosophy. A challenge to the rationalist assertions of modernity and science must lie at the centre of a new politics, and in many passages of *Risk Society* Beck's critique of scientific rationality sounds distinctly conservative: he writes, 'the sciences are *entirely incapable* of reacting adequately to civilizational risks, since they are prominently involved in the origins and growth of those very risks' (Beck, 1992: 59).

The guiding dictum of contemporary politics should be what Beck calls the 'art of doubt'; the optimism of human solutions to global problems found in the enlightenment ideologies of liberalism and socialism must be replaced by a new scepticism. Indeed, for Beck, 'the political programme of radicalised modernity is scepticism' (Beck, 1997: 168). This scepticism must in turn be informed by the distinctively conservative idea of human beings' harmony with nature. As Beck puts it, reflexive modernity involves 'the end of the antithesis between nature and society' (Beck, 1992: 80). The modernist ethos of mastering nature must give way to an ethic of nurture, repair and conservation.

Political renewal must, argues Beck, take place at the level of what he calls *sub-politics*. Beck does not only mean the protection of established institutions of civil society such as the media (which provide much needed balance to the state), but more profoundly he suggests that the politics of late modernity must involve an ethos of self-criticism permeating all public and private bodies (Beck, 1992: 232). Beck argues that a new spirit of democracy is present in the actions of social movements, but is also appearing in businesses, where the need to respond in increasingly flexible ways to changing markets means that the opportunity exists for a 'fusion of democratic reforms and capitalistic rationalisation' (Beck, 1997: 48). All of this means the politicisation of civil society. As Beck writes, 'politics breaks open and erupts *beyond* the formal responsibilities and hierarchies' (Beck, 1997: 99). This also involves a shift from an authoritarian state to the state acting as a facilitator of political behaviour in civil society. The authoritarian state and its associated political parties have lost their *raison d'être*: with the end of the Cold War the threat of an alternative and subversive enemy in the form of communism has disappeared, while class-based political parties search in vain for a class support that has melted away (Beck, 1997: 140). Consequently, 'sub-politics has taken over the leading role from politics in shaping society' (Beck, 1992: 14).

With the development of risk society, and the associated redefinition of politics, Beck argues that individuals are being 'set free from the social forms of industrial society' (Beck, 1992: 87). NSMs are pivotal in connecting processes of the self-actualisation of individuals with the 'new risk situations' (Beck, 1992: 90). In opposition to state and corporate interference in the private sphere, NSMs (argues Beck), may create new bases for governance, founded not upon ascribed social roles, but emerging from self consciously designed identities.

A Critical Assessment of Giddens and Beck

The work of Giddens and Beck provides insightful analyses of the problems of governance in the light of what they both recognise as profound social change. While sharing much of the post-modernist critique of modernity, and its associated political forms, both thinkers avoid the conclusion that nothing constructive can be done to redefine politics in the light of radically transformed circumstances. Central to both Giddens and Beck is an emphasis upon democracy as developmental and deliberative, rather than defensive and dogmatic. In the shadow of 'man'-made risks, we must morally regenerate our politics in ways that move beyond the destructive impulses of productionism and the assertion of centralised solutions to questions of governance.

However, a number of tensions can be identified in Giddens's and Beck's works, most of which relate to our central question of the state–civil society relationship.

In their emphasis upon individualisation, both thinkers underplay the structural reasons for continuing inequalities and political problems. In particular, the contradictions inherent both to a civil society structured by capitalism and the tensions of the states system continue to exercise a malign effect on the formation of active trust and constructive deliberation to resolve disputes. The ongoing problems of capitalism and class division within civil society are at the heart of the arguments of socialists like Miliband, and will be discussed below. However, as well as understating the negative effects of capitalism, Giddens and Beck fail to give enough attention to the problem of the state.

Giddens in particular is eager to avoid dismantling the divisions between state and civil society, since he assumes that the only alternative to this liberal dualism is a totalitarian 'communism' state. Consequently, Giddens is left with a distinctly liberal view of the state–civil society relationship. He argues that the liberal state creates 'general conditions of legitimacy' but, as was argued in Chapter 1, a state that rests its legitimacy upon violence is highly problematic. Indeed, in another context Giddens recognises that there is an inherent contradiction between violence and legitimacy because legitimacy implies ongoing communication and consent. Commenting upon the need to democratise gender relations he writes, 'men's violence against women . . . can be understood as a generalised refusal of dialogue' (Giddens, 1994: 242). On this point Giddens is surely right. But how can this be squared with a defence of a state which has as its bottom line the doctrine of 'might is right'?

Giddens also assumes that 'most aspects of life' should be kept strictly out of 'the public domain' otherwise the 'state tends to reach down into them and become an autocracy' (Giddens, 1994: 116). This ignores the argument that just such a split in liberal society, between a political sphere centred upon the state and a society run on 'a-political' principles such as market forces, is itself a deeply political and ideological division. This defence of a liberal understanding of the state is also in tension with the view, made powerfully by Beck, that the social conditions of late modernity require a radical politicisation of civil society.

Giddens's implicitly liberal theory of the state makes him wary of a civil society free from the ordering capacities of the state. However, this is in tension with his advocacy of generative politics and deliberative democracy. This contradiction arises in Giddens's theory because he conceives of civil society only in liberal terms, as the other face of the state (Giddens, 1994: 124). Thus, once the state is removed from the equation, Giddens assumes that latent tensions, in the past 'pacified' by the state, would result in 'an upsurge of fundamentalism, coupled to an increased potentiality for violence' (Giddens, 1994: 125). This judgement is based upon Giddens's view that the order created internally by the state is closely linked to its 'preparation for external war'. However, exactly the opposite point could be made. The willingness of the state to resort to violence in its international affairs renders the use of physical force, both against and within civil society, more rather than less acceptable and likely. There is a Hobbesian logic here which rests upon a highly abstract view of individualism, which sees human relations without the state being characterised only by self-interest and domination.

In apparent contrast to Giddens, Beck's argument is that the state becomes increasingly less differentiated from the domain of sub-politics. Indeed the logic of Beck's arguments is a gradual withering away of the liberal state. Promisingly, Beck begins to see the problem of the state's potential to resort to violence when he argues that the link between violence and the state 'is definitely dubious' (Beck, 1997: 142). However, in his desire to critique the dysfunctions of science, he undertheorises the relationship between technology, capitalism and the state. The key to understanding the appalling side effects of the often unaccountable actions of scientists is the irrationalities of both capitalist production and the state's military machine, with their relentless search for new methods of profitability and destructive weaponry. Because of the reciprocal relationship between the state and the economy, these irrationalities cannot therefore be seen as unconnected: a critique of science must be linked to the relationship between civil society and the state. However, in his dismissal of the socialist critique, and with his assertion of individualisation, Beck under-stresses structural contexts, which are central to the failure of the liberal capitalist state. He therefore fails to develop the logic of his position fully. In the place of a socialist alternative, Beck is left defending institutions like the media as channels of resistance, and placing his faith in the transformative influence of NSMs (Beck, 1992: 234; 1997: 41–2). As was argued in Chapter 5, the ability for these often opposed and fragmented social movements to mount a sustained challenge to statist and capitalistic structures is problematic, while the mass media is bound up with the wider inequalities of civil society. Given the high concentration of ownership, the lack of minority access and the conservative nature of much of the media, their status as genuine champions of deliberative democracy is questionable.

Despite their novel attempts to draw upon aspects of conservative philosophy to transcend the limitations of modernist ideologies, Giddens and Beck fail to move beyond a problematic liberal perspective on the relationship between the state and civil society. Consequently they face the accusation that in rightly identifying and rejecting the dysfunctions of the socialist alternative to capitalism they are nevertheless in danger of throwing the baby out with the bath water. I will now turn to the question of whether socialism can be revived to meet the challenges social change has posed for governance.

Rethinking the Left

For Miliband in *Socialism for a Sceptical Age* (1994) and Wainwright in *Arguments for a New Left* (1994), it is the inequities of capitalism that still make socialism the only coherent and truly radical alternative to liberalism. Following the collapse of communism in Eastern Europe, symbolised by the destruction of the Berlin Wall, many theorists saw the end of such a socialist alternative. For Miliband, however, the failures of Soviet-style 'socialism' should not blind us to the continuing problems of capitalism. Indeed he argues that this 'socialism' was a 'thorough repudiation of classical Marxism' and points to the dangers of a new hegemony of resignation whereby we learn to live with an inherently flawed liberal system and fail to seek alternative ways to run our lives (Miliband, 1994: 11, 49). In attempting to revitalise classical socialist thought in the light of social change, Miliband seeks to provide an alternative vision of governance.

Indeed Miliband's whole argument can be seen to be addressing the key questions of governance: how can we maintain social order? And how do we distribute resources fairly? A capitalistic civil society cannot solve these dilemmas because 'capitalism is essentially driven by the micro-rationality of the firm, not by the macro-rationality required by society' (Miliband, 1994: 13). Miliband defines the socialist alternative in simple terms. It involves the continued democratisation of society, an ethic of equality and the socialisation of the economy. Interestingly, Miliband (1994: 18) appears to accept many of the criticisms of the Marxist theory of the state, when he acknowledges that 'the executive power of the state often acts quite autonomously . . . without reference to its corporate partner'.

Politically, therefore, Miliband defends many of the mechanisms of liberal democracy as necessary to any democratic state. He argues for the rule of law, a separation of powers, and a reformed, but independent judiciary. He also points to the importance of effective opposition parties to provide criticisms of what Miliband hopes would be a socialist government. However, he envisages building upon and expanding liberal devices of democracy by decentralising power to reduce the divide between representatives and citizens. Crucially he argues that civil society too must be democratised to include all institutions where power is exercised, such as factories, unions and schools. An ethos of participation must replace the doctrine of oligarchy championed by elitists.

However, it is the economic exploitation of the majority of the population, even within advanced industrial countries, that does most to undermine the effects of political reform, and constantly threatens gains made politically, such as citizenship rights. Moreover, the ecological crises discussed by Giddens and Beck are not, for Miliband, the result of modernity *per se*, but are due to the hegemony of the profit motive that sees not only people but also the environment as of secondary importance. It is therefore crucial that political change is married to economic reform, because 'political democracy . . . is not compatible with the oligarchic control of the means of power' (Miliband, 1994: 92). Miliband therefore favours large elements of industry being under the control of public bodies. It is the hostile context of capitalism that has falsely discredited public ownership rather than problems intrinsic to a socialised economy. An important 'means of power' that Miliband identifies as a target for radical reform is the mass media. The control of mass communications by a handful of media barons is incompatible with democracy. Personal ownership must therefore be strictly controlled and more public media corporations created.

For Miliband, the reconstruction of political and economic forms has as its goal a greater equality of 'citizen power'. He rejects the thesis that late modernity is classless. Instead he argues for a concentration on the division between wage earners, still the bulk of the population in industrial societies, and the ruling class, which controls the means of economic and communicative power. Conflicts of gender, 'race' and ethnicity are for Miliband bound up with this primary division. Insecurities of unemployment and income, intrinsic to capitalism, fuel antagonisms against those who appear 'different' and threatening (Miliband, 1994: 22). Removing discriminatory barriers to constitute an equality of opportunity is for Miliband to miss the exploitative logic of even a 'meritocratic' capitalism. Equal opportunity implies an abstract individualistic account of economic production, which denies the fact that all such production is socially created. It is the simplistic logic of the free market advocated by neo-liberals that tells us that an equal opportunity to exploit or to be exploited is any equality at all.

Only a socialist government can begin to heal the antagonisms of civil society and create a stable system of governance. However, Miliband rejects the idea that governance, at least for the foreseeable future, can occur without the state: the state would be an 'essential element in the construction of a new social order' (Miliband, 1994: 62). In the context of an increasingly internationalised economy, Miliband accepts that difficult decisions would need to be made by a socialist state concerning policy towards foreign-run companies. While not ruling out the forced nationalisation of such companies, the preferred strategy would involve a pluralist economy, combining a 'predominant' public sector, an expanded co-operative sector and a 'sizeable' privately owned sector (Miliband, 1994: 110). The social as well as economic advantages of such a system would gradually change the prevailing 'common-sense' view of the advantages of production for profit to one that favours production for need (Miliband, 1994: 121). However, global economic pressures would mean the road to a developed socialism would be a long and rocky one.

Miliband endorses the need for a socialist political party as the main agent of these changes. While accepting that the innovations of NSMs have been able to make important changes to political culture, and have placed new issues at the centre of debate, Miliband argues that their contribution can only be a partial one. This is because such movements are often narrowly focused and are wary of engaging in a more generalised struggle with the capitalist system. Parties of the left need to find ways to integrate the claims of such movements, but nonetheless must seek a more profound structural shift than is possible through the protest politics of such movements alone. With the failures of neo-liberalism becoming clearer by the day, as inequalities between rich and poor grow ever-wider, and social cohesion continues to break down, the prospects for the left, if not rosy, are at least reasonable. Given the incoherence of conservatism, and the nihilism of post-modernism, socialism is, for Miliband, still the only realistic alternative to capitalism (Miliband, 1994: 157).

The attractions of a socialist solution are endorsed by Wainwright (1994). However, she offers a vision of governance more centred upon the contribution of social movements and more sceptical of the role of the state than Miliband's theory. She contends that such an approach is particularly relevant in the context of Eastern Europe, where the experiences of state-centred communism have tempted many to turn to the neo-liberal critique of the state and to advocate unfettered markets as the road out of serfdom.

The central thread of Wainwright's argument is a critique of the theory of knowledge advocated by neo-liberals like Hayek (1960). For

Hayek, human knowledge is produced primarily through the practical interactions of individuals in the market place and is often a product of the unintended consequences of such interactions. Innovation and progress in human affairs are therefore best achieved in a civil society free from interference by the state. In attempting to centralise the sum of human knowledge, statist solutions to human problems are bound to be dictatorial. Wainwright agrees that there are dangers with an 'all-knowing' and unaccountable state imposing its will upon civil society. However, she rejects the abstract and individualistic view of knowledge advocated by Hayek. Indeed, the introduction of markets in health care and education in the USA and Britain has helped to destroy networks of trust and communication between professionals, voluntary groups and consumers, which are central to generating knowledge about the effectiveness of such services. In the place of market mechanisms, Wainwright argues for 'a democratization of the state that involves direct expression of the expertise of grassroots organisations' (Wainwright, 1994: 11).

NSMs, argues Wainwright, highlight the essentially social production of knowledge. Through localised campaigns, decentralised and unhierarchical power structures and deliberative decision making, movements not only build the confidence of their members, they produce new forms of knowledge and create novel ways of thinking about the problems of governance. As such, NSMs radicalise leftist politics in more profound ways than Miliband suggests. Miliband is wrong to classify NSMs as narrow in focus since their concentration on particular issues is less important than the challenge they pose to notions of power and the state. They challenge not only the simple-minded logic of neo-liberals, but also the bureaucratic and rationalist 'engineering state' and the authority of its associated 'experts' in the welfare system (Wainwright, 1994: 83). However, while sharing some affinity with post-modern notions of the stifling effects of the power discourses of the medical, administrative and penal systems, Wainwright highlights the limits of a post-modern politics. She writes:

> While for the radical right the incompleteness of our knowledge means that society is the outcome of the blindfold and therefore haphazard activity of the individual, for the post-modern theorist, society is an equally haphazard plethora of solipsistic statements of various sorts. The only significant difference is that while the neo-liberal is interested in social order, the post-modernist celebrates chaos. Where the right's dilemma is to explain the social order that pertains despite the haphazard outcomes of individual activity, the

post-modern dilemma is to identify the criteria for the value judgements without which even their own activities would be impossible.
(Wainwright, 1994: 100)

The way forward for Wainwright is decentralisation of power structures
to allow for much greater self-management of politics and the economy. The innovative knowledge of NSMs must also be built into the
wider systems of representation. Although clearly pluralist in its emphasis, Wainwright's theory does represent a restatement of socialism
in that, like Miliband, she stresses the need for democratisation of civil
society, as well as the state, and puts emphasis upon an egalitarian view
of knowledge that is strictly bottom up and resistant to the hierarchical
tendencies of the old left. Like Miliband she envisages a role for parties,
but by necessity these parties need to be of 'a new kind' (Wainwright,
1994: Ch. 7).

Using the example of the collapse of communism in Eastern Europe,
Wainwright shows how social movements in civil society failed to
organise political parties to fill the power vacuum left by the communists. The democratisation of Eastern Europe was therefore stalled by
the lack of an understanding of the need for complementary reform of
the state and civil society and the need for party organisation to
mediate between the two (Wainwright, 1994: 190–1). However, a true
socialist party is, for Wainwright, one that helps to co-ordinate the
wider movement of which it is but a part, and that draws upon as many
sources of knowledge as possible. Only in this way does socialism
become free from its past tendencies to impose solutions from above,
which are by definition undemocratic, and which fly in the face of the
grass-roots origins of human knowledge.

A Critical Assessment of Miliband and Wainwright

In contrast to Beck and Giddens, Miliband offers a more structured
context for the problems of late modernity. The blame is laid firmly at
the door of capitalism. Miliband is surely right to stress the dehumanis-
ing aspects of capitalism that sees individuals, and indeed nature, as
dispensable commodities to be bought and sold in the market place.
However, his account, while to some extent recognising the importance of the interdependent relationship between state and civil society, underestimates the irrationalities of the states system as a crucial
factor in creating divisions both within and between states.

In particular, there are tensions in his argument that Marxism is
unconnected to the practice of the communist state in the Soviet
Union and Eastern Europe. He recognises the dangers of an author-

itarian state, Soviet style, but fails to explain why such a state has emerged in all states that have claimed Marxism as their guiding light. If this is due to individuals misusing or misinterpreting Marx, then what is to say this would not happen again? Such a view in any case ignores the weaknesses of Marx's account of politics and method of transition to communism highlighted in Chapter 2. The problem of conception of the state in Miliband's work is illustrated in his discussions of Nazi Germany and the Cold War.

While recognising that the Nazis' plans 'were based on many different impulses', Miliband contends that the close relationship between National Socialism and business 'endured to the end of the Nazi regime' (Miliband, 1994: 36). Much of the historiography of the period, however, suggests that Miliband underestimates the tensions between the goals of the Nazi state and the interests of business. As Kershaw (1993: 49) writes, 'the ultimately self-destructive irrational momentum of the Nazi regime [negated] . . . the potential of the socio-economic system to reproduce itself'. The relationship between business and the state regime was highly complex and involved a shifting power dynamic between different wings of the Nazi party and various sections of business before and during the war. However, the last years of the war witnessed 'the growing paramountcy of Nazism's radical nihilism over "rational" economic interest' (Kershaw, 1993: 58). This suggests that Nazism was a phenomenon bound up with the problem of state power, rather than the problems of capitalism: issues of state militarism and state racism are central to understanding the Nazi phenomenon.

Similarly, in his argument that the Cold War was essentially a struggle for the maintenance of 'free enterprise', Miliband underestimates the power–security concerns of the main antagonists that are inherent in any states system, whether deep ideological divisions exist or not (Miliband, 1994: 36–42). In the case of the Cold War, as in his analysis of the Nazi regime, Miliband is in danger of economism, which has contributed to the lack of a developed theory of the state and of governance in Marxism (see Chapter 2).

That there is a void in Marxism concerning governance in a post-capitalist society is implicitly acknowledged when Miliband asserts that the 'rejection of the separation between legislative and executive' by Marx and Lenin is 'unrealistic' (Miliband, 1994: 82). Miliband's answer to this problem is a defence of the mechanisms (albeit greatly reformed) of liberal democracy. His hopes for socialism ultimately rest upon a shift in industrial societies towards electoral support for a socialist party. Miliband discusses the possibility for the creation of a biased media machine and the use of emergency powers if necessary, to quell unlawful resistance, once socialism is in power. Miliband's statist solution to these problems would be sure to alienate many of the radical groups on the left identified by Wainwright as representing a potentially new, decentralised method of socialist governance.

One of the reasons why Miliband's hope for an elected and radical socialist government seems unlikely is the failure of socialist parties to take account of the need for a new kind of 'generative' politics theorised by Giddens, and supported by Wainwright's assertion of the social nature of human knowledge. As Wainwright makes clear, it is individual agents who must take responsibility for the creation of an alternative society (Wainwright, 1994: 122). Socialists who continue to privilege the state underestimate the alienation felt by ordinary people in their experience with state services in welfare, health and education.

However, in her enthusiastic endorsement of the achievements of NSMs, Wainwright is in danger of overstating their impact. For example, her contention that the peace movement was a major element in the ending of the Cold War is an exaggeration (Wainwright, 1994: 241). The economic and political difficulties for the Soviet Union in sustaining a huge military arsenal far outweighed any pressure by groups like the Campaign for Nuclear Disarmament.

Nonetheless, Wainwright's socialism is interesting in its clear convergence towards elements of pluralism and in its partial acceptance of the critique of the state made by neo-liberals and NSMs. The dilemmas of NSMs, who wish to both effect radical social change, while at the same time staying outside traditional political structures, suggests, however, that some method for combining the decentralised structures of such movements with more centralised systems of governance is necessary.

Radical Pluralism: Towards Theoretical Convergence?

Wainwright's arguments for socialism explicitly entail the need for a reconsideration of the relationship between liberalism and socialism and between the state and civil society. She writes of the need for 'a new kind of left: in which a liberalism that had moved beyond individualism co-operated and contested with a form of socialism that no longer relied primarily on the nation state' (Wainwright, 1994: 16). Such an argument represents a general trend amongst many political sociologists to be more eclectic in their approach to the question of the state's relationship with civil society. The failures of state socialism, the emergence of NSMs, post-modernism and neo-liberalism as radical challenges to statism and the acknowledgement of processes of internationalisation, if not globalisation, have been some of the main reasons for this theoretical convergence.

Marsh (1995: 270) has argued that this convergence has been 'towards an elitist position'. Certainly, few would deny that elites do retain control over the state and exercise a high degree of power within the institutions of civil society. Elitist assumptions still underpin the practice of citizenship and political participation in liberal democracies. Some authors, notably Etzioni-Halevy (1993), have even made a strong defence on normative, as well as practical grounds, for the protection of elite autonomy, which she argues has been the basis of the success of liberal democracies. However, all of the theorists explored in this chapter have either implicitly or explicitly challenged such a defence of elite rule. Even in the work of Giddens and Miliband, where the conception of the state is particularly problematic in their arguments, there is an acceptance of the need for a more bottom-up approach to problems of governance, where individuals play a much more active and responsible part. Most thinkers now accept that it is a mistake to identify power as residing in a single section of civil society, and they embrace a pluralist defence of diversity, as a bulwark against authoritarian statism. I would argue therefore that the trend amongst many prominent political sociologists has been towards a reconceptualisation of pluralism.

As a consequence of rapid social change the appropriate relationship between the state and civil society has become particularly problematic. The result has been a greater interest in democracy, not just as a means to an end, but as a good in itself. For example, Giddens and Wainwright stress how democratic debate and participation can build confidence and trust between individuals. As we have seen, even Miliband (in his constitutional recommendations) accepts the potential tension between Marxism and democracy. Thus most contemporary thinkers play down democracy as a search for a single 'truth' and emphasise instead the process of deliberation and consensus building as valuable in themselves.

All the thinkers we have explored also support a pluralist approach to the economy. Even Marxists nowadays tend to advocate a mixed or at least a highly decentralised economy, and most have rejected a simple deterministic view of the relationship between economic and other types of power. The work of one of the most sophisticated neo-Marxists, Bob Jessop, provides a good example of the recent convergence of aspects of pluralism and Marxism. Jessop argues that what is required is an analysis of the relationship between state and society where neither is given a priori significance. Jessop argues that state power, 'cannot be reduced to a simplistic realization of the purported needs or interests of capital' (Jessop, 1990: 354). In his 'strategic relational' approach, Jessop consciously moves away from economism and towards a radical pluralist account of the state–civil society dynamic. Both the state and the institutions of civil society possess independent resources that make their total dominance by the other impossible. Therefore, 'states shape society and social forces shape the state' (Jessop, 1990: 361–2). Because of the complexities of this relationship, any state strategy, which seeks to govern in a new way, must attempt to draw support from several sections of civil society. Moreover, past events, conflicts, crises, compromises and struggles mean that some projects of social change are more likely to be successful than others. The main point is that because power is always to some extent fragmented, no strategy can ever be totally dominant: 'the state's powers always comes up against structural constraints and resistance which inevitably limit its ability to master the social formation' (Jessop, 1990: 361–2). Consequently, Jessop puts a great deal of emphasis upon the actions and calculations of political actors in shaping the nature of the state. This allows for the possibility of a greater variety of state forms than is present in the more structural and deterministic theories associated with classical Marxism.

Jessop, then, perceives the state and civil society to be in a tense and often contradictory relationship. These contradictions manifest themselves not only through class conflict, but also in struggles based on gender, 'race' and generation, etc. This 'primary paradox' of the stat–civil society dynamic, as we have seen throughout this book, is inherent to liberalism and for Marxists is a source of alienation and oppression. The task taken up by radical pluralists like Hirst (1994) is to attempt to overcome such a paradox by partially dissolving the relationship between the state and civil society.

In his *Associative Democracy* (1994), Hirst makes one of the most interesting attempts to reconcile state and civil society through advocating a fundamental shift in their relationship. The challenge, Hirst argues, is to build on the strengths of liberal ideals such as individual autonomy, freedom and diversity by making such values real for all members of society. Hirst therefore accepts the criticisms of classical pluralism discussed in Chapter 2. In particular, the destructive impact of poverty and powerlessness upon individuals' lives needs to be addressed. At the same time, however, Hirst notes the dangers of socialist solutions that seek to solve such problems through state intervention. This statist approach has meant 'the imposition of common rules and standard services on the increasingly diverse and pluralistic objectives of the members of modern societies' (Hirst, 1994: 6). Hirst therefore agrees with Beck and Giddens on the need to recognise the existence of a reflexive population in industrial societies, and therefore the necessity to adopt a model of generative politics. What Hirst offers is an attempt to constitute generative politics through the notion of associationalism:

> Associationalism makes accountable representative democracy possible again by limiting the scope of state administration, without diminishing social provision. It enables market-based societies to deliver the substantive goals desired by citizens, by embedding the market system in a social network of coordinative and regulatory institutions. (Hirst, 1994: 12)

Hirst suggests that the way forward is to reconstruct political institutions to allow for groups of individuals to 'build their own self-governing communities in civil society' (Hirst, 1994: 14). Associations in civil society should be the main vehicle for democratic decisions and the key providers of welfare. This necessarily entails a federal and decentralised state that provides public funds for these associations. Some tasks, such as national defence, would still need to operate at the level of the state. However, governance would increasingly involve citizens making their decisions, with the state providing a framework of general regulations and standards (Hirst, 1994: 24). For Hirst, the problem with representative systems of politics is not representation as such, but rather its scope. In Hirst's plan, the decentralisation of democracy would help to prevent the tyranny of a majority at a state level. It would also increase the communication between different levels of government, thereby tapping locally generated knowledge that is either ignored or bypassed in a more centralised system. Voluntary associations, empowered by public money, may also be a more suitable way of intensifying links with similar groups in other states. Associationalism may therefore be better equipped than are antagonistic states to deal with the challenges of a more interdependent world (Hirst, 1994: 71). The associations advocated by Hirst would be highly diverse, involving church organisations, voluntary groups and NSMs. Each would be able to organise themselves in any manner they chose, provided they did not infringe upon the basic rights of individuals, including the right to exit from the group.

A foundation stone of Hirst's system is the idea of a guaranteed income for citizens, again funded through central taxation. At a stroke this would make the voluntarism principle real, by removing the compulsion to seek poorly paid and undignified work just to survive, and by freeing the citizen from dependence upon a bureaucratic and arbitrary welfare state (Hirst, 1994: 134). Such a policy, as well as reflecting the social nature of economic production, would likely result in a richer and more diverse civil society, as individuals were freed from the burden of having to earn a basic living and could instead choose to pursue cultural pursuits, undertake voluntary work or set up innovative co-operatives.

In terms of the economy, Hirst envisages the democratisation of corporations which would be encouraged to become 'self-governing associations' (Hirst, 1994: 146). Hirst suggests a wide range of inter-esting measures of funding and tax incentives that would deliver greater control over companies to the workforce. Limits of space do not permit me to outline these here, but the key point is that an associative economy would be one where 'a more decentralized doc-trine of economic governance that relies on political mechanisms of seeking coordination and compliance in regulation through the co-operation of economic actors' would help to reduce the tensions between state and civil society (Hirst, 1994: 96).

Hirst's theory is not without its problems. In particular, critics may point to the strength of resistance to the attack on privilege that a shift to associationalism would involve, and which Hirst perhaps under-estimates. Traditional elites would be likely to attempt to block more co-operative and egalitarian methods of governance, particularly radi-cal measures such as a guaranteed income. Socialists may also wish to argue that the inequalities on a global level could only be countered by a commitment to a more radical socialisation of the economic struc-tures than that envisaged by Hirst. However, the form of association-alism theorised by Hirst does present the most promising version of radical pluralism. Radical pluralism entails a greater stress upon human agency, a recognition of the problem of the state, and the need for economic and political structures that reflect the diversity of civil society. Such ideas mark a point of theoretical convergence for many contemporary political sociologists.

Conclusion

In this chapter we have looked at how contemporary political sociol-ogists have understood the relationship between the state and civil society and have attempted to tackle the problems this relationship raises for human governance. Post-modernism offers no answer to this perennial question of governance. Instead of embracing the fatalism that post-modernism seems to imply, political sociology must continue to search for ways to achieve more just and effective systems of governance that build upon the insights of classical political sociology. Contemporary sociologists have grappled with the problem of how the state–civil society relationship can be reformed to meet more effectively the social changes which we explored in Parts II and III of this book. Such theorising has resulted in some important insights, which I have argued have meant a convergence towards radical pluralism. In particular, three of these insights are worth emphasising.

First, the democratisation of the institutions of the state and civil society is a crucial step in reconciling the increasingly diverse demands and needs of citizens. Given the growth of social reflexivity, patronising and elitist assumptions about the masses, which are central to elite theory and behaviouralism, need to be dispensed with. But in working to remove elitist structures of power, and in contrast to classical Marxism, the aim is not to transcend conflict, which is impossible and undesirable, but to find ways to manage conflict through structures of governance which encourage active participation and deliberation.

Second, the requirements of the economic associations of civil society must be secondary to the requirements of social order and the just distribution of resources. Thus neo-liberalism's reliance upon the market to solve these two problems of governance are rightly rejected by radical pluralists. Classical pluralist assumptions about the neutrality of the state and the unity and liberty of civil society must be acknowledged as having failed to perceive how structures of power, such as class and gender, have underpinned political institutions and undermined the active participation in governance by many citizens.

Thirdly, Giddens and Beck's stress upon the growth of global risks and the implications of such risks for governance is particularly insightful. Whatever positive democratic reforms of individual state–civil society relationships are made, governance will remain unstable if these risks are not met at a global level. In the final chapter of this book, therefore, I address the development of governance beyond the state.

10

Global Governance

In the previous chapter, we noted how the growth of global risks is rapidly changing the context of governance. In terms of the main theme of this book, it would appear that the growth of such risks marks the most important social change that is impacting upon the state's relationship to civil society. While the state is fully implicated in the creation of such risks, for example through its search for ever-more destructive weaponry and its promotion of economic 'liberalisation' which has resulted in global inequality and ecological deterioration, the state also remains the political actor most capable of countering such risks. If the governance of global problems is to be effective, however, states will have to reconcile themselves to sharing their power with other states, international organisations and an emerging global civil society.

In this chapter I expound this argument by first outlining some of the weaknesses of international relations theory, which is the academic discipline most concerned with global politics. Many of its assumptions, particularly concerning the nature of state sovereignty and security, are analytical barriers to understanding the contemporary realities of international politics, which are increasingly being shaped by new security dilemmas that individual states can no longer manage effectively.

In the second section of the chapter the extent to which institutions of global governance have begun to evolve is explored. I shall consider some of the ways states co-operate through international regimes, such as the United Nations (UN), and in regional organisations such as the European Union (EU). The emergence of a global civil society, through which non-state actors are increasingly influencing world governance, will also be discussed.

Sustainable institutions of global governance are at an embryonic stage, and it is by no means certain that diverse societies will be able to work together effectively to meet the challenges of global risks. However, theories of cosmopolitan democracy offer the hope that discernible trends towards greater global co-operation do create the possibility for a new form of governance that gradually moves beyond the state. The chapter will therefore conclude with a discussion of cosmopolitan democracy and its implications for the future of governance.

International Relations Theory and Global Risk

International relations theory is concerned with the forces that shape politics beyond the boundaries of individual states. In the post-war period, the dominant theoretical strand within the discipline has been Realism. For realists, the state is the primary actor in world affairs. It is struggles between states, for power and security, that determine the nature of global politics. For classical realists, such as Morgenthau (1948), conflict is an ever-present feature of the states system because it is an ever-present feature of human nature. The best that we can hope for is to contain this conflict by constructing strategic alliances between states. This can be achieved through the pursuit of diplomacy and by the great powers taking a lead in deterring the use of force by rogue states.

The picture Morgenthau paints of the anarchic relations of the international system is similar to Hobbes's theory of the state of nature, which describes the insecurities of a society without a state. For Hobbes (1973), individuals, like states, are driven by the pursuit of self-interest and therefore there always exists the possibility of what Hobbes described as a 'war of all against all'. This can only be prevented if individuals make a contract with a higher power to protect them from each other. The analogy between the states system and the interaction between individuals is, however, said by realists to be a limited one: states have a greater longevity than do individuals because they cannot so easily be destroyed by an act of force, and will resist the temptation to sign away their autonomy to a higher authority. Global governance is therefore a utopian illusion that denies the reality of state sovereignty, which remains the cornerstone of international affairs.

Sovereignty then is the primary concept of realism. It is taken as given that states enjoy unchallenged jurisdiction within their own boundaries. Realists make little attempt to theorise the impact a state's relationship with its civil society has upon its relations with other states. Waltz expresses this simplistic view when he writes that 'students of international politics will do well to concentrate on separate theories of internal and external politics until someone figures out a way to unite them' (cited in Rosenberg, 1994: 5). Waltz is able to argue this because of his view of how the states system operates. Waltz (1979) rejects explanations of international conflict which stress flaws in human nature. Rather it is the structure of the international system that creates tension between states: in the absence of a higher authority, states compete with each other to ensure their security. This may trigger an arms race, perhaps leading to full-scale war. This structure will determine a state's foreign policy, regardless of its internal political arrangements or the nature of the dominant belief system within civil society.

The strength of realism is that it highlights the irrationalities that underpin the logic of a world divided into states. The conflicts between states, which are well documented by history, and which often transcend apparent commonalties of 'race' or ideology, present compelling evidence in support of the realist argument. It is increasingly clear, however, that realism's assumptions are inadequate to the task of explaining the nature of contemporary world politics. The problems of mainstream international relations theory lie mainly in its understanding of state sovereignty and security.

State sovereignty has been the foundation of the states system ever since the Treaty of Westphalia established a doctrine of non-interference in the internal affairs of states in 1648. The classic realist image of the states system is of a number of independent and solid billiard balls, which occasionally collide and that are incapable of building common interests beyond those dictated by the doctrine of self-help. With the globalisation of risk, this abstract conception of sovereignty is increasingly problematic.

The solid billiard ball image is giving way to the metaphor of the 'hollowed out' state, as forces beyond and below the state threaten its claims to territorial control. As has been argued in this book, however, the state is still a powerful actor and the notion of a 'hollowed out' state is of little more use than the abstract realist image. Instead, states, like individuals, should be understood as socially embedded actors. The state must therefore not be viewed in atomistic terms, as it is understood by realists, but rather in relation to both its own civil society and to states and societies beyond its boundaries. Furthermore, processes of globalisation are increasingly connecting societies' problems. These demand collective action by states to meet the new dangers that go beyond the realist conception of security as being purely the protection of territory.

The New Security Dilemmas

The primary promise states make to their citizens is the protection of their security. In the past, security has been narrowly defined in terms of the defence of state boundaries, the application of immigration policy to maintain national coherence, and the protection of citizens from the use of violence by their fellow citizens, aliens or foreign states. Of course, the extent to which any one state could fulfil these promises has always varied enormously according to its command over the resources of power. A great deal of hypocrisy has also surrounded this view of security. Liberal democracies have prided themselves on their protection of rights and popular participation internally, but in the international arena they have happily supported states that deny these rights to their citizens, or they have economically exploited countries where such freedoms are at best fictions. Morally, this dualism between internal and external affairs has always been questionable. In this regard, the concept of sovereignty has provided dictators with a veil of international legality behind which they can 'hide' human rights abuses. Sovereignty has also allowed powerful states a convenient get-out-clause, whereby they could wash their hands of any responsibility for the plight of their fellow human beings who have the misfortune to be born in highly unstable regions of the world.

However, such a narrow view of security is becoming redundant in the face of the growth of numerous and interconnected risks, which no single state can successfully counter. As Elkins (1992: 1) observes, we are now facing 'interlocking crises of unprecedented magnitude'. The moral argument for a global perspective to governance is increasingly becoming merged with an argument based upon self-interest. If states ignore the problems of their neighbours, the result is likely to be instability for all states. At the heart of these new security dilemmas is the issue of global inequality.

The levels of global inequalities are astonishing. It is estimated that 1.3 billion people live in absolute poverty and lack access to basic resources such as water, food and shelter. The gap between rich and poor has actually been growing in recent years: around 85 per cent of the world's income goes to the richest 20 per cent, while the poorest 20 per cent receive just 1.4 per cent (Real World Coalition, 1996: 41–2). Global poverty is primarily located in the developing world and is particularly concentrated in Africa and parts of Asia. In contrast, in Western countries a huge number of people are overweight and vast amounts of food are wasted, either inadvertently by individual con-sumers or deliberately by states and businesses wishing to maintain world prices. The growth of the mass media means that awareness of this inequality is increasing rapidly. However, events such as famine, as occurred in Sudan in the summer of 1998, are often portrayed by the media as natural disasters and therefore unavoidable. This masks the human causes of inequalities. They primarily result from the structure of the states system, which favours the interests of developed states over those of the developing world. There is good reason for thinking, however, that the West can no longer remain complacent about this problem.

Global inequality has a number of consequences which are impacting upon rich as well as poor states. One of the most dramatic of these is the explosion in the numbers of refugees seeking sanctuary from their poverty-stricken and war-torn countries. The United Nations (UNHCR, 1997: 2) identified a total of 13.2 million refugees in January 1997; millions more have been the victims of forced displacement within their own country. These 'internal refugees' have grown enormously as the result of ethnic cleansing and civil wars in places such Bosnia and Kosovo in Europe and Sudan and Rwanda in Africa. Such events underline another weakness of traditional conceptions of sovereignty and security: 'Most people are more in danger from their own governments than from foreigners' (Brown, 1997: 132). But for the developed countries these refugees also pose a potential threat to their stability, as political and economic migrants attempt to flee to more prosperous states through either legal or illegal methods. The displacement of millions of people from their homes is also a focal point of regional instability that may threaten the long-term security of the world.

The proliferation of nuclear arms means that regional conflicts can less easily be contained. In May 1998 India and Pakistan exploded several nuclear devices, thus signalling their nuclear status in the face of world opposition, and setting in motion a dangerous arms race between two countries which have already fought three wars since partition and are engaged in an ongoing dispute in Kashmir. These events frighteningly highlight the inability of even the most powerful states to prevent the spread of weapons that could spell annihilation for all of us. In the face of the destructive power of nuclear warfare, the realist reliance on great powers or strategic alliances lending stability to world affairs is becoming outmoded. Even the 'weak' can now threaten the survival of the strong (Bull, 1977: 48).

The problems of large-scale migration and nuclear proliferation are also connected to transnational organised crime. Carter (1997) argues that political instability in Eastern Europe and Africa, the deregulation of world trade and the sophistication of transport and communication technologies are amongst the factors which have globalised organised crime. Highly organised criminals such as the Italian Mafia and Chinese triads conduct a thriving trade in illegal immigrants, arms and drugs. The UN (1996b) estimates that crime syndicates take in $1000 billion every year. The illegal drugs market alone makes up 10 per cent of all global trade, which is second only to the trade in oil (Real World

Coalition, 1996: 55). Even more worrying is the evidence that increasingly sophisticated arms are being sold to governments and terrorist groups by criminals. In July 1994 German police, while investigating an organised counterfeiting operation, found one-fifth of an ounce of weapons-grade plutonium. Such developments support Carter's (1997: 146) observation that 'issues of global crime are the new genre of national security threats'.

Like many of the new security dilemmas, global inequality is at the root of many of the most damaging criminal activities. A good example is the drug trade, where almost invariably the basic product is grown in very poor countries such as Columbia and Pakistan, where prices for other crops such as cocoa and rice are extremely low and therefore unprofitable. As the Real World Coalition (1996: 55) contends, 'the story of narcotics production and the drugs trade is a by-product of the failure of our international agricultural trading system'.

Poverty and inequality also increase the deterioration of the natural environment. Attempts to place restrictions on industrial output are often viewed suspiciously by developing countries who see this as an attempt by developed countries to prevent the development of competition. In turn, developed economies have tended to resist restrictions on economic production on the grounds that these will not be implemented by poorer countries (Elliott, 1998). However, in no other area is sovereignty so fictitious. Writers like Beck (1992) have highlighted the meaninglessness of geography in the face of ecological problems such as global warming and the depletion of the ozone layer.

What is required to tackle environmental damage, as well as the other security dilemmas identified here, is a global approach to governance. However, this would need to recognise that good governance is only possible if global inequalities are addressed. In the developing world, practices such as deforestation and high rates of births often result from poverty. Poor people destroy the rainforests upon which all life depends, not through wanton neglect of the environment but in order to make a living, while high birth rates in the developing world often result from the need to create another pair of hands to help feed starving families. This last point raises the question of demography.

Population growth has been of concern since at least the eighteenth century. What is new, however, is the intensity of this growth in the late twentieth century. In 1990, the world's population was 5.3 billion; by 2100 it is estimated that it will be more than 10 billion (Kennedy, 1994: 23). Again, what is striking about this problem is its connection to global inequality: 95 per cent of population growth is in the developing world. This growth is linked, not only to material poverty, but also to lack of education and access to birth control. This last factor raises the issue of women's rights, and more generally the whole question of human rights. State sovereignty has often been a barrier to the promotion of a set of basic rights enjoyed by all peoples of the world. Women suffer disproportionately in this regard, representing 70 per cent of the global poor and two-thirds of those who are illiterate (Real World Coalition, 1996: 29). However, it is becoming ever more obvious that the denial of rights such as basic education and birth control to women in the developing world helps to fuel population growth, which in turn increases global inequalities, encourages desta-bilising migration and fuels transnational crime. Extra strain is also placed upon the ecostructure, as developing countries are forced to try to offset these problems by pursuing short-term economic gains rather than prioritising sustainable development. Additionally, ecological damage combines with poverty and the denial of human rights to increase instability in the poor regions of the world. It may be, for example, that many future military conflicts, in regions such as the Middle East, will involve struggles over access to basic resources such as water (Elliott, 1998: 224). Population growth also has implications for levels of global unemployment, which the International Labour Orga-nisation estimated was 30 per cent of the world's labour force in January 1994 and which is yet another source of political instability (Chomsky, 1997: 188).

The interconnected nature of these new security dilemmas, only some of which have been highlighted here, cannot be understood through the statist assumptions of traditional international relations theory. For this reason, writers such as Martin Shaw (1994) have advanced a political sociology of world politics. Shaw addresses the lack of a concept of society in international relations theory by ex-tending the notion of the state–civil society relationship to the global sphere. Thus Shaw identifies the emergence of global state (a term Shaw uses to refer to the development of global governance) and a global civil society, and analyses these in relation to what he calls post-militarism.

The beginnings of the creation of a global 'state' can be found in institutions such as the UN, while an embryonic global civil society can be detected in the development of global social movements, the activities of multinational companies (MNCs) and in the growing awareness of global risks. The concept of post-militarism is significant in two ways. First, it does not mean the end of military threats as such, but it does entail the recognition that most security issues now faced by states are not of a directly military nature, but involve transnational issues of inequality, migration and environmental damage. Second, a post-military society is one where citizenship is detached from its close association with military duty. With the growing technological nature of weapons systems, mass conscription armies are unlikely to be a feature of future armed conflict. These two aspects of post-militarism allow at least the possibility of breaking the link between citizenship and the state, and the fostering of an ethic of global responsibility to meet the challenges posed by global threats. The 'demilitarisation' of citizenship may also help to encourage political rather than violent methods of reconciling differences globally.

Having established the urgent need for global governance, and identified some trends which may foster it, in the next section I shall explore the extent to which we are witnessing its actual development.

Towards Global Governance

In May 1998 the G8 met in Birmingham (England) to debate a series of pressing global problems, many of which reflected the new security dilemmas outlined above. The main points of discussion included the implementation of the 1997 Kyoto agreement (which aimed to reduce emissions of greenhouse gases), the problem of global unemployment, the promotion of sustainable development and integration of developing countries into the world economy, the need for reform of global financial architecture to deal with such crises as the collapse in Asian currencies that began in 1997, and the condemnation of India's recent nuclear tests (*Guardian*, 1998b). The global nature of these problems illustrates the growing need for a coherent international response. However, in the absence of a world government, the success of global governance rests mainly upon co-operation between states. The institution of the G8 is itself, however, an example of the undemocratic and unaccountable nature of many institutions of international governance, which are invariably dominated by elites from Western countries. The principles that drive global governance have, therefore, not surprisingly been those of neo-liberalism and state sovereignty.

Nevertheless, it is clear, as Shaw (1994: 21) argues, that even powerful states have begun to realise the limitations of their sovereignty and have sought greater co-operation with other states. Although, in one sense, realists are right to identify a high degree of self interest driving these developments, in fact, as has already been indicated, the dichotomy between self-interest and morality is increasingly a false one. The more states realise that a global approach to world problems is the most likely to secure order, and that this order must be underpinned by an ethic of justice and shared responsibility, the more we are likely to see the diversification of institutions of governance. This process is already underway and is illustrated by the growth of international organisations and the emergence of an embryonic global civil society. We cannot, however, simply plot a clear path from a governance centred on the state to a new kind of governance at a global level. These organisations and actors have developed largely in an *ad hoc* manner, are full of contradictions, and often lack a vision of governance beyond short-term gain and crisis management.

International Regimes

International organisations have always been a feature of world politics. Examples from the past include the Concert of Europe, constituted after the defeat of Napoleon, and the League of Nations, set up after the First World War. The participants in such organisations, however, were almost invariably states. The modern concept of an international regime, in contrast, denotes a form of governance which, though dominated by states, is multi-actor in composition and involves a consultative role for global civil society. For liberals, it is through such governmental institutions that world problems can be regulated without resorting to more radical changes to the international system (Hurrell, 1995: 61–4).

The most important regime 'manages' the world economy. A plethora of organisations exists to monitor and promote trade and financial stability. The G8 has already been mentioned, but there is also the World Bank, the International Monetary Fund, the World Trade Organisation (WTO) and the Organisation for Economic Co-operation and Development (OECD). Although these organisations have a certain independence from states, and interact with non-state actors such as MNCs, it is the most powerful states that provide the linkages between them. Taken together, these organisations form an economic management regime (EMR) which is so influential in shaping the world economy that one commentator has referred to it as the 'de facto world government' (Morgan, cited in Chomsky, 1997: 178). The problem with the EMR is that it is dominated by neo-liberal ideology which for Chomsky (1997: 178) is 'designed to serve the interests of TNCs, banks and investment firms'.

Certainly, the EMR does appear to be driven by the requirements of Western corporate and state interests. It has jealously guarded the West's rights to intellectual property, thereby maintaining the developed world's all important control of advanced technologies. At the same time, it has promoted the liberalisation of trade in areas of benefit to the developed world. Two recent attempts at liberalisation illustrate the underlying motives of the EMR and lend weight to the arguments of critics such as Chomsky.

First, Wade and Venerovo (1998) argue that the reaction of the West to the Asian financial crisis, which saw a sharp fall in currency and share values in countries such as Singapore, Indonesia, South Korea and Japan in 1997–8, was misplaced and triumphalist. These crises threatened to send the region, if not the world, into recession. However, the EMR's reaction was to attempt to force countries like South Korea, through stringent conditions being placed upon financial 'rescue' packages, to adopt a neo-liberal system of financial deregulation, despite the fact that it was a lack of effective regulation in this and other sectors of the economy that caused the problems in many Asian countries in the first place (Weiss, 1998: xi–xv). For Wade and Venerovo (1998: 19), such tactics reflect the ongoing conflict between competing economic systems, with the EMR seeking to 'institute a world-wide regime of capital mobility' in the interests of the Anglo-American dominated neo-liberal economic system.

Second, the EMR has sought to liberalise foreign investment in a most dramatic fashion through the promotion of Multilateral Agreements on Investments (MAIs). These were first discussed by the OECD in 1995, but stalled in 1998, partly because of pressure from environmental groups and the fears of some developing states. MAIs have been called a Bill of Rights for MNCs (Friends of the Earth, 1998). They would 'strip nations of their power to screen against unsustainable foreign investments and give multinational corporations and other investors unprecedented rights' (Friends of the Earth, 1998). If implemented, these agreements would shift the balance of power between developing states and MNCs firmly in the direction of the latter. States would be unable to discriminate against foreign companies and, as such, MAIs may preclude development of small-scale local enterprises in poorer countries, which may provide the only realistic path to sustainable development. It is also feared that, under MAIs, foreign companies would be exempted from minimum wage and consumer protection legislation. Social movements have also expressed concerns about the weakening of environmental regulation, as well as the negative implications of MAIs for democracy.

The EMR is typical of the failure of powerful states to look beyond their own narrowly conceived interests and to reform and utilise such regimes to effectively govern the planet. In particular, the dominance of neo-liberal ideology in economic policy has prevented the successful management of many points of tension within the global system such as the debt crisis, world unemployment, instability in the world's financial systems and environmental damage. The elitist and undemocratic nature of such regimes has also raised questions about their right to govern any aspect of world affairs.

The United Nations

The UN offers more promising raw material with which to construct a system of global governance than do other international regimes. This is due in part to it being the only international body that enjoys almost universal membership of the world's states (Bailey and Daws, 1995: 109). The UN, in contrast to most other international organisations, also has a significant participatory element to it. The General Assembly of the UN operates on the principal of one state-one vote and all members have the opportunity to voice their opinion on world affairs. However, the UN is a contradictory institution which increasingly symbolises the uncertain direction of global governance.

On the one hand, the UN Charter reinforces the doctrine of state sovereignty. Article 2 (7) commits the UN to a doctrine of non-interference in the domestic affairs of states and the most important body of the UN, the Security Council, is dominated by its five permanent members: the USA, China, Russia, Britain and France. Its state-centred structure reflects the UN's initial and primary purpose of providing a means by which military aggression by one state against another can be dealt with collectively. On the other hand, however, the UN is potentially subversive to the states system through its role as a promoter of human rights, which is enshrined in its Universal Declaration of Human Rights of 1948.

The tension between these contradictory aspects of the UN has become more pronounced in the 1990s because of changes in the nature of world politics. The Cold War effectively placed the UN in a straightjacket because either the Western capitalist states or the communist powers would use their veto to oppose the other side's resolutions. With the collapse of communism the use of the veto by the permanent members of the Security Council declined considerably and the opportunity was created for the UN to play a more proactive role in world affairs. Recently, the UN has intensified its operations in areas that blur the distinction between its promotion of human rights and its supposed respect for state sovereignty.

Since 1990, the UN has ventured into territory that is not clearly covered in its Charter. In particular, it has developed a new role in peacekeeping in countries like Somalia and Yugoslavia, which have been torn apart by civil wars. However, the concept of peacekeeping is not even mentioned in the UN's founding document. This new doctrine of peacekeeping has even been extended to the unprecedented move of creating safe havens in the North of Iraq in 1991 to protect the Kurdish people who have suffered persecution at the hands of Saddam Hussein's government (Luard with Heater, 1994: 180–1). The doctrine of peacekeeping reflects the reality of the new security dilemmas, which increasingly involve the development of threats to peace within state boundaries. However, the UN is hamstrung in its new role by a number of constraints. In particular, the UN suffers from deficiencies in its legitimacy and its resources.

The main problem with the concept of peacekeeping is that it has been applied selectively. UN resolutions condemning abuses of human rights by Indonesia in East Timor and Israel in Palestine have been consistently vetoed by Security Council members. The suspicion that the UN will only act when it serves the interests of the most powerful states is heightened when states like the USA act unilaterally, as in its invasion of Panama in 1989, which was condemned by the General Assembly of the UN as a 'flagrant violation of international law and of the independence, sovereignty and territorial integrity of states' (Chomsky, 1997: 12–13).

The legitimacy of the UN is also called into question by the composition of the Security Council. The domination of the Council by the West could be diluted by increasing the number of permanent members, through the inclusion of representatives from the developing world: Nigeria, Brazil and India are often cited as possibilities. However, more fundamentally, the UN needs to address the changing nature of security issues and rewrite its Charter to clearly determine its objectives. For some commentators, the process of reforming the UN must include a greater role for global civil society (Falk, 1995: Ch. 7). Suggestions have been made for a forum of non-governmental organisations, or even some kind of democratically elected people's assembly, to work alongside the General Assembly: such an elected body would have at least a consultative role concerning the UN's activities (Commission of Global Governance, 1995: 258; Held, 1995: 273).

The huge growth in the UN's activities has not been matched by increased funds from member states. In fact, some states, and in particular the USA, have failed to pay their contributions to the UN budget: in August 1997 the USA owed $1.4 billion (United Nations, 1997b). This has been withheld for somewhat dubious reasons. For example, the Republican dominated Senate has cited the UN's support for abortion, advocated in some circumstances as part of the UN's efforts to counter the global population explosion, as the reason for non-payment (Keesings, 1998: 42167).

The UN also consistently lacks the necessary human resources to carry out its peacekeeping activities. Following the failure of peacekeeping operations in states like Somalia, governments are reluctant to commit their personnel for fear of casualties, which may damage their popularity at home. Indeed, in May 1994, President Clinton declared that the USA would only participate in those UN operations where its own interests were involved (Pugh, 1997: 146). If UN peacekeeping is to be viable, it may be that the creation of an independent rapid reaction force, made up of volunteers from member states, is required. This would greatly increase the UN's reaction time to international crises, which has tended to be slow and half hearted; in 1994, for example, the Security Council decided unanimously that 5500 troops needed to be sent to Rwanda, but it took six months for member states to supply the troops (United Nations, 1997a). Such a permanent force would also help to resolve the problems of command structures and strategic decision making, when UN troops are placed in the field. In the past, this has been complicated by the reluctance of states to place their troops under the direct command of the UN (Ruggie, 1998: 253–5).

The UN does offer an important focal point for global governance and it has had some notable successes in restoring stability in countries such as Cambodia and Angola in the 1990s (Ratner, 1997). Reforms to its Charter, and a rationalisation of its organisation, would undoubt-edly help to improve its coherence and perhaps encourage states to pay their outstanding financial contributions. However, the future role of the UN will be determined above all by the will of states and, in particular, the USA's perception of its own ability to deal with the new security dilemmas identified in this chapter. While it may be true that in relation to other states the USA, with its powerful economy and vast array of military hardware, is stronger than ever before, it is also true that, in important areas of security, all states are in a weakened position and will therefore need to seek more successful methods of co-operation in the future.

Regionalism

Another way in which states have attempted to manage global insecu-rities is through greater co-operation with their regional neighbours. Organisations such as the North Atlantic Treaty Organisation (NATO) and Association of Southeast Asian Nations (ASEAN) were created, in part, to try to operate a more collective approach to regional military conflicts. With the UN handing over responsibility for its operations in Bosnia to NATO in 1995, and declaring the desire for a more integrated relationship with regional bodies, it appears that regional security organisations will have a greater role in maintaining international order in the future (Henrikson, 1995: 124). However, the extent to which the world can rely on regional solutions is limited by the military tensions that exist within regions, the fear that one regional hegemon will dominate regional affairs, the difficulties of reaching agreement between neighbours on how a particular issue should be resolved, and, most importantly, the relative lack of military power in many regions of the world, such as Africa (Fawcett and Hurrell, 1995: 316).

Of perhaps greater significance than regional security arrangements has been the growth of trading blocs such as the European Union (EU), the North American Free Trade Agreement (NAFTA) and the Asia-Pacific Economic Co-operation Forum (APEC). The number of such agreements has grown enormously in the post-war period: between 1948 and 1994, 109 were signed (Dicken, 1998: 102). On the question of the significance of regionalism for global governance, a number of possible interpretations have been advanced. The most persuasive view, expressed by Gamble and Payne (1996: 248), is that regionalism is as an aspect of, rather than a reaction against, political globalisation.

Despite the great variety of forms that regional organisations have taken, they have all conformed to the global movement towards economic liberalisation, driven by the EMR. There is, so far, little evidence to suggest that regionalism will entail increased economic protectionism and in that way exacerbate tensions between the three power centres of East Asia, Europe and the USA. Most regional agreements, in any case, lack the level of institutionalisation necessary to implement extensive economic regulation. Instead, regionalisation involves states co-operating to create a regional framework for their companies to operate in and, where possible, to exploit economies of scale and enhance co-ordination of the free movement of capital, services and labour. In some regions, tensions between states undermine the potential for greater regional governance. In East Asia, the presence of two competing regional powers, Japan and China, as well as ongoing disputes between other states within the region, limits the extent to which a close regional identity can be generated (Brook, 1998: 244). Vast inequalities of power between the USA, Canada and Mexico also make it unlikely that more extensive co-operation can be constituted within NAFTA in the near future. Moreover, one of most cited reasons for the creation of NAFTA is that the USA believed it would be a useful lever with which to persuade other countries to conform to neo-liberal economics on a global scale (Wyatt-Walter, 1995: 85).

The only regional organisation that has made significant progress beyond the facilitation of free trade is the EU. What is significant about the EU is that it has created genuinely supranational bodies. The European Commission and European Parliament possess important powers that impact upon the governance of member states. The latter is particularly significant, as it is organised on a democratic basis. The Council of Ministers is still the key decision-making body of the EU and is controlled by national governments. However, the number of policy areas where decisions in the Council are made on the basis of qualified majority voting grew considerably after the signing of the Single European Act in 1986. Through the provisions of the 1992 Maastricht Treaty, the EU has created a Single European Currency (1999) and this will necessarily entail greater political union with the possibility of common tax and spending policies (Barón, 1997: Ch. 7).

The EU has clearly much more potential to develop into a genuinely governmental body beyond the state than do all other contemporary regional agreements. However, the lack of certainty over the direction that the EU should take reflects the difficulties of regionalised governance more generally. Despite the democratic nature of the European Parliament, the priorities of the EU have been those of national elites: trade liberalisation has been prioritised over worker's rights and unemployment; European monetary union, rather than the democratisation of the EU has been given precedent; and policies towards both developing states outside Europe and non-European 'guest' workers within Europe have created the fear of a European superstate that is as exclusive and discriminatory as any nation-state. The failure of the EU to agree a common policy towards regional problems such as the Yugoslavia crisis or the question of the enlargement of the EU to include parts of Eastern Europe also illustrates the lack of a common European identity or shared political culture (Faulks, 1998: 187–97).

Generally, regionalisation has been driven by the interests of state elites and has overwhelmingly been concerned with economic liberalisation. The violent riots in Mexico and the rise of populist politicians such as Ross Perot in the USA that greeted the signing of NAFTA serve to illustrate the alienation many ordinary citizens have felt towards such undemocratic agreements. As such, regional organisations are unlikely by themselves to be able to form the democratic building blocs of a federal system of global governance. A more likely scenario is expressed by Fawcett and Hurrell (1995: 327) who write, 'at best it can be argued that regionalism may come to constitute one of many pillars supporting an evolving international order'.

Global Civil Society

Advocates of global governance have often pinned their hopes as much on the development of a global civil society as they have upon the formation of international organisations. Important institutions of an emerging global civil society include the mass media and MNCs. The mass media have helped make public opinion a central factor in shaping the actions of democratic states on the world stage, as witnessed by the important part the media played in encouraging humanitarian intervention by Western states in the Somalia and Bosnia crises in the early 1990s. MNCs have generally been perceived more negatively. They have often been analysed in terms of their conflicts with other actors in civil society and as symbols of the need for an enhanced global governance to manage the often harmful side effects of unregulated capitalism (Sklair, 1995). Thus, MNCs have been in conflict with trade unions over the unemployment that results from the shifting of production to cheaper and less unionised locations, and also with environmental groups concerning the toxic wastes that are dumped in developing countries, such as by the *maqiladoras*, which are export assembly plants, set up by Western MNCs on the Mexico–USA border to avoid economic and environmental regulation (Dwyer, 1994: 4–5).

However, it is upon non-governmental organisations (NGOs) that much of the discussion concerning global civil society has focused. In terms of sheer numbers, NGOs have grown apace in recent years. In 1909 there were around 109 NGOs that operated in at least three countries; by 1993 their numbers were 28,900 (Commission on Global Governance, 1995: 32). The growth in communication technology and the relative openness of post-Cold War politics have both facilitated this growth.

Examples of NGOs include environmental groups, such as the World Wildlife Fund and Greenpeace, human rights groups such as Amnesty and Human Rights Watch, and organisations concerned with under-development and poverty, such as Christian Aid and Oxfam (See box 10.1). Their shared goal is a humanitarian one, aiming to promote a healthy environment for peace and a sustainable life. They have tended to be non-profit making and to remain distant from the state. Indeed, it has been argued that 'NGO activity presents the most serious challenge to the imperatives of statehood in the realms of territorial integrity, security, autonomy and revenue' (Fernando and Heston, 1997: 8).

NGOs possess considerable communicative power and have played an important role in raising awareness of global inequalities, ecological crises and human rights abuses across the globe. They have gained a significant presence at many international conferences, playing a crucial part, for example, in UN conferences on population in Cairo in 1994 and the Beijing International Women's Conference in 1995. The World Bank and the WTO have increasingly invited NGOs to act as consultants and observers at their meetings. Through such interactions with international organisations, NGOs have successfully campaigned for legislation as varied as international sanctions against the apartheid regime in South Africa, a code of conduct for the marketing of baby milks and the creation of the UN's Convention Against Torture in 1984 (Clark, 1992: 197).

Box 10.1 Amnesty International: An Example of a NGO

Amnesty was founded in 1961 after a London lawyer, Peter Benenson, wrote to the *Observer* newspaper to highlight the abuse of human rights in Portugal. This sparked a more extensive campaign targeting 'prisoners of conscience' who were imprisoned across the globe for their political, religious or social beliefs. Amnesty was initially based upon the efforts of individual members, who wrote letters to officials in countries where such prisoners were being held urging their release. Its activities have grown in the last three decades and now encompass research and publications on human rights abuses, as well as a number of specialist networks concerned with encouraging human rights in businesses and the professions. By the 1990s there were over 4000 local groups affiliated to the organisation, and in 1993 the organisation had 1 million members in over 150 countries. Amnesty has an excellent reputation for impartiality and for the accuracy of its information. It seeks to free all prisoners of conscience, ensure fair trails for political prisoners, abolish the death penalty and torture, and end extrajudicial executions. By the end of 1997, Amnesty was working on nearly 4000 individual cases of human rights violations. However, research by Jordan and Maloney (1997) has shown that 72.1 per cent of Amnesty members felt that being active politically was not a 'very important reason' or 'played no role whatsoever' in explaining why they were members. For Jordan and Maloney, such evidence shows that NGOs such as Amnesty are not examples of a new 'superior' form of political activism. Such organisations remain hierarchical and involve little direct participation by members. They are therefore unlikely to replace more traditional forms of participation such as political parties.

Sources: Amnesty International (1998); Jordan and Maloney (1997)

NGOs also increasingly play an economic role in global politics and receive a growing percentage of public development aid, as well as large revenues from private donors. This money has been used to relieve suffering in the short term and, in the longer term, NGOs have acted as sources of credit and investment in rural and urban development. Their supporters argue that the fact that they operate outside the geo-political considerations of Western states and are more in touch with the grass roots allows them to better support developing countries. Their greater impartiality has also enabled them to act as mediators between communities in conflict, such as, for example, between the Tamil minority and the Sinhalese majority in Sri Lanka (Fernando and Heston, 1997: 13). Despite these notable achievements, NGOs are not without their critics.

NGOs have often been created by a single charismatic figure and have subsequently failed to build proper democratic structures within their own organisation. This, it is argued, often makes them excessively bureaucratic and unaccountable. This is a particular problem amongst Western NGOs who play a developmental role in the poor regions of the world. The impression is that NGOs have exhibited a paternalistic relationship with the recipients of their aid and are 'keener to deliver services than build participation' (Streeten, 1997: 196).

The argument has also been made that NGOs have grown gradually closer to the interests of their donors and consequently have become less responsive to the long-term needs of developing countries. Hulme and Edwards contend that the reason states have made greater use of NGOs since the 1980s is linked to the dominance of a neo-liberal approach to governance, which prioritises market and voluntary solutions to poverty over state intervention. In effect, NGOs have become the subcontractors of states and 'implementers of donor policies' (Hulme and Edwards, 1997: 8). This has allowed states to withdraw from their obligations to the global community. The problem is, however, that the un-coordinated and *ad hoc* actions of NGOs are no substitute for collective governmental action to relieve the root causes of global inequality.

The un-coordinated nature of NGO activity is compounded by the fact that their reliance upon donors drives them to compete with each other for funding. This necessarily demands a physical presence in trouble spots across the world, so that donors can see that their money is being used immediately to tackle the latest famine or environmental disaster. However, given the complexities of many global problems, a hurried response by NGOs may exacerbate rather than solve a crisis. NGOs competing for coverage in the world's media, in order to reassure donors they are 'doing *something*', is clearly not the most productive approach to adopt. The need to demonstrate results also means that NGO relief operations are targeted, not at the poorest, but at those just on the poverty line, whose problems can more easily be resolved. Consequently, 80 per cent of the world's most poorest 1.3 billion people remain largely untouched by NGO activity (Streeten, 1997: 197).

NGOs may also help sustain the very crises they seek to relieve. In a discussion of the role of NGOs in delivering humanitarian aid to

Rwandan refugees during the mid-1990s, Storey (1997: 386) argues that 'some NGOs . . . lent support to the forces of the deposed genocidal regime'. This was due in part to the choice many NGOs made to focus their attention upon refugee camps in neighbouring Zaire, which were 'predominantly under the control of the forces of the former regime, which had been responsible for the genocide', rather than upon aid to the victims of the former government within Rwanda itself (Storey, 1997: 387). Many NGOs also demonstrated shocking *naïveté* concerning the nature of the conflict in Rwanda and gave ill-informed accounts of the roots of the conflict to the mass media, which in turn carried a distorted message back home. In short, the image NGOs often portray of themselves as 'the embodiment of disinterested humanitarianism' (Stirrat and Henkel, 1997: 69) is simply unsustainable. Moreover, this illusion of neutrality helps to weaken the resolve of the global community to meet such crises as occurred in Rwanda with a firm and well co-ordinated response that cannot in reality be neutral in its objectives or effects.

NGOs have undoubtedly played an important role in raising awareness of global threats, but they cannot be the main actors in resolving them. In some cases, their good intentions can unwittingly sustain global risks and weaken the chances of dealing with their root causes. Therefore, writers such as Hulme and Edwards (1997) have argued that NGOs would be well advised to concentrate their efforts on pressuring their own states through the mobilisation of public opinion and lobbying at conferences and international organisations, and less on short-term relief work, where, 'no matter how hard they try to avoid it, they inevitably become players in a world of patronage and political manipulation' (Stirrat and Henkel, 1997: 74).

From Liberal Democracy to Cosmopolitan Democracy?

The prospects then for the creation of sustainable institutions of global governance are uncertain. Existing international organisations suffer from severe democratic deficits and are driven by the interests of the elites of the most powerful states, while non-state actors within global society lack the coherence and legitimacy to successfully exercise governance by themselves. Moreover, the dominance of neo-liberalism over the world's economy has increased global inequalities, which lie at the root of many world problems. The potential therefore exists for violent reactions to the uncertainties of the post-Cold War world. Could it be that, as in the 1930s, the failures of economic liberalisation and the instability of the states system will prompt the formation of the modern equivalents of fascism and communism, as marginalised communities seek moral 'certainty' in the form of religious or ethnic fundamentalism centred upon the militaristic state?

Certainly, political globalisation has been accompanied by fragmentation. In this sense, we are witnessing an upsurge in the popularity of the state, rather than its demise. The break up of the Soviet Empire and Yugoslavia, the rise of fundamentalist Islam in the Middle East and tensions over post-colonial state boundaries in Africa have all helped to make the struggle for control of territory and the demand for statehood a primary feature of the contemporary world. One highly influential interpretation of these events has been advanced by Samuel Huntington (1998).

Huntington argues that far from creating common interests, and therefore a basis for global governance, globalisation has instead heightened long-established cultural differences, such as between Christianity and Islam. For Huntington, nation-states will increasingly come to define their interests in relation to their allegiance to one of the world's great civilisations. Relationships between these civilisations will be 'almost never close, usually cool, and often hostile' (Huntington, 1998: 207). The most significant division is between 'the West and the rest' (Huntington, 1998: 183). In response to this, the leading power of the West, the USA, should rid itself of the notion that it can reproduce its culture globally, at the expense of other civilisations, and should instead concentrate its efforts internationally on building alliances where possible and domestically on 'rejecting the divisive siren calls of multiculturalism', so that its Western identity can be reasserted (Huntington, 1998: 307).

Huntington's thesis is flawed in many ways. It fails to explain the tensions that exist between states within the same 'civilisation', as witnessed by Iraq's invasion of Kuwait in 1990, and, although he acknowledges that civilisations are 'dynamic', the understanding of culture that underpins his thesis is a highly static one; after all, what is American culture if it is not 'multicultural'? What is most important to our discussion, however, is that Huntington's policy prescriptions are simply unrealistic. In the context of the global risks highlighted throughout this chapter, a strategy that advocates a retreat behind the walls of the state to defend the illusion of a shared civilisation would be disastrous. If this fate is to be avoided, a way must be found to give greater coherence to the idea of global governance. It needs to be recognised that the tensions identified by Huntington are not rooted in the incompatibilities of diverse cultures, but instead result from the neglect of the needs of the majority of societies by powerful states, acting in the name of 'national interest'. The central argument of this chapter has been, however, that, because of a shared vulnerability to global risks, true national interest is becoming indistinguishable from the interests of humanity as a whole. The arrogant denial of the needs of others will therefore become increasingly self-defeating.

The theory of cosmopolitan democracy, advanced by writers such as Held (1995) and Linklater (1998), is the most important attempt to construct a theory of global governance. This theory is crucial to contemporary political sociology because it again highlights the contradictions of the state–civil society relationship and seeks to explore how contemporary social change may be creating the opportunity for their transcendence. A discussion of cosmopolitan democracy therefore returns us to the roots of our subject and the preoccupations of its most important thinker; for it was always Marx's intention to understand the state's relationship with civil society so that one day its paradoxes could be dispensed with. To conclude, I shall consider how a consideration of cosmopolitan democracy enhances our understanding of the state's problematic relationship to violence, democratic citizenship and the market. Although not all advocates of cosmopolitan democracy will accept my interpretation of the implications of the concept, nonetheless it is true to say that all would agree that the relations between the state and civil society lie at the heart of the problem of global governance.

First the objective of cosmopolitan democracy is to build upon the development of international organisations and global civil society, and find ways to knit these elements together in a coherent system of global governance. The key, in contrast to Huntington, is to see different cultures as complementary rather than competitive and to find ways in which global governance can be rendered inclusive through processes of democratisation. Linklater (1998) uses the term 'immanent critique' to describe this strategy, for it seeks to ground its theoretical prescriptions firmly upon developments in the real world. As has been emphasised in this chapter, the most important motivating force for global governance is global risk, which cannot be managed effectively by states acting in isolation. Advocates of cosmopolitan democracy do not argue, however, for the creation of a world government, in the form of a centralised global state. In the shadow of nuclear annihilation, the Westphalian concept of 'might is right' is redundant. Therefore, the creation of a global state would be counterproductive. Instead, differences between communities need to be resolved politically where possible, through multiple yet integrated and democratic sites of governance. This necessarily means a diminished role for violence. Thus, although some supporters of cosmopolitan democracy allow for the use of force as a last resort, their arguments further highlight the problem of the state which grounds its legitimacy on the use of violence. Unlike the state, which is defined in terms of its use of violence, cosmopolitan governance implies the use of force only on tactical grounds, to remove barriers to the entrenchment of democratic methods for the resolution of future conflicts.

Second, cosmopolitan democracy is a post-liberal theory. It seeks to utilise key liberal concepts such as democratic citizenship and make them real for all people, regardless of their membership of a particular state. This therefore demands that such concepts are uncoupled from the state, which has created its identity through exclusionary practices, and extended to the global level. As Held (1995: 228) contends, cosmopolitan law, which has at its heart democratic and citizenship rights, should apply to the 'universal community'. This exposes the hypocrisy of liberal states who have argued for rights at home (for privileged groups at least), but defended the use of might abroad. It also highlights the relational nature of concepts of citizenship and democracy: unless the rights associated with these notions are extended globally, they are always partial and therefore vulnerable.

Finally, cosmopolitan democracy challenges the dualistic logic of liberalism, which stresses that politics is to be confined to the state and that civil society should be dominated by the market. All too often this has meant the needs of the market have subverted the democratic will. Recognising this fact does not mean that we need to abandon the market altogether. It does mean, however, that we acknowledge that the market is a good servant but a bad master. If a meaningful global governance, based upon democratic principles, is to be created, 'the market system has to be entrenched in the rights and obligations clusters of democratic law' (Held, 1995: 250).

Conclusion

It is crucial to stress that the extent of global governance in the future will very much depend upon the choices states make. Clearly resistance to global governance will be great, and there are no inevitable historical forces at work which will guarantee its success. Moreover, developments in global communications have enhanced the potential for greater conflict as well as co-operation between the very diverse peoples of the world.

It has been demonstrated in this chapter, that global risks are creating a basis for universal common interests, if only in avoiding mutual annihilation through war, or extinction through the destruction of the planet's life support systems. The interconnected nature of these new security dilemmas, which are rooted in global inequalities and the instability of the states system, means that they can only be successfully managed at a global level.

For this reason political sociologists have sought ways in which the gradual growth of global institutions such as the UN can be built upon to constitute systems of governance that move beyond the state. The challenge to political sociology posed by these theories of cosmopolitan democracy is for political sociology to focus its attention upon the interactions between societies and states, as well upon the power relations that exist within states. Indeed, an understanding of any single state can only be complete within this global context. There is still a place, however, for the analysis of individual state–civil relations, for it is here that the transformation to global governance, or points of resistance to it, will emerge. It has been argued in this book that it is the state, more than any other human institution, which is able to concentrate power, and which remains largely the 'master' of its own destiny. Different state strategies of economic management, democracy and citizenship are therefore as crucial as ever: how states respond to global challenges and how civil society might resolve tensions of cultural and material differences remain important questions in political sociology. Contrary to rumour, history is not at an end and political sociology, with its unique focus upon the problematic of the state–civil society relationship, will be crucial to understanding its future directions.

Conclusion

In this book I have argued that the primary focus of political sociology is the interdependent power relationship between the state and civil society. The conclusion will be both a review of the main elements of this argument and a brief discussion of the ways in which political sociology is addressing the contemporary problems of governance.

A Review of the Book's Argument

In the Introduction, it was noted that the question to which political sociology will always return to is this: how is power distributed and institutionalised within society? If we are to begin to answer this question, then this text has contended that it is vital to acknowledge the centrality of the state. This is because it is the state which is the political institution most capable of concentrating those resources necessary to the exercise of economic, communicative and military power. However, the importance of the state has not been accepted by all political sociologists.

In Part I, we saw how for much of the post-war period political sociology was dominated by perspectives which ignored or denied the state, or treated the state as unproblematic or as less significant than other institutions. For behaviouralists, the state was too difficult and abstract an entity to define. It was therefore unhelpful in explaining the distribution of power. In elite theory the state was not especially significant, representing just one institution amongst many where elites inevitably hold sway over the masses. Classical pluralism saw the state as no more than a neutral arbiter between the competing forces within civil society. According to classical Marxism, the state was of secondary importance. The question of how power is distributed is answered instead by reference to who controls the economic means of production.

In the 1970s, however, the state took centre stage in political sociology. This was due mainly to the fact that in the real world the state was more robust than ever. Especially in communist countries, which had theoretically and briefly promised the state's transcendence, the state was enormously powerful. The unique ability of the state to centralise power therefore became widely acknowledged within political sociology. In particular, scholars influenced by Marx and Weber began to take the state more seriously. In the 1980s and 1990s contemporary political sociologists have contributed much to our understanding of the state. Crucially, writers such as Giddens (1985) and Mann (1986; 1993) reminded us of the importance of Max Weber's definition of the state, which emphasised the significance of the state's domination of coercive power. In Chapter 2 of this book I therefore argued that the state's role as the symbol of 'national' communities, its powers of surveillance over civil society, and its importance as a military actor within the context of an inherently tense states system, all give the state an autonomy from the institutions of civil society which classical theories of political sociology failed to acknowledge. The state has a logic and imperatives of its own which do sometimes transcend the interests of any single section of civil society.

In Part I however, it was made clear that the state has to be understood in relation to the associations of civil society and in the context of processes of social change occurring within and beyond its own boundaries. Moreover, it is not enough to merely acknowledge the power of the state. It is important to challenge the state as well. Marx's willingness to look beyond the state therefore retains a relevance today.

For Marx, the modern liberal state was a significant development, precisely because it enshrined a sharp divide between itself and the institutions of civil society. The liberal state, for the first time in history, claimed to protect the 'universal rights' of its citizens. Thus within its own logic lay the seeds of its downfall. This is because in reality, the inequalities of civil society (what I have referred to as structures of power) ensure that the liberal rights of life, liberty and property are enjoyed only by a privileged minority. The legitimacy of the liberal state is therefore inevitably challenged by those groups which are unable to assert the rights that liberalism promises them. Building upon Marx's critique, I have argued that the state–civil society relationship cannot effectively resolve the inherent human problem of governance, which I define as the management of the perennial problems of social order and the distribution of resources. I have contended that Marx is therefore correct to look beyond the liberal state for a resolution to these problems.

Since the 1980s, rapid social changes have for some scholars undermined the state to the extent to which alternative systems of governance may now well be more appropriate. I agree that social change has further highlighted the problem of the state and the need to move beyond it. However, in my discussions of the challenges of globalisation, neo-liberalism and new social movements in Part II, I concluded that rumours of the death of the state have been greatly exaggerated. Extreme theories of globalisation have overestimated the development of a truly global culture and economy which are rootless and un-bounded by the state. In reality, cultural globalisation accents differences between peoples as much as it transcends these differences, while economic globalisation is the product of the interactions between the state and economic associations of civil society. The key point, which Hirst and Thompson (1996) make so well, is that if the political will existed states could regulate the world economy more effectively. The truth is that such regulation does not currently suit many powerful states. This is where the ideology of neo-liberalism, discussed in Chapter 4, has been so important. Neo-liberalism has been highly influential in structuring the world economy because it has stressed the need to 'roll back the state' and instead let the laws of supply and demand create social order and distribute resources. However, wherever neo-liberalism has been applied in practice, the result has been an enhanced role for the state, as the 'free market' creates not opportunity for all, but vast inequality; not order, but social conflict. Ironically, it has been left to a strong 'law and order state' to pick up the pieces.

Chapter 5 explored the very different challenge to the state presented by new social movements. Such movements have been very important in enhancing political participation amongst sections of society dis-illusioned with the statist assumptions of conventional political parties and pressure groups. However, too many of their supporters, such as Touraine and Melucci, have urged NSMs to adopt a romanticised detachment from the state. NSMs they contend will transform society through by-passing the state altogether, or by challenging its authority through 'symbolic acts of resistance'. In reality, NSMs are caught in the dilemma of either maintaining their autonomy and thereby remaining politically marginal, or, alternatively, compromising some of their principles and becoming largely indistinct from traditional forms of political organisation in an effort to gain greater influence. Either way, NSMs are unable to significantly reduce the power of the state by themselves.

Part III was a discussion of the optimistic assumptions that have underpinned many accounts of civil society. In Chapters 6–8 it was shown that the nature of political culture, citizenship and political participation are being transformed by social change in ways which suggest the need to re-evaluate our systems of governance. The key development seems to be what Giddens (1994) has christened social reflexivity. This concept acknowledges the development of more globally aware, critical and diverse populations, particularly within liberal democracies. Social reflexivity means that citizens are increasingly alienated from elitist forms of governance within civil society and the state. Demand for greater opportunities for participation in governance, however, cannot be met in civil society alone.

What is required is a rethinking of the totality of the state–civil society relationship. Moreover, the greater global awareness which Giddens notes is strongly linked to fears that the institutions of the state and civil society will be unable to meet the challenges presented by the growth of global risk. These issues were addressed in Part IV: the problem of achieving sustainable governance is sure to remain a critical question in political sociology.

Future Directions in Political Sociology

In Chapter 9, I explored some influential contemporary theories of the state–civil society relationship, all of which have sought ways to improve the foundations of governance. Not all of course agree with Marx's argument that rethinking the problem of governance means moving beyond the state. It was noted, for example, how writers such as Giddens and Miliband are wary of the notion that effective governance can be constituted without some form of state. However, there is general agreement amongst the thinkers we considered that the state must be rendered more democratically accountable, its use of force minimised, and many of its powers transferred to alternative political institutions. If all of these reforms could be achieved, we would surely be on a path towards constructing systems of governance which greatly diminish the role of the state. Furthermore, in Chapter 10 it was suggested that such power sharing may well also develop between states, as well as within states. If globalisation has a useful meaning, I have argued that it is within a primarily political context: that is, globalisation refers to the growing fusion of global problems. These new security problems require solutions at a global level. If such global governance moves beyond the embryonic forms it currently takes then the state's jealously guarded 'monopoly' of force will become increasingly problematic and unsustainable.

The concept that best unites the concerns explored in Part IV is that of democracy. It is this concept, above all others, which political sociologists have turned to in their efforts to rethink the problem of governance. The democratisation of governance may be the key to achieving social order and distributing resources fairly, because democracy implies consent, justice and the primacy of politics over economic profitability. Theories of cosmopolitan democracy, introduced in Chapter 10, have been crucial in exposing the problems facing systems of governance based on the state–civil society divide. Liberals have been keen to sustain a polarisation between state and civil society partly because they are so enchanted by the power of the market to create opportunity and liberty. However, as our awareness of the causes of global risks grows, it is becoming clear that economic 'liberalisation', which has been a very selective and state-driven process, is at the root of many of these problems. Also, by exploring how democracy can be applied at the global level, we necessarily expose the limitations of a democracy centred upon the exclusive state. How can democracy, citizenship and rights be meaningful and lasting if they do not apply to all people wherever they may reside? None of this is to deny the extreme difficulties of securing more stable forms of governance. Huntington's (1998) clash of civilisations thesis, despite its many flaws, does highlight some of the many obstacles to global governance. However, in the context of new security threats, which do not respect state or cultural boundaries, some form of cosmopolitan democracy seems a more realistic approach than Huntington's scenario, which would sooner or later lead to zero sum conflicts between uncompromising 'civilisations'.

I would suggest, therefore, that much useful research and theorising remains to be done within political sociology around the issue of democracy and political participation. First, we need more studies on the possibilities new technologies create for democracy. As was noted in Chapter 8, not all such developments may be as beneficial as they first appear. More empirical studies into the practicalities of governing through information and communication technologies are therefore much needed. Second, the work of radical pluralists such as Paul Hirst has been useful in exploring the way in which a shift from state-centred governance towards self-governing associations in civil society can be constituted and facilitated. Such work can be built upon. Thus extensive studies of citizens' juries, workplace democracy and other systems of direct democracy, which empower citizens within civil society, are vital. Finally, a great deal more theoretical work is required to establish how democratic principles can be broadened and properly constituted at the global level. A key question which needs to be resolved is whether global governance can be based upon a set of institutions and rights which are Western in origin.

The democratisation of the state–civil society relationship and the gradual extension of democratic principles at a global level nonetheless represents the best chance humanity has of governing itself and the planet effectively. The founder of political sociology, Karl Marx, was right therefore to point to the limits of the state. Furthermore, in the context of the profound social changes discussed in this book, the prospects for a world beyond the state have never been better. Marx was nevertheless wrong to assume that we could rely upon the evolutionary forces of history to propel us beyond the state. This book has argued that the state retains enormous power, and can thwart as well as enhance future developments in governance. In the face of mutual annihilation, it is the responsibility of democrats everywhere to help the state to realise where its true interests lie. As Hoffman (1995: 192) contends, paradoxically this means that states must be 'willing accomplices in their own transcendence'.

Guide to Further Reading

Chapter 1. Approaches and Key Concepts in Political Sociology

For a classic example of the behaviouralist approach to political sociology see Easton (1953). Kavanagh (1983) provides a sympathetic overview of many aspects of behaviouralism. On the concept of power, Lukes (1974) remains a key starting point for debate, while Hindess (1996) introduces a variety of approaches to power, from Hobbes to Foucault. The difficulties associated with defining the state are discussed at length in Hoffman (1995). For an introduction to the historical development and nature of the modern state, see the works by Poggi (1978, 1990) and Giddens (1985), the latter being particularly interesting on the issue of military power and its relationship to state formation. The early chapters of Mann (1986), as well as introducing an influential theory of power, provide a stimulating discussion of the origins of the state. An excellent anthropological text on the nature of politics and the state is Gledhill (1994). For recent analyses of the relationship between the state and civil society see Keane (ed.) (1988) and Cohen and Arato (1992). A useful collection of essays on the legacy of Hegel's theory of the state and civil society is Pelczynski (ed.) (1984).

Chapter 2. Classical Theories of the State and Civil Society

McLellan (1977) provides a wide selection of the writings of Marx, including many of his important treatments of the state and civil society. Both Carnoy (1984) and Thomas (1994) offer clear and sympathetic overviews of the important developments in Marxist state theory. Mosca (1939), Pareto (1968) and Michels (1962) are important statements of classical elite theory. Bottomore (1993a) presents a critical overview of elite theory and Bachrach (1967) is a good summary of democratic elitism. On pluralism, see the classic studies by Dahl (1961) and Truman (1951), and Dunleavy and O'Leary (1987: Ch. 6) for a detailed overview of recent trends in pluralist thinking. Mann (1988) and Skocpol (1979) are excellent examples of the recent interest shown by political sociologists in the state. Schwarzmantel (1994) and Marsh and Stoker (eds) (1995: Chs 11–13) provide reasonably detailed summaries of the work of many of the theorists touched upon in this chapter.

Chapter 3. Globalisation

The best short, yet comprehensive, introduction to globalisation, which discusses its cultural, economic and political aspects, is Waters (1995). Albrow (1996) and Axford (1995) are both wide-ranging overviews of recent changes in the spheres of economy, society and politics associated with processes of globalisation. Robertson (1992) is an intelligent discussion of the cultural aspects of globalisation. Particularly useful sources on the growing influence of multinational corporations are Korten (1995) and Dunning (1993). Good sources on technological change and its impact upon economic markets and the state can be found in Dicken (1998: Ch. 5) and Camilleri and Falk (1992: Ch. 5). On the development of the 'global market' see Ohmae (1990, 1995) and O'Brien (1992). Hirst and Thompson (1996) is the best critique of the thesis that the world economy can be described as global. Michie and Smith (eds) (1995) is a useful collection of essays on how the world economy has developed and how it might be managed. The edited work by Scott (ed.) (1997) is particularly strong on the limits of a 'global culture'. Gray (1998) is a pessimistic vision of the impact globalisation is having upon the autonomy of local communities and states.

Chapter 4. Neo-Liberalism

Neo-liberal theory is normally discussed as an aspect of the so-called New Right, which is often said to combine elements of both liberal and conservative thought. General accounts of the New Right can be found in Green (1987) and Barry (1987). However, the best source of neo-liberal ideas can be found in the work of its most important advocate: Hayek (1944, 1960) is particularly readable and Gamble (1996) provides an excellent critical assessment of Hayek's theory. On the impact of neo-liberalism in Britain see Wilson (1992), Gamble (1994) and in particular Gilmour (1992). The last was a minister in the first Thatcher cabinet, and he manages to be simultaneously eloquent and scathing on the Thatcher legacy. I discuss the relationship between Thatcherism, conservatism and neo-liberalism in the British context in Chapter 5 of Faulks (1998). Perhaps because neo-liberal ideas have formed part of the political mainstream for many years in the USA, there is less recent material exploring the American experience. However, Friedman and Friedman (1980) and Anderson (1988) are worth consulting as influential sources of neo-liberal ideas. Some comparisons of the American and British experience of the New Right can be found in Adonis and Hames (eds) (1994). For assessments of the impact of neo-liberalism on Africa see in particular Brown (1995), Dixon et al. (1995) and Watkins (1995).

Chapter 5. New Social Movements

For general overviews of the impact of NSMs see Scott (1990), which is particularly good on NSMs' relationships to 'conventional' political structures, and Eder (1993), which discusses the relationship between NSMs and social class. Garner (1996) provides comprehensive coverage of many of the most important social movements, including many examples drawn from the USA. Bryne (1997) addresses the British situation, and Kriesi et al. (1995) is useful on NSMs in Western Europe. For a comparative analysis of the nature of movements in non-Western states, Foweraker (1995) is excellent on the Latin-American experience. NSMs theory is notoriously hard going. However, Maheu (ed.) (1995) offers a collection of accessible essays that introduces many of the main theoretical issues and includes contributions by key figures such as Touraine and Melucci. A strong collection of essays which addresses the relationship between NSMs activity and political opportunity is McAdam et al. (eds) (1996). For critical approaches to NSMs, the article by Calhoun (1993) on pre-twentieth-century movements argues that there is little that is new about NSMs while Jordan and Maloney (1997) contend that many so-called NSMs are indistinguishable from pressure groups.

Chapter 6. Political Culture

A good place to start investigating the relationship between culture and politics is Almond and Verba's original work on political culture (1963) and their follow-up study (1980). Rosenbaum (1975) and Welch (1993) provide useful overviews of the political culture approach, while Eatwell (ed.) (1997) is a collection of informative essays on political culture in various European countries. Interesting studies of the significance of culture for political sociology are Street (1997) and Lloyd and Thomas (1998). On theories of crisis in the 1970s see Held (1996: Ch. 7), Hay (1996: Ch. 5) and Crozier et al. (1975). For further reading on recent theories of moral and cultural decline see Tester (1997) on Himmelfarb and Mingione (1996) on the underclass, which collects together a number of useful contributions to the debate. Hutton (1996) provides, amongst other things, a readable addition to the culture of contentment thesis. Overviews of post-modernist accounts of our present cultural condition and its relationship to political and economic change can be found in Kumar (1995) and Lash and Urry (1994).

Chapter 7. Citizenship

Marshall's very readable 1950 essay on citizenship and social class, reprinted in Marshall and Bottomore (1992), is the best-known modern account of citizenship, and is still well worth reading. Works that criticise Marshall's legacy and develop alternative approaches to citizenship include Barbalet (1988), Roche (1992) and Faulks (1998). Turner and Hamilton (eds) (1994) brings together a large number of excellent articles and extracts exploring theories of citizenship from antiquity to the modern period, including the work of Turner and Mann discussed in this chapter. Other useful collections of essays on aspects of citizenship are Bulmer and Rees (eds) (1996) and Andrews (ed.) (1991). For a feminist analysis of citizenship see Lister (1997). A well-organised overview of the communitarian debate can be found in Mulhall and Swift (1996). Regular contributions to citizenship theory, exploring in particular the impact of recent social and economic changes, can be found in the excellent journal *Citizenship Studies*, published by Carfax, and edited by Bryan Turner.

Chapter 8. Political Participation

For a thorough overview of the most influential theories of democracy see Held (1996). Etzioni-Halevy (1993) and Sartori (1987) make the case for a democracy run by political elites. Green and Shapiro (1994) provides an intricate critique of rational choice as applied in political analysis, while the work of Olson (1971) remains one of the most influential attempts to utilise the model to analyse political behaviour.

For advocates of direct democracy, see Pateman (1970), Barber (1984) and the very accessible Budge (1996). Parry et al. (1991) and Verba et al. (1995) are the most comprehensive accounts of political participation in Britain and the USA respectively. Kaase and Newton (1995) and, most impressively, Dalton (1996) are the best sources for trends in participation in Western Europe, with the latter also covering the USA. A wealth of material is now appearing on the impact of ICT on democracy. Particularly interesting are McLean (1989) and Tsagarousianou, et al. (eds) (1998). Mulgan (ed.) (1997) is a very useful collection of essays that discuss how liberal democracies may adapt to the demands of an increasingly disillusioned citizenry, and contains material on recent innovations such as citizens' juries.

Chapter 9. Contemporary Theories of the State and Civil Society

On post-modernity, Lyon (1994) provides a good, short overview. Jameson (1991) is an influential Marxist interpretation of post-modernism, while Harvey (1990) sets post-modernism in its theoretical and social context. For a critique of Giddens's political sociology, see Meštrović (1998: especially Ch. 5). Further discussion of Beck's notion of 'risk society' can be found in Franklin (ed.) (1998). Good sources on the rethinking of the left include Wright (1996) and the edited collections, Mouffe (ed.) (1992) and Osborne (ed.) (1991). Jessop (1990) and Hay (1996) are both good examples of neo-Marxist attempts to transcend the problems of economism. McLennan (1989, 1995) contain useful discussions of the revival of pluralism and its relationship to Marxism. See Young (1990) for an interesting example of one of the directions contemporary pluralist theory is moving. Etzioni-Halevy (1993) addresses the question of theoretical convergence from an elite theory perspective.

Chapter 10. Global Governance

For concise introductions to the international relations discipline, see Brown (1997) and Bayliss and Smith (eds) (1997). More critical approaches to international relations theory are Ruggie (1998) and Rosenberg (1994) which is a critique of realism from a Marxist perspective. Hoffman (1998) offers a stimulating discussion of the problems and contradictions of state sovereignty. On global risk, both Kennedy (1994) and the Real World Coalition (1996) offer excellent discussions of many of the new security issues touched upon in this chapter. On international regimes, see Chapter 12 of Bayliss and Smith (eds) (1997) and, for more advanced reading, Zacher and Sutton (1996) is a liberal account of international regimes in the fields of transport and communications. Readable accounts of the United Nations are Luard with Heater (1994) and Bailey and Daws (1995). Ratner (1997) deals specifically with the issue of UN peacekeeping. Excellent discussions of regionalisation can be found in Gamble and Payne (eds) (1996) and Fawcett and Hurrell (eds) (1995) which both contain essays exploring individual case studies and wider historical and theoretical issues. On global civil society, see Shaw (1994) for a theoretical overview, and Hulme and Edwards (eds) (1997) for a thorough collection of essays exploring the pros and cons of NGOs. The two most successful attempts to construct a theory of cosmopolitan democracy are Held (1995) and Linklater (1998). Their views on the forces shaping global governance can usefully be contrasted with the pessimism of Huntington (1998).

Bibliography

Abercrombie, N., Hill, S., and Turner, B. (1980) *The Dominant Ideology Thesis* (London: Allen and Unwin).

Adonis, A., and Hames, T. (eds) (1994) *A Conservative Revolution: The Thatcher – Reagan Decade in Perspective* (Manchester: Manchester University Press).

Adonis, A., and Mulgan, G. (1997) 'Back to Greece', pp. 227–45 in Mulgan, G. (ed.) (1997).

Ahmed, A., and Donnan, H. (1994) 'Islam in the Age of Post-modernity', pp. 1–20 in Ahmed, A., and Donnan, H. (eds) (1994) *Islam, Globalisation, and Post-modernity* (London: Routledge).

Albertoni, E. (1987) *Mosca and the Theory of Elitism* (Oxford: Blackwell).

Albrow, M. (1996) *The Global Age* (Cambridge: Polity Press).

Almond, G. (1956) 'Comparative Political Systems', *Journal of Politics* vol. 18 (3) pp. 391–409.

Almond, G., and Verba, S. (1963) *The Civic Culture* (Princeton: Princeton University Press).

Almond, G., and Verba, S. (eds) (1980) *The Civic Culture Revisited* (Boston: Little Brown).

Amin, S. (1996) 'The Challenge of Globalisation', *Review of International Political Economy* vol. 3 (2) pp. 216–59.

Amnesty International (1998) 'Facts and Figures about Amnesty International' (http://www.amnesty.org/aboutai/factfigr.htm).

Anderson, B. (1983) *Imagined Communities* (London: Verso).

Anderson, J. (1995) 'The Exaggerated Death of the Nation-State', pp. 65–112 in Anderson, J., Brook, C. and Cochrane, A. (eds) (1995) *A Global World* (Oxford: Oxford University Press).

Anderson, M. (1988) *Revolution* (San Diego: Jovanovich).

Andrews, G. (ed.) (1991) *Citizenship* (London: Lawrence and Wishart).

Archer, R. (1996) 'Towards Economic Democracy in Britain', pp. 85–96 in Hirst, P., and Khilnani, S. (eds) (1996).

Armstrong, P., Glyn, A., and Harrison, J. (1984) *Capitalism since World War Two* (London: Fontana).

Avineri, S. (1972) *Hegel's Theory of the Modern State* (Cambridge: Cambridge University Press).

Axford, B. (1995) *The Global System* (Cambridge: Polity Press).

Axtmann, R. (1996) *Liberal Democracy into the Twenty-First Century* (Manchester: Manchester University Press).

Bachrach, P. (1967) *The Theory of Democratic Elitism: A Critique* (Boston: Little Brown).

Bailey, S., and Daws, S. (1995) *The United Nations: A Concise Political Guide* (3rd edn) (London: Macmillan).

Barbalet, J. (1988) *Citizenship* (Milton Keynes: Open University).

Barber, B. (1984) *Strong Democracy: Participatory Politics for a New Age* (Berkeley: University of California Press).

Barón, E. (1997) *Europe at the Dawn of the Millennium* (London: Macmillan).

Barry, B. (1978) *Sociologists, Economists and Democracy* (Chicago: University of Chicago Press).

Barry, N. (1987) *The New Right* (London: Croom Helm).

Bayliss, J., and Smith, S. (eds) (1997) *The Globalization of World Politics* (Oxford: Oxford University Press).

Beck, U. (1992) *Risk Society* (London: Sage Publications).

Beck, U. (1997) *The Reinvention of Politics* (Cambridge: Polity Press).

Bell, D. (1976) *The Cultural Contradictions of Capitalism* (London: Basic Books).

Bennett, S. (1997) 'Knowledge of Politics and Sense of Subjective Political Competence', *American Politics Quarterly* vol. 25 (2) pp. 230–40.

Benyon, J., and Edwards, A. (1997) 'Crime and Public Order', pp. 326–41 in Dunleavy, P., et al. (eds) (1997).

Berridge, G. (1992) *International Politics* (2nd edn) (London: Harvester and Wheatsheaf).

Beyer, P. (1994) *Religion and Globalisation* (London: Sage Publications).

Birch, A. (1993) *The Concepts and Theories of Modern Democracy* (London: Routledge).

Bottomore, T. (1993a) *Elites and Society* (2nd edn) (London: Routledge).

Bottomore, T. (1993b) *Political Sociology* (2nd edn) (London: Pluto Press).

Bourdieu, P., and Passeron, J. (1977) *Reproduction in Education, Society and Culture* (London: Sage Publications).

Brittan, P. (1987) 'Fighting Fascism in Britain: The Role of the Anti-Nazi League', *Social Alternatives* vol. 6 (4) pp. 42–6.

Brittan, S. (1976) 'The Economic Contradictions of Democracy', pp. 96–137 in King, A., Coates, D., St John-Stevas, N., Mackintosh, J., and Brittan, S. (1976) *Why is Britain Becoming Harder to Govern?* (London: BBC).

Brook, C. (1998) 'Regionalism and Globalism', pp. 230–46 in McGrew, A. and Brook, C. (eds) (1998) *Asia-Pacific in the New World Order* (London: Routledge).

Brown, C. (1997) *Understanding International Relations* (London: Macmillan).

Brown, M. (1995) *Africa's Choices: After Thirty Years of the World Bank* (London: Penguin).

Bryan, C., Tsagarousianou, R., and Tambini, D. (1998) 'Electronic Democracy and the Civic Networking Movement in Context', pp. 1–17 in Tsagarousianou, et al. (1998).

Bryne, P. (1997) *Social Movements in Britain* (London: Routledge).

Budge, I. (1996) *The New Challenge of Direct Democracy* (Cambridge: Polity Press).

Bull, H. (1977) *The Anarchical Society* (London: Macmillan).

Bulmer, M., and Rees, A. (eds) (1996) *Citizenship Today* (London: UCL Press).

Butler, D. and Ranney, A. (eds) (1994) *Referendums around the World* (London: Macmillan).

Buxton, W. (1985) *Talcott Parsons and the Capitalist Nation-State: Political Sociology as a Strategic Vocation* (Toronto: University of Toronto).

Cable, V. (1995) 'The Diminished Nation-State: A Study in the Loss of Economic Power', *Daedalus* vol. 124 (2) pp. 23–53.

Cable, V. (1996) 'Globalisation: Can the State Strike Back?' *The World Today* May pp. 133–7.

Calhoun, C. (1993) 'New Social Movements of the Early Nineteenth Century', *Social Science History* vol. 17 (3) pp. 385–427.

Camilleri, J., and Falk, J. (1992) *The End of Sovereignty?* (Aldershot: Edward Elgar).

Campbell, J., and Oliver, M. (1996) *Disability Politics* (London: Routledge).

Carnoy, M. (1984) *The State and Political Theory* (Princeton: Princeton University Press).

Carter, D. (1997) 'International Organised Crime', pp. 131–51 in Ryan, P., and Rush, G. (eds) (1997) *Understanding Organised Crime in Global Perspective: A Reader* (London: Sage Publications).

Chomsky, N. (1997) *World Orders, Old and New* (revised edn) (London: Verso).

Clapham, D., Kintrea, K. and Kay, H. (1996) 'Direct Democracy in Practice: The Case of "Community Ownership" Housing Associations', *Policy and Politics* vol. 24 (4) pp. 359–73.

Clark, J. (1992) 'Policy Influence, Lobbying and Advocacy', pp. 191–202 in Edwards, M., and Hulme, D. (eds) (1992) *Making a Difference: NGOs and Development in a Changing World* (London: Earthscan).

Coates, D. (1991) *Running the Country* (London: Hodder and Stoughton).

Cohen, J., and Arato, A. (1992) *Civil Society and Political Theory* (Cambridge: MA/ MIT).

Commission of the European Communities (1997) *Eurobarometer: Public Opinion in the European Union* no. 47 (Brussels: Commission of the European Communities).

Commission on Global Governance (1995) *Our Global Neighbourhood* (Oxford: Oxford University Press).

Coote, A., and Lenaghan, J. (1997) *Citizens' Juries: Theory into Practice* (London: IPPR).

Coxall, B., and Robins, L. (1994) *Contemporary British Politics* (2nd edn) (Basingstoke: Macmillan).

Crozier, M. (1975) 'Western Europe', pp. 11–57 in Crozier, M., Huntington, S., and Watanuki, J. (1975) *The Crisis of Democracy* (New York: New York University).

Curtice, J., and Jowell, R. (1997) 'Trust in the Political System', pp. 89-109 in *British Social Attitudes: The 14th Report* (Aldershot: Ashgate).

Dahl, R. (1956) *A Preface to Democratic Theory* (Chicago: University of Chicago Press).

Dahl, R. (1961) *Who Governs? Democracy and Power in an American City* (New Haven: Yale University Press).

Dahl, R. (1991) *Modern Political Analysis* (5th edn) (New Jersey: Prentice-Hall).

Dalton, R. (1996) *Citizen Politics* (2nd edn) (New Jersey: Chatham House).

De Jasay, A. (1985) *The State* (Oxford: Blackwell).

Denning, D. (1997) 'The Future of Cryptography', pp. 175–190 in Loader, B. (ed.) (1997).

Dicken, P. (1998) *Global Shift* (3rd edn) (London: Paul Chapman).

Dixon, C., Simon, D. and Narman, A. (1995) *Structurally Adjusted Africa: Poverty, Debt and Basic Needs* (London: Pluto Press).

Doherty, B. (1998) 'Opposition to Road Building', *Parliamentary Affairs* vol. 51 (3) pp. 370–83.

Downs, A. (1957) *An Economic Theory of Democracy* (New York: Harper).

Dunleavy, P., Gamble, A., Holliday, I., and Peele, G. (eds) (1997) *Developments in British Politics 5* (Basingstoke: Macmillan).

Dunleavy, P. and O'Leary, B. (1987) *Theories of the State* (London: Macmillan).

Dunning, J. (1993) *Multinational Enterprises and the Global Economy* (Wokingham: Addison-Welsey).

Durham, M. (1985) 'Suffrage and After: Feminism in the Early Twentieth Century', pp. 179–91 in Langan, M. and Schwarz, B. (eds) (1985).

Dwyer, A. (1994) *On the Line* (London: Latin American Bureau/Central Books).

Easton, D. (1953) *The Political System: An Enquiry into the State of Political Science* (New York: Alfred A. Knopf).

Eatwell, R. (ed.) (1997) *European Political Cultures* (London: Routledge).

Eder, K. (1993) *The Politics of Class: Social Movements and Cultural Dynamics in Advanced Societies* (London: Sage Publications).

Eder, K. (1995) 'Does Social Class Matter in the Study of Social Movements? A Theory of Middle-class Radicalism', pp. 21–54 in Maheu, L. (ed.) (1995).

Elkins, P. (1992) *A New World Order* (London: Routledge).

Elliott, L. (1998) *The Global Politics of the Environment* (London: Macmillan).

Etzioni, A. (1995) *The Spirit of Community* (London: Fontana).

Etzioni, A. (1997) *The New Golden Rule* (London: Profile Books).

Etzioni-Halevy, E. (1993) *The Elite Connection* (Cambridge: Polity Press).

Eurostat, (1995) *The Globalization Newsletter* no. 1, April.

Evans, M. (1995) 'Elitism', pp. 228–247 in Marsh, D., and Stoker, G. (eds) (1995).

Evans, M. (1997) 'Political Participation', pp. 110–25 in Dunleavy, P., et al. (eds) (1997).

Evans, P., Rueschemeyer, D., and Skocpol, T. (eds) (1985) *Bringing the State Back in* (Cambridge: Cambridge University Press).

Falk, R. (1995) *On Human Governance* (Cambridge: Polity Press).

Faulks, K. (1998) *Citizenship in Modern Britain* (Edinburgh: Edinburgh University Press).

Fawcett, L. and Hurrell, A. (eds) (1995) *Regionalism in World Politics* (Oxford: Oxford University Press).

Fernando, J., and Heston, A. (eds) (1997) 'The Role of NGOs: Charity and Empowerment', The Annals of the American Academy of Political and Social Science vol. 554.

Financial Times (1998) 'The Day the Miracle Came to an End' 12 January.

Foucault, M. (1980) Power/Knowledge (Brighton: Harvester).

Foweraker, J. (1995) Theorizing Social Movements (London: Pluto Press).

Francissen, L. and Brants, K. (1998) 'Virtually Going Place: Square-Hopping in Amsterdam's Digital City', pp. 18–40 in Tsagarousianou, et al. (eds) (1998).

Franklin, J. (ed.) (1998) The Politics of Risk Society (Cambridge: Polity Press).

Frazer, N., and Gordon, L. (1994) 'Civil Citizenship Against Social Citizenship', pp. 90–107 in Van Steenbergen, B. (ed.) (1994) The Condition of Citizenship (London: Sage Publications).

Friedman, M., and Friedman, R. (1980) Free to Choose (London: Secker and Warburg).

Friends of the Earth (1998) 'A Bill of Rights for Multinationals?' (http://www.foe.co.uk/foei/tes/link14b.htm).

Fuchs, D. and Klingemann, H. (1995) 'Citizens and the State: A Relationship Transformed', pp. 419–443 in Klingeman, H. and Fuchs, D. (eds) (1995).

Fukuyama, F. (1992) The End of History and the Last Man (London: Hamilton).

Galbraith, J. (1992) The Culture of Contentment (London: Penguin).

Gamble, A. (1994) The Free Economy and the Strong State (2nd edn) (London: Macmillan).

Gamble, A. (1996) Hayek (Cambridge: Polity Press).

Gamble, A. and Payne, A. (eds) (1996) Regionalism and World Order (London: Macmillan).

Garner, R. (1996) Contemporary Movements and Ideologies (New York: McGraw-Hill).

George, S. (1993) 'Uses and Abuses of African Debt', pp. 59–72 in Adedeji, A. (ed.) Africa within the World (London: Zed Books/ACDES).

Giddens, A. (1985) The Nation-State and Violence (Cambridge: Polity Press).

Giddens, A. (1990) The Consequences of Modernity (Cambridge: Polity Press).

Giddens, A. (1994) Beyond Left and Right (Cambridge: Polity Press).

Gilmour, I. (1992) Dancing with Dogma (London: Simon and Schuster).

Gledhill, J. (1994) Power and its Disguises: Anthropological Perspectives on Politics (London: Pluto Press).

Gramsci, A. (1971) Selections from the Prison Notebooks (London: Lawrence and Wishart).

Gray, J. (1997) Endgames (Cambridge: Polity Press).

Gray, J. (1998) False Dawn (London: Granta Books)

Green, D. (1987) The New Right (Brighton: Wheatsheaf).

Green, D., and Shapiro, I. (1994) Pathologies of Rational Choice: A Critique of Applications in Political Science (New Haven: Yale University Press).

Guardian (1998a) 'Apathy Grips US Students', 13 January.

Guardian (1998b) 'World Leaders Bask in Summit Glow', 18 May.

Habermas, J. (1976) Legitimation Crisis (London: Heinemann).

Hadjimichael, M., Nowak, M., Sharer, R. and Tahari, A. (1996) Adjustment for

Growth: The African Experience Occasional Paper no. 143 (Washington DC: International Monetary Fund).

Hall, J., and Ikenberry, J. (1989) *The State* (Milton Keynes: Open University).

Hall, S. (1995) 'New Cultures for Old', pp. 175–213 in Massey, D., and Jess, P. (1995) *A Place in the World* (Milton Keynes: Open University).

Hall, S., and Schwarz, B. (1985) 'State and Society: 1880–1930', pp. 7–32 in Langan, M., and Schwarz, B. (eds) (1985).

Harris, M. (1993) *Culture, People, Nature: An Introduction to General Anthropology* (London: HarperCollins).

Harvey, D. (1990) *The Condition of Post-modernity* (Oxford: Blackwell).

Hay, C. (1996) *Re-Stating Social and Political Change* (Milton Keynes: Open University).

Hay, C. (1997) 'Divided by a Common Language: Political Theory and the Concept of Power', *Politics* vol. 17 (1) pp. 45–52.

Hayek, F. (1944) *The Road to Serfdom* (London: Routledge).

Hayek, F. (1960) *The Constitution of Liberty* (London: Routledge).

Haynes, J. (1996) *Third World Politics: A Concise Introduction* (Oxford: Blackwell).

Hebdige, D. (1982) 'Towards a Cartography of Taste 1935–1962' pp. 194–218 in Waites, B. (ed.) *Popular Culture: Past and Present* (London: Croon Helm).

Hegel, F. (1942) *The Philosophy of Right* (London: Oxford University Press).

Held, D. (1995) *Democracy and the Global Order* (Cambridge: Polity Press).

Held, D. (1996) *Models of Democracy* (2nd edn) (Cambridge: Polity Press).

Henman, P. (1997) 'Computer Technology – a Political Player in Social Policy', *Journal of Social Policy* vol. 26 (3) pp. 323–40.

Henrikson, A. (1995) 'The Growth of Regional Organizations and the Role of the United Nations', pp. 122–168 in Fawcett, L. and Hurrell, A. (eds) (1995).

Himmelfarb, G. (1995) *The De-Moralization of Society* (London: IEA Health and Welfare Unit).

Hindess, B. (1996) *Discourses of Power* (Oxford: Blackwell).

Hirst, P. (1994) *Associative Democracy* (Cambridge: Polity Press).

Hirst, P., and Khilnani, S. (eds) (1996) *Reinventing Democracy* (Oxford: Blackwell).

Hirst, P., and Thompson, G. (1995) 'Globalisation and the Future of the Nation State', *Economy and Society* vol. 24 (3) pp. 408–42.

Hirst, P., and Thompson, G. (1996) *Globalization in Question* (Cambridge: Polity Press).

Hobbes, T. (1973) *Leviathan* (London: Dent).

Hoffman, J. (1988) *State, Power and Democracy* (Brighton: Wheatsheaf).

Hoffman, J. (1995) *Beyond the State* (Cambridge: Polity Press).

Hoffman, J. (1998) *Sovereignty* (Buckingham: Open University).

Hofstede, G. (1981) 'Culture and Organisations', *International Studies of Management and Organisation* vol. 10 (4) pp. 15–41.

Horowitz, Z. (1972) *Foundations of Political Sociology* (New York: Harper and Row).

Horsman, M. and Marshall, A. (1995) *After the Nation-State* (London: Harper-Collins).

Hulme, D., and Edwards, M. (eds) (1997) *NGOs, States and Donors: Too Close for Comfort?* (London: Macmillan).

Huntington, S. (1998) *The Clash of Civilisations and the Remaking of the World Order* (London: Touchstone).

Hurrell, A. (1995) 'Regionalism in Theoretical Perspective', pp. 37–73 in Fawcett, L., and Hurrell, A. (eds) (1995).

Hutton, W. (1995a) 'The Familiar Shape of Things to Come', *Guardian*, 28 December.

Hutton, W. (1995b) 'Myth That Sets the World to Right', *Guardian*, 12 June.

Hutton, W. (1996) *The State We're in* (revised edn) (London: Vintage).

Ilting, K.-H. (1984) 'Hegel's Concept of the State and Marx's Early Critique', pp. 93–113 in Pelczynski, Z. (ed.) (1984) *The State and Civil Society: Studies in Hegel's Political Philosophy* (Cambridge: Cambridge University Press).

Inglehart, R. (1990) *Culture Shift in Advanced Industrial Society* (Princeton: Princeton University Press).

Jameson, F. (1991) *Post-modernism or the Cultural Logic of Late Capitalism* (Durham, NC: Duke University).

Jessop, B. (1974) *Traditionalism, Conservatism and British Political Culture* (London: Allen and Unwin).

Jessop, B. (1982) *The Capitalist State* (Oxford: Martin Robertson).

Jessop, B. (1990) *State Theory: Putting the Capitalist State in its Place* (Cambridge: Polity Press).

Jordan, G. and Maloney, W. (1997) *The Protest Business? Mobilising Campaign Groups* (Manchester: Manchester University Press).

Kaase, M., and Newton, K. (1995) *Beliefs in Government* (Oxford: Oxford University Press).

Kaiser, P. (1996) 'Structural Adjustment and the Fragile Nation: The Demise of Social Unity in Tanzania', *The Journal of Modern African Studies* vol. 34 (2) pp. 227–37.

Kavanagh, D. (1983) *Political Science and Political Behaviour* (London: Allen and Unwin).

Keane, J. (ed.) (1988) *Civil Society and the State* (London: Verso).

Keesings (1998) *Keesings Record of World Events* vol. 44 (Cambridge: Keesings Worldwide).

Kennedy, P. (1994) *Preparing for the Twenty-First Century* (London: Fontana).

Kershaw, I. (1993) *The Nazi Dictatorship* (3rd edn) (London: Edward Arnold).

Kiely, R. (1995) *Sociology and Development* (London: UCL Press).

King, R. (1986) *The State in Modern Society: New Directions in Political Sociology* (London: Macmillan).

Kirdar, U. (ed.) (1992) *Change: Threat or Opportunity?* (New York: United Nations).

Klingemann, H., and Fuchs, D. (eds) (1995) *Citizens and the State* (Oxford: Oxford University Press).

Koopmans, R. (1996) 'New Social Movements and Changes in Political Participation in Western Europe', *West European Politics* vol. 19 (1) pp. 28–50.

Korten, D. (1995) *When Corporations Rule the World* (Connecticut: Kumarian).

Kozul-Wright, R. (1995) 'Transnational Corporations and the Nation State', pp. 135–172 in Michie, J., and Smith, J. (eds) (1995).

Kriesi, H. (1996) 'The Organisational Structure of New Social Movements in a Political Context', pp. 152–84 in McAdam, D. et al. (eds) (1996).

Kriesi, H., Koopmans, R., Dyvendak, J. and Giugni, G. (1995) *New Social Movements in Western Europe: A Comparative Analysis* (London: UCL Press).

Kumar, K. (1995) *From Post-industrial to Post-modern Society* (Oxford: Blackwell).

Langan, M., and Schwarz, B. (eds) (1985) *Crises in the British State 1880–1930* (London: Hutchinson).

Lanjouw, G. (1995) *International Trade Institutions* (London: Longman).

Lash, S. and Urry, J. (1987) *The End of Organised Capitalism* (Cambridge: Polity Press).

Lash, S. and Urry, J. (1994) *Economies of Signs and Space* (London: Sage Publications).

Lenin, V. (1965) *The State and Revolution* (Peking: Foreign Languages Press).

Leonard, D. (1994) *Guide to the European Union* (4th edn) (London: Hamish Hamilton).

Lijphart, A. (1997) 'Unequal Participation: Democracy's Unresolved Dilemma', *American Political Science Review* 91 (1) pp. 1–14.

Linklater, A. (1998) *The Transformation of Political Community* (Cambridge: Polity Press).

Lister, R. (1997) *Citizenship: Feminist Perspectives* (London: Macmillan).

Lloyd, D., and Thomas, P. (1998) *Culture and the State* (London: Routledge).

Loader, B. (ed.) (1997) *The Governance of Cyperspace: Policy, Technology and Global Restructuring* (London: Routledge).

Locke, J. (1924) *Two Treatises of Government* (London: Dent).

Logan, I., and Mengisteab, K. (1993) 'IMF-World Bank Adjustment and Structural Transformation in Sub-Saharan Africa', *Economic Geography* vol. 69 (1) pp. 1–24.

Luard, E., with Heater, D. (1994) *The United Nations* (2nd edn) (London: Macmillan).

Lukes, S. (1974) *Power: A Radical View* (London: Macmillan).

Lyon, D. (1994) *Post-modernity* (Buckingham: Open University).

Lyotard, J. (1984) *The Post-modern Condition* (Manchester: Manchester University Press).

McAdam, D. (1996) 'Conceptual Origins, Current Problems, Future Directions', pp. 23–40, in McAdam, D. et al (eds) (1996).

McAdam, D., McCarthy, J. and Zald, M. (eds) (1996) *Comparative Perspectives on Social Movements* (Cambridge: Cambridge University Press).

McKay, D. (1997) *American Politics and Society* (4th edn) (Oxford: Blackwell).

McLean, I. (1989) *Democracy and New Technology* (Cambridge: Polity Press).

McLellan, D. (1977) (ed.) *Karl Marx Selected Works* (Oxford: Oxford University Press).

McLennan, G. (1984) 'Capitalist State or Democratic Polity? Recent Developments in Marxist and Pluralist Theory' pp. 80-109 in McLennan, G., Held, D. and Hall, S. (1984) *The Idea of the Modern State* (Milton Keynes: Open University).

McLennan, G. (1989) *Marxism, Pluralism and Beyond* (Cambridge: Polity Press).

McLennan, G. (1995) *Pluralism* (Buckingham: Open University).

McMichael, P. (1996) *Development and Social Change* (California: Pine Forge).

Maheu, L. (ed.) (1995) *Social Movements and Social Classes* (London: Sage Publications).

Mair, L. (1962) *Primitive Government* (Harmondsworth: Penguin).

Mann, M. (1970) 'The Social Cohesion of American Liberal Democracy', *American Sociological Review* vol. 35 (3) pp. 423–39.

Mann, M. (1986) *The Sources of Social Power* vol. 1 (Cambridge: Cambridge University Press).

Mann, M. (1988) *States, War and Capitalism: Studies in Political Sociology* (Oxford: Blackwell).

Mann, M. (1993) *The Sources of Social Power* vol. 2 (Cambridge: Cambridge University Press).

Mann, M. (1996) 'Ruling Class Strategies and Citizenship', pp. 125–144 in Bulmer, M., and Rees, A. (eds) (1996) *Citizenship Today* (London: UCL Press).

Marable, M. (1997) 'Rethinking Black Liberation: Towards a New Protest Paradigm', *Race and Class* vol. 38 (4) pp. 1–13.

Marsh, D. (1995) 'The Convergence Between Theories of the State', pp. 268–87 in Marsh, D. and Stoker, G. (eds) (1995).

Marsh, D., and Stoker, G. (eds) (1995) *Theory and Methods in Political Science* (London: Macmillan).

Marshall, G., Roberts, S., and Burgoyne, C. (1996) 'Social Class and Underclass in Britain and the USA', *British Journal of Sociology* vol. 47 (1) pp. 22–44.

Marshall, T. H., and Bottomore, T. (1992) *Citizenship and Social Class* (London: Pluto).

Marshall, T. H. (1981) *The Right to Welfare and Other Essays* (London: Heinemann).

Marx, K. (1994) 'On the Jewish Question', pp. 28–56 in Marx, K. (1994) *Early Political Writings* (Cambridge: Cambridge University Press).

Marx, K., and Engels, F. (1962) *Selected Works* vol. 1 (Moscow: Foreign Languages Publishing House).

Melucci, A. (1989) *Nomads of the Present: Social Movements and Individual Needs in Contemporary Society* (London: Hutchinson).

Melucci, A. (1995) 'The New Social Movements Revisited: Reflections on a Sociological Misunderstanding', pp. 107–19 in Maheu, L. (ed.) (1995).

Mešrović, S. (1998) *Anthony Giddens* (London: Routledge).

Michels, R. (1962) *Political Parties* (New York: Free Press).

Michie, J. and Smith, J. (eds) (1995) *Managing the Global Economy* (Oxford: Oxford University Press).

Miliband, R. (1968) *The State in Capitalist Society* (London: Weidenfeld and Nicolson).

Miliband, R. (1970) 'The Capitalist State: Reply to Nicos Poulantzas', *New Left Review* no. 59 January/February pp. 53–66.

Miliband, R. (1994) *Socialism for a Sceptical Age* (Cambridge: Polity Press).

Mingione, E. (ed.) (1996) *Urban Poverty and the Underclass: A Reader* (Oxford: Blackwell).

Morgan, E., and Thomas, W. (1969) *The Stock Exchange* (London: Elek).

Morgenthau, H. (1948) *Politics among Nations* (New York: Alfred P. Knopf).

Morris, L. (1995) *Social Division* (London: UCL Press).

Mosca, G. (1939) *The Ruling Class* (New York: McGraw-Hill).

Moser, G., Rogers, S., and van Til, R. (1997) *Nigeria: Experience with Structural Adjustment* Occasional Paper no. 148 (Washington DC: International Monetary Fund).

Mouffe, C. (ed.) (1992) *Dimensions of Radical Democracy* (London: Verso).

Mulgan, G. (ed.) (1997) *Life After Politics: New Thinking for the Twenty-First Century* (London: Fontana).

Mulhall, S., and Swift, A. (1996) *Liberals and Communitarians* (2nd edn) (Oxford: Blackwell).

Murray, C. (1996) *Charles Murray and the Underclass: The Developing Debate* (London: Institute of Economic Affairs).

New Internationalist (1993) 'Multinationals: The Facts', no. 246 August.

Nisbet, R. (1986) *Conservatism* (Milton Keynes: Open University).

O'Brien, R. (1992) *Global Financial Integration: The End of Geography* (New York: Council on Foreign Relations Press).

Oakeshott, M. (1975) *On Human Conduct* (Oxford: Clarendon Press).

Observer (1997) 'Switzerland Freezes Ousted Dictator's Assets', 18 May.

OECD (1996) *Globalisation: What Challenges and Opportunities for Governments?* (www.oecd.org/puma/gvrnance/strat/pubs/glo96/parts.htm).

Ohmae, K. (1990) *The Borderless World* (New York: HarperCollins).

Ohmae, K. (1995) *The End of the Nation-State* (New York: Free Press).

Olson, M. (1971) *The Logic of Collective Action* (2nd edn) (Cambridge, MA: Harvard University).

Oppenheim, F. (1975) *The State* (Montreal: Black Rose).

Osborne, P. (ed.) (1991) *Socialism and the Limits of Liberalism* (London: Verso).

Pareto, V. (1966) *Sociological Writings* (London: Pall Mall Press).

Pareto, V. (1968) *The Rise and Fall of the Elites* (New Jersey: Bedminister Press).

Parry, G., Moyser, G. and Day, N. (1991) *Political Participation and Democracy in Britain* (Cambridge: Cambridge University Press).

Parsons, T. (1969) *Politics and Social Structure* (Harvard University Archive: Parsons Papers).

Pateman, C. (1970) *Participation and Democratic Theory* (Cambridge: Cambridge University Press).

Pateman, C. (1988) *The Sexual Contract* (Cambridge: Polity Press).

Pateman, C. (1989) *The Disorder of Women* (Cambridge: Polity Press).

Pelczynski, Z. (ed.) (1984) *The State and Civil Society* (Cambridge: Cambridge University, Press).

Pienaar, J. (1997) 'A New Word in Public Standards', pp. 187–195 in *BBC News General Election Guide* (London: Harper Collins).

Pierson, C. (1991) *Beyond the Welfare State?* (Cambridge: Polity Press).

Poggi, G. (1978) *The Development of the Modern State* (London: Hutchinson).

Poggi, G. (1990) *The State: Its Nature, Development and Prospects* (Cambridge: Polity Press).

Poulantzas, N. (1978) *State Power and Socialism* (London: Verso).

Pugh, M. (1997) 'Peacekeeping and Humanitarian Intervention', pp. 134–56 in White, B., Little, R., and Smith, M. (eds) (1997) *Issues in World Politics* (London: Macmillan).

Raab, C. (1997) 'Privacy, Democracy, Information', pp. 155–74 in Loader, B. (ed.) (1997).

Ramesh, M. (1995) 'Economic Globalisation and Public Policy Choices: Singapore', *Governance* vol. 8 (2) pp. 243–60.

Raphael, D. (1990) *Problems of Political Philosophy* (2nd edn) (London: Macmillan).

Ratner, S. (1997) *The New UN Peacekeeping* (London: Macmillan).

Ravetz, J. (1997) 'Citizenship and Information Technology', paper presented at the conference *Citizenship for the 21st Century* at the University of Central Lancashire.

Real World Coalition (1996) *The Politics of the Real World* (London: Earthscan).

Richardson, J., and Jordan, A. (1979) *Governing under Pressure* (London: Martin Robertson).

Robertson, R. (1992) *Globalization* (London: Sage Publication).

Roche, M. (1992) *Rethinking Citizenship* (Cambridge: Polity Press).

Rosenbaum, W. (1975) *Political Culture* (London: Nelson).

Rosenberg, J. (1994) *The Empire of Civil Society* (London: Verso).

Ruggie, J. (1998) *Constructing the World Polity* (London: Routledge).

Ruzza, C. (1997) 'Institutional Actors and the Italian Peace Movement: Specialising and Branching Out', *Theory and Society* vol. 26 (1) pp. 87–127.

Sahlins, M. (1988) *Stone Age Economics* (London: Routledge).

Sanders, D. (1995) 'Behavioural Analysis', pp. 58–75 in Marsh, D., and Stoker, G. (eds) (1995).

Sartori, G. (1987) *The Theory of Democracy Revisited* (New York: Chatham House).

Schatz, S. (1994) 'Structural Adjustment in Africa: A Failing Grade So Far', *The Journal of Modern African Studies* vol. 32 (4) pp. 679–92.

Schmitt, H., and Holmberg, S. (1995) 'Political Parties in Decline?', pp. 95–133 in Klingemann, H., and Fuchs, D. (eds) (1995).

Schuller, D. (1996) *New Community Networks: Wired for Change* (New York: ACM).

Schumpeter, J. (1942) *Capitalism, Socialism, and Democracy* (New York: Harper).

Schwarzmantel, J. (1994) *The State in Contemporary Society* (London: Harvester and Wheatsheaf).

Scott, A. (1990) *Ideology and the New Social Movements* (London: Routledge)

Scott, A. (ed.) (1997) *The Limits of Globalization* (London: Routledge).

Shaw, M. (1994) *Global Society and International Relations* (Cambridge: Polity Press).

Sklair, L. (1995) *Sociology of the Global System* (2nd edn) (Harvester and Wheatsheaf).

Skocpol, T. (1979) *States and Social Revolutions* (Cambridge: Cambridge University Press).

Smith, A. (1995) *Nations and Nationalism in a Global Era* (Cambridge: Polity Press).

Smith, M. (1995) 'Pluralism', pp. 209–27 in Marsh, D., and Stoker, G. (eds) (1995).

Spybey, T. (1996) *Globalization and World Society* (Cambridge: Polity Press).

Stirrat, R. and Henkel, H. (1997) 'The Development Gift: The Problem of Reciprocity in the NGO World', pp. 66–80 in Fernando, J. and Heston, A. (eds) (1997).

Storey, A. (1997) 'Non-Neutral Humanitarianism: NGOs and the Rwanda Crisis', *Development in Practice* vol. 7 (4) pp. 384–94.

Street, J. (1997) *Politics and Popular Culture* (Cambridge: Polity Press).

Streeten, P. (1997) 'NGOs and Development', pp. 193–210 in Fernando, J. and Heston, A. (eds) (1997).

Studzinski, K. (1994) *Lesbians Talk Left Politics* (London: Scarlet).

Sunday Times (1997) 'Thatcher's Children to Boycott Polling Booths', 23 March.

Tester, K. (1997) 'Making Moral Citizens: On Himmelfarb's De-moralization Thesis', *Citizenship Studies* vol. 1 (1) pp. 57–71.

Therborn, G. (1989) 'The Two-Thirds, One-Third Society', pp. 103–115 in Hall, S., and Jaques, M. (eds) (1989) *New Times* (London: Lawrence and Wishart).

Thomas, P. (1994) *Alien Politics: Marxist State Theory Retrieved* (London: Routledge).

Thomassen, J. (1995) 'Support for Democratic Values', pp. 383–416 in Klingemann, H., and Fuchs, D. (eds) (1995).

Thompson, D. (1970) *The Democratic Citizen* (Cambridge: Cambridge University Press).

Thomson, A. (Forthcoming) *Introduction to African Politics* (London: Routledge).

Tocqueville, A. de (1945) *Democracy in America*, 2 volumes (New York: Alfred Knopf).

Topf, R. (1989) 'Political Change and Political Culture in Britain, 1959–87', pp. 52–80 in Gibbins, J. (ed.) (1989) *Contemporary Political Culture* (London: Sage Publications).

Touraine, A. (1981) *The Voice and the Eye: An Analysis of Social Movements* (Cambridge: Cambridge University Press).

Truman, D. (1951) *The Governmental Process* (New York: Alfred A. Knopf).

Tsagarousianou, R., Tambini, D., and Bryan, C. (eds) (1998) *Cyberdemocracy: Technology, Cities and Civic Networks* (London: Routledge).

Turner, B. (1994) 'Outline of a Theory of Citizenship', pp. 199–226 in Turner, B., and Hamilton, P. (eds) (1994) *Citizenship* (London: Routledge).

UNHCR (1997) *The State of the World's Refugees* (Oxford: Oxford University Press).

United Nations (1996a) *Globalisation and Liberalization* (New York: United Nations).

United Nations (1996b) *The United Nations and Crime Prevention* (New York: United Nations).

United Nations (1996c) *World Economic and Social Survey* (New York: United Nations).

United Nations (1997a) 'Peacekeeping redux . . . but still indispensable' (http://www.un.org/Depts/dpko/yir97/peacekp.htm).

United Nations (1997b) 'Setting the Record Straight' (http://www.un.org/News/facts/setting.htm).

Verba, S., Schlozman, K., and Brady, H. (1995) *Voice and Equality: Civic Voluntarism in American Politics* (London: Harvard University).

Wade, R., and Venerovo, F. (1998) 'The Asian Crisis: The High Debt Model Versus the Wall Street-IMF Complex', *New Left Review* no. 228 March/April pp. 3–23.

Wainwright, H. (1994) *Arguments for a New Left* (Oxford: Blackwell).

Walby, S. (1990) *Theorising Patriarchy* (Oxford: Blackwell).

Waltz, K. (1979) *Theory of International Politics* (Reading, MA: Addison-Wesley).

Walzer, M. (1992) 'The Civil Society Argument', pp. 89–107 in Mouffe, C. (ed.) (1992) *Dimensions of Radical Democracy* (London: Verso).

Waters, M. (1995) *Globalization* (London: Routledge).

Watkins, K. (1995) *The Oxfam Poverty Report* (Oxford: Oxfam)

Weber, M. (1947) *The Theory of Social and Economic Organisation* (New York: Free Press).

Weber, M. (1948) *From Max Weber: Essays in Sociology* (London: Routledge and Kegan Paul).

Weiss, L. (1998) *The Myth of the Powerless State* (Cambridge: Polity Press).

Welch, S. (1993) *The Concept of Political Culture* (London: Macmillan).

Whiteley, P., Seyd, P., and Richardson, J. (1994) *True Blues: The Politics of Conservative Party Membership* (Oxford: Clarendon Press).

Widfeldt, A. (1995) 'Party Membership and Party Representatives', pp. 134–82 in Klingemann, H., and Fuchs, D. (eds) (1995).

Willis, P. (1977) *Learning to Labour* (Farnborough: Saxon House).

Wilson, E. (1992) *A Very British Miracle* (London: Pluto Press).

Wilson, W. (1987) *The Truly Disadvantaged* (Chicago: University Press of Chicago).

World Bank (1994) *Adjustment in Africa: Reforms, Results and the Road Ahead* (Washington DC: World Bank).

World Development Movement (1993) *Trade: How International Trade Keeps the Third World Poor* (London: World Development Movement).

Wright, T. (1996) *Socialisms: Old and New* (2nd edn) (London: Routledge).

Wyatt-Walter, A. (1995) 'Regionalism, Globalization, and World Economic Order', pp. 74–121 in Fawcett, L., and Hurrell, A. (eds) (1995).

Young, I. (1990) *Justice and the Politics of Difference* (Princeton: Princeton University Press).

Zacher, M. and Sutton, B. (1996) *Governing Global Networks* (Cambridge: Cambridge University Press).

Zhao, D. (1997) 'Decline of Political Control in Chinese Universities and the Rise of the 1989 Chinese Student Movement', *Sociological Perspectives* vol. 40 (2) pp. 159–82.

Index